AFTER THE FLOOD

The Irish Abroad

GENERAL EDITOR: RUÁN O'DONNELL, UNIVERSITY OF LIMERICK

The series publishes short biographies and collected writings studying Irish men and women who made their mark outside their native country. Accounts of those who settled permanently overseas are published along with the life stories of temporary residents and involuntary emigrants. Expatriates of all types are considered whether explorers, travellers, military personnel, colonial pioneers, members of religious orders, professionals, politicians, revolutionaries, exiles or convicts. Most titles concern the Irish in North America, the former territories of the British Empire (including Australasia) and Great Britain, although biographies of those who journeyed to Spanish America, the West Indies, Africa, Continental Europe and other non-English speaking sectors will form part of the series.

Already published in the Irish Abroad series from Irish Academic Press:

Thomas Francis Meagher
The Making of an Irish-American
John M. Hearne and Rory T. Cornish (Eds)

Through American and Irish Wars
The Life and Times of Thomas W. Sweeny
Jack Morgan

Bishop in the Dock
The Sedition Trial of James Liston in New Zealand
Rory Sweetman

Irish Republicanism in Scotland 1858-1916
Fenians in Exile
Máirtín Seán Ó Catháin

Ireland, Australia and New Zealand
History, Politics and Culture
Laurence M. Geary and Andrew J. McCarthy (Eds)

Irish 'Ingleses'
The Irish Immigrant Experience in Argentina 1840–1920
Helen Kelly

AFTER THE FLOOD

Irish America 1945–1960

Editors

JAMES SILAS ROGERS

University of St Thomas

MATTHEW J. O'BRIEN

The Franciscan University of Steubenville

IRISH ACADEMIC PRESS

DUBLIN • PORTLAND, OR

First published in 2009 by Irish Academic Press

2 Brookside	920 NE 58th Avenue, Suite 300
Dundrum Road	Portland, Oregon,
Dublin 14, Ireland	97213-3786, USA

This Edition © 2009 Irish Academic Press
Individual chapters © Contributors

www.iap.ie

British Library Cataloguing in Publication Data
An entry can be found on request

978 0 7165 2987 3 (cloth)
978 0 7165 2988 0 (paper)

Library of Congress Cataloging-in-Publication Data
An entry can be found on request

Printed by the MPG Books Group in the UK

For our children
Frank, Margaret and Anne Rogers
and
Thomas and Julia O'Brien

Contents

About the Authors   xi

Introduction
James Silas Rogers and Matthew J. O'Brien   1

PART ONE: THE SEARCH FOR CONTINUITIES

1. Dance Halls of Romance and Culchies in Tuxedos:
   Irish Traditional Music in America in the 1950s
   Gearóid Ó hAllmhuráin   9

2. Playing 'Irish' Sport on Baseball's Hallowed Ground:
   The 1947 All-Ireland Gaelic Football Final
   Sara Brady   24

3. 'The Irish Movement in this Country is Now Moribund':
   The Anti-Partition Campaign of 1948–1951 in the United States
   Troy D. Davis   38

PART TWO: RESPONSES TO SOCIAL CHANGE

4. 'Hibernians on the March': Irish–American Ethnicity
   and the Cold War
   Matthew J. O'Brien   57

5. Shamrocks and Segregation: The Persistence of
   Upper-Class Irish Ethnicity in Beverly Hills, Chicago
   Margaret Lee   71

6. Irish New Yorkers and the Puerto Rican Migration
   Eileen Anderson   87

7. From 'Peace and Freedom' to 'Peace and Quiet':
   The Quiet Man as a Product of the 1950s
   Edward A. Hagan   100

8. Ahead of Their Time: Irish–American Women Writers, 1945–1960
Sally Barr Ebest   114

PART THREE: REARTICULATING THE MEANINGS OF IRISHNESS

9. Ireland as a Past Life: Bridey Murphy and Irish–American Tourism to Ireland, 1945–1960
Stephanie Rains   131

10. Ignorable Irishry: Leprechauns and Postwar Satire
James Silas Rogers   146

11. Unnatural Law: William McGivern's Rogue Cops
Tony Tracy   160

12. Beyond St Malachi's, There is Nothing: Edward McSorley and the Persistence of Tradition
Christopher Shannon   174

13. Present at the Creation: John V. Kelleher and the Emergence of Irish Studies in America
Charles Fanning   189

Notes   204

Index   211

About the Authors

Eileen Anderson is a Teaching Assistant Professor at North Carolina State University in the Department of Foreign Languages and Literature. She graduated from the University of North Carolina, Chapel Hill in May 2008. Her dissertation is titled 'Resisting Anglicization: Irish and Puerto Rican Intersections in New York in the Twentieth Century'. She recently published 'An Alternative View to the Propaganda: The Irish–American Press and the Spanish American War' in the Society for Irish Latin American Studies' journal, *Irish Migration Studies in Latin America* (November 2007). Her research interests lie in exploring the convergences of Latino and Irish studies in the United States.

Sara Brady is Lecturer in Drama Studies at Trinity College Dublin. Her writing has appeared in *TDR: The Drama Review*, *American Theatre* magazine, *New York Irish History* and *New Hibernia Review*. She is co-editor of *Crossroads: Performance Studies and Irish Culture* with Fintan Walsh (Palgrave, 2009).

Troy D. Davis is an Associate Professor of History and Chair of the History Department at Stephen F. Austin State University in Nacogdoches, Texas. He is the author of *Dublin's American Policy: Irish–American Diplomatic Relations, 1945–1952* (Washington, DC, 1998) and of a number of articles and book chapters on Irish and Irish–American history. He has also presented several papers on these topics at professional conferences. His research focuses primarily on twentieth-century Irish and Irish–American political and diplomatic history.

Sally Barr Ebest is Professor of English at the University of Missouri, St Louis. Her primary research interests are contemporary Irish–American women writers and the conjunction between feminism and Catholicism.

She has presented on these topics at regional and national meetings of the American Conference on Irish Studies, contributed chapters on the subject, and published in *New Hibernia Review*. Her books include: *Reconciling Catholicism and Feminism?* (University of Notre Dame Press, 2003), *Changing the Way We Teach* (Southern Illinois University Press, 2005), *Writing From A to Z* (McGraw-Hill 2005), and *Too Smart to be Sentimental: Contemporary Irish American Women Writers* (University of Notre Dame Press, 2008). She is currently working on a feminist literary history of contemporary Irish–American women writers, titled 'True Confessions'.

Charles Fanning is Professor of English and History and Distinguished Scholar Emeritus at Southern Illinois University Carbondale, where he was founding director of the Irish studies program. His books include: *The Irish Voice in America*, *The Exiles of Erin*, and *Finley Peter Dunne and Mr Dooley: The Chicago Years*. Most recently he has edited the University of Southern Illinois Press republication of James T. Farrell's five O'Neill–O'Flaherty novels.

Edward A. Hagan is Professor of Writing at Western Connecticut State University. His most recent book is *Goodbye Yeats and O'Neill: Contemporary Irish and Irish–American Fiction and Memoir*, forthcoming in 2009 from Editions Rodopi. He edited and introduced three volumes in the University College Dublin Press's Classics of Irish History series: *To the Leaders of Our Working People* and *Sun and Wind* – both by Standish James O'Grady – and *The Green Republic* by W.R. MacDermott. Hagan has published articles recently in the *Connecticut Review*, *Nua*, *The Recorder* and *New Hibernia Review*. He is the author also of *High Nonsensical Words: A Study of the Works of Standish James O'Grady*.

Margaret Lee is currently pursuing a Ph.D. in American History at the University of Wisconsin at Madison. Her dissertation focuses on the process of community formation among ethnic populations in suburban Chicago from the 1920s to the 1960s. Her research interests include ethnicity and immigration, urban and suburban studies, and environmental history.

A fourth-generation Clare concertina player, **Gearóid Ó hAllmhuráin** is the Smurfit-Stone Professor of Irish Studies and Professor of Music at the University of Missouri at St Louis. A graduate of University

College Cork, Trinity College Dublin, Université de la Sorbonne and Université de Toulon, he holds a Ph.D. in Social Anthropology and Ethnomusicology from Queen's University Belfast. Author of *A Pocket History of Irish Traditional Music* (1998), his recordings include: *Traditional Music from Clare and Beyond* (1996), *Tracin – Traditional Music from the West of Ireland* (1999), and *Paddy Murphy: Field Recordings from a Pioneer of the Irish Concertina* (2007). A consultant for documentaries on Irish music in the US, Canada and the EU, he is a former member of the Kilfenora Céilí Band, Ireland's oldest traditional ensemble.

Matthew O'Brien is an Associate Professor at the Franciscan University of Steubenville, Ohio, with a Ph.D. in history from the University of Wisconsin. He has published several articles on Irish–American ethnicity in *Eire-Ireland*, the *US Catholic Historian* and *Revue Etudes Irlandaises*. He is currently working on a comparative study of Irish ethnicity in Britain and the United States between 1920 and 2000.

Stephanie Rains works in the Centre for Media Studies at the National University of Ireland at Maynooth. She received her Ph.D. from Dublin City University in 2003, and her book, *The Irish–American in Popular Culture*, was published by Irish Academic Press in 2007. She has also published articles on Irish tourism and popular culture and is currently working towards a book on the history of consumer culture in nineteenth-century Ireland.

James Silas Rogers edits *New Hibernia Review: A Quarterly Record of Irish Studies*, published by the University of St Thomas in Minnesota. His articles on Irish–American fiction, autobiography and journalism have appeared in such journals as *Studies, The Recorder, US Catholic Historian* and also in the volume *New Perspectives on the Irish Diaspora* (2000). He is an elected officer of the American Conference for Irish Studies.

Christopher Shannon is Associate Professor of History at Christendom College in Front Royal, Virginia. He received his Ph.D. in American Studies from Yale University and is the author of two books on American cultural/intellectual history: *Conspicuous Criticism: Tradition, the Individual and Culture in Modern American Social Thought* (Johns Hopkins University Press, 1996) and *A World*

Made Safe for Differences: Cold War Intellectuals and the Politics of Identity (Rowman and Littlefield, 2001). He is currently completing a study of Irish Catholics in American film, titled *Bowery to Broadway: The Irish City in Classic Hollywood Cinema,* to be published by the University of Scranton Press.

Tony Tracy is Lecturer in Film Studies and Associate Director of the Huston School of Film and Digital Media at the National University of Ireland, Galway. He has taught at schools in Japan, France and the United States, is a former senior education officer at the Irish Film Institute and is currently pursuing a Ph.D. on Irish–American cinema from 1939 to 1959 at Trinity College Dublin.

Introduction

JAMES SILAS ROGERS and MATTHEW J. O'BRIEN

To begin at the beginning, we have chosen to name this volume of thirteen widely varied essays *After the Flood: Irish America, 1945–1960*. The metaphor is presumably obvious, the 'flood' being the heroic age, or ages, of Irish emigration into America. More than a generation of immigration historians – following such decisive researchers as Marcus Hansen and Oscar Handlin – have now revised and added detail to the causative and demographic dimensions of that vast transatlantic migration. Less obvious, perhaps, is our stress on the post-diluvian aspect; the consequence of a flood is, it should be noted, a changed landscape.

This volume provides a new set of perspectives to what is already a changed landscape in the study of Irish America, an endeavour in which the last two decades have occasioned a number of groundbreaking projects. Regional studies, ranging from the West Coast to the Deep South, have challenged the conventional fixation on north-eastern versions of Irish–American identity. Scholars have also expanded their chronological scope beyond the traditional focus on the nineteenth century – and the facile assumption that years of the Famine migration set the paradigm for all that followed – with provocative work on Protestant Irish settlers in colonial America, as well as more recent expressions of Irish heritage. Furthermore, scholarship on Irish America has been joyously interdisciplinary. The best researchers have always integrated various academic fields to fashion a more comprehensive understanding of the Irish–American experience.

The unifying theme among these efforts has been the divergent expression of Irish heritage during the course of American history. The unruly republicanism of Scots–Irish rebels, the desperate fatalism of the San Patricio Brigade and the marginalized insecurities of the undocumented New Irish have dispatched any sanguine notions about the fulfilment that awaited Irish immigrants in the so-called Land of Opportunity. As scholars have uncovered these less conventional expressions of Irishness in America, they have also highlighted the protean character of ethnic memory, noting not only the selective nature of immigrants' recollections about the 'old country', but also the ongoing process of revision that is taken up by later generations of American-born ethnics.

And yet, while the trajectory of research in the Irish–American experience has run toward regionalism, nuance and diversity, such multiplicity of hues appears to be lost by a number of recent approaches. Social scientists – sometimes forgetting the humanistic nature of their subject – have too often sought to describe the Irish–American experience through the backwards projection of recent achievement and affluence. For the adherents of the 'ethnic fade' approach, the definitive moment came not long after the Irish had disembarked in the American ports, committing themselves (or so it is assumed) to a straight-line course of assimilation that would reduce ethnicity to a romanticized affectation. Based on quantitative measures such as intermarriage and the chronological gap between immigrant ancestors and later generations, this school of thought remains fixed on the notion of ascribed characteristics in its dismissal of Irish–American ethnicity during the last seventy or eighty years. It was this presumed deliquescence that lay behind the harsh opening chapter of Michael Novak's influential *Rise of the Unmeltable Ethnics* (1971), which launched a diatribe that effectively accused the Irish of having traded their heritage for a mess of pottage – a reductionist misstep that Novak himself later retracted.

The ethnic fade school during the 1970s and 1980s was soon followed by a more polemical appraisal from the 'whiteness studies' movement. The adherents of this school – charitable and progressive as their goals may be – have characterized Irish–American identity as a façade meant to conceal ethnic accommodation with a racist society. By the time that this movement reached its rhetorical crescendo a decade later, advocates of the approach were quite comfortable in insinuating that the commemoration of Irish heritage was almost necessarily an exercise in crypto-racism, an attempt to legitimate the imperiled category of whiteness.

The energy and creativity during the mid-twentieth century offers a compelling case for scholars to go beyond demographic trends, and to resist teleological superstructures, in their study of Irish America. The years that this volume claims for its purview represent a distinct historical and cultural moment. Twenty years removed from the last substantial inflow of arrivals from Ireland, and nearly forty years distant from the massive influx of the post-Famine Irish, American-born ethnics redefined their tradition and revitalized their identity. Rising to prominence as the postwar champions of ethnic patriotism, and celebrated as a driving force behind the integration of Catholic Americans within the larger nation, this generation reinforced the confessional identification of Irish America.

Which is not to say that this milieu was monolithic. Years before a young John F. Kennedy would mount his first congressional campaign, a new generation of Irish Americans began an ethnic sea change, the success of which would be belatedly recognized in the 1960 presidential election. The 'great men' involved in this transformation included women writers and folk musicians, as well as national organizers and Hollywood directors. It was only after these relatively obscure and unglamorous figures had redefined Irish–American ethnicity that the Kennedy campaign would be able to overcome long-standing suspicions about the background of their candidate.

The pivotal significance of Irish–American ethnicity in the late 1940s and 1950s offers a controlling focus to each of the three sections within this collection. The first group of essays addresses three campaigns to sustain, or revive, connections between Ireland and Irish America. According to Gearóid Ó hAllmhuráin's comprehensive account of Irish music across the United States, such efforts not only preserved the past, they breathed new life into the medium through regional combinations of traditional music and contemporary American folk. Sara Brady's account of the relocated 1947 All-Ireland football match, played at the hyper-American venue of New York's Polo Grounds, offers a mixed verdict. While recognizing the monumental nature of the relocated match, the author offers a less certain view of its long-term significance, especially given the event's failure to generate a sustained revival of Gaelic sports in New York. Finally, Troy Davis pairs the modest popular reception afforded to Irish nationalists during the late 1940s with the underwhelming displays of opposition to visiting unionist leaders in order to illustrate the degree to which the once-vaunted spirit of Irish–American 'exiles' had dissipated.

The decline of transatlantic networks did not necessarily curtail Irish–American activity, however. In the second section, our contributors turn their attention toward the internal changes of ethnic groups, as they adapted to American trends. Matthew O'Brien's essay on the Cold War and the Ancient Order of Hibernians details how a new generation of leadership managed to revive the institution through an emphasis on ethnic patriotism, linking the Irish with American civil religion. Soon, Irish–American ethnicity would find itself drawn into the national conversation on race relations. Margaret Lee's account of Irish–Catholic parishes on the South Side of Chicago details vibrant expressions of Irish–American culture during Saint Patrick's Day festivities, at the same time as long-standing denominational tensions thwarted attempts to enlist Irish–Catholic parishes in the wider cause of residential segregation. Irish–American ethnics appear less charitable in Eileen Anderson's essay, which describes the complicated and variegated relations between Irish–American ethnics and Puerto Rican migrants in New York City. This account also offers another example of how Irish–American communities attempted to rewrite the past in light of postwar circumstances, with ethnic antagonism undermined by the uneasy recognition of a shared immigrant experience.

Rescuing John Ford's 1950s films from the scorn of subsequent critics, Edward A. Hagan plumbs below the director's superficial depiction of 'the old country' to discover the way in which Ford offered Irish–American viewers a means to process traumatic memories from World War Two. Hagan suggests, too, that Ford's films reflect the *zeitgeist* of the decade's sociological thought, specifically that of David Riesman. Finally, Sally Barr Ebest features a number of ground-breaking Irish–American women writers. The enforced silences and rigid gender roles of the time required many of these women to tell their stories retrospectively, as memoir. In some accounts, scandalous themes and personal lives contest notions of Irish–American conformity and offer an often overlooked foreshadowing of the larger liberation movements of the 1960s.

The last section of this volume focuses on the creation of iconic images within Irish America at mid-century. Stephanie Rains's exposition of the 'Bridey Murphy' phenomenon finds an implicit connection between the efforts of the Irish tourist industry and popular American notions of Irish mysticism, or at least, escape. James Silas Rogers engages with the popularization of a mythological figure as well, attributing the surprising prominence of the leprechaun in popular culture to the hidden anxieties that accompanied Irish–American upward mobility – the Irishman as a mocking Shakespearean fool. The now common figure of the hardened Irish–American detective also gained new prominence during this period, which the film scholar Tony Tracy attributes to the difficult practice of reconciling traditional adherence to institutional authority with the more individualized conscience that emerged around mid-century. But all was not dissent or discontentment: Christopher Shannon's account of spirituality and self-discovery in the work of Edward McSorley, a nearly forgotten Irish–American writer from this era, offers the message that fulfilment can be achieved within the bonds of tradition and community. Finally, Charles Fanning's account of John V. Kelleher's early contributions to Irish studies, including Irish America, presents a fitting conclusion to this section. Kelleher's contemporary remarks on this subject were both unsentimental and elegiac, but perhaps even more significant were his seminal efforts in shaping the approach of the American Committee for Irish Studies, and by extension, of the project of Irish studies.

Understanding the Irish–American experience in the postwar years is, of course, inseparable from the larger American experience. It is no longer possible to conceive of American society in these years as in any way complacent: there was no 'return to normalcy'. Alongside enormous economic, demographic and cultural shifts, the postwar years were a time of unceasing self-examination and debate over the future shape of American society.

The fifteen years after World War Two might also be the most important single period for twentieth-century Irish-American ethnicity – a time that witnessed the death of certain traditional elements, the adaptation of others, and the forging of images that would define the Irish American for the rest of the century. In many ways, this was a period that defied the determinism of straight-line assimilation and reasserted the vitality and salience of Irish ethnicity in the United States. Each of our contributors offers a vignette of why and how their subject attempted to do this: by searching for continuity, by injecting contemporary energies into ethnic issues or by creating iconic images – often serendipitously – that would come to dominate popular conceptions of 'Irishness' in American eyes.

Nearly half a century later, another movement offers a complementary opportunity. With its focus on variations of expatriate identity, the diasporic model of Irish migration rejects the long-standing treatment of the Irish in the United States as *sui generis*. The future of Irish–American studies will depend on those writers who are able to distinguish between expatriate tendencies in general and American influences in particular. Twentieth-century Irish America can be fully understood only by placing its conflicts and contradictions in the larger context of the universal and inescapable pressures that accompany resettlement for expatriates. Such considerations will inevitably provide opportunities for comparative analyses, and in so doing will extend the pertinence of Irish America to that of other groups worldwide.

In this next step of analysis, focusing on the complementary tensions of tradition and accommodation within the diaspora, the study of mid-twentieth-century Irish America has much to offer, as well as much more to learn. The contributors to this volume have established themselves as willing to engage with the attenuated connections, internal modifications and indigenous creativity that redefined Irishness in America during the middle decades of the twentieth century. It will be necessary to understand the mosaic nature of Irish America – to insist that the 1950s were about much more than Joe McCarthy and Jack Kennedy – if we truly want to integrate Irish America into the larger framework of the diaspora.

PART ONE
THE SEARCH FOR CONTINUITIES

Dance Halls of Romance and Culchies in Tuxedos: Irish Traditional Music in America in the 1950s

GEARÓID Ó HALLMHURÁIN

The prosperity and abundance of postwar America with its *el dorado* of Hollywood movies, liberal benefits and wages, interstate highways, and cosy suburban lifestyles proved powerful magnets for Irish immigrants seeking a new life beyond the poverty and inertia of postcolonial Ireland. Packing the boarding-houses and job markets of Boston, New York, Chicago and San Francisco, Irish labourers, nurses, factory workers and domestic servants arrived beaming with optimism and hungry for work, yet lonesome for the familiar sounds of home. While a vibrant network of friends, relations and foremen took care of the work, a connection to the familiar sounds of home was often sought through the intercession of the music-makers who were part of the mass emigration from Ireland in the postwar years.[1] In contrast to social life at home in Ireland, American popular culture – an alchemy of musical comedies, television sitcoms, rebellious teenagers and rock 'n' roll – moved into overdrive in the 1950s. Simultaneously, Irish dance-halls, county organizations and parish clubs all over America filled with the music and dance of new immigrants. In this nexus of Old World music and New World glitz, traditional musicians – Yanks, Narrowbacks and Culchies just off the boat – seized opportunities to form new orchestras and céilí bands, create record labels, seek out 'big gigs' and tout their own music on their own radio shows in cities across the nation.

In the New World the economic doldrums that had prevailed for Irish traditional musicians since the Great Depression were finally over. For a whole generation of immigrant musicians, the 1950s epitomized the American Dream at its best. After serving their apprenticeships in galvanized ballrooms of romance in the small towns and villages of Galway, Roscommon and Clare, country lads such as Joe Cooley, Martin Wynne, Seán McGlynn, Joe Madden and Paddy O'Brien now donned tuxedos to play with orchestral sax and bass players in the snazzy ballrooms of urban America. Elsewhere, in a sea of artistic exchange, small-town singers such as the Clancy brothers from Tipperary and Tommy Makem from Armagh were about to forge an unlikely link between the American folk boom and the Irish vernacular ballad.

TRACING THE MUSICAL IMMIGRANT

Most traditional musicians who arrived in the United States in the 1950s were young, eager to work and willing to chance their luck in a variety of unfamiliar urban environments. While some had played professionally with céilí and modern dance-bands in Ireland, the prospect of becoming professional musicians in America hardly seemed feasible to most immigrant players. In reality, music was secondary to the challenge of finding 'real work' in America (O'Keefe, interview with author, 1999).

Once in America, however, part-time opportunities beckoned for many, among them accordion icon Joe Cooley from Peterswell, in the musical heartland of east Galway. Cooley's departure from Ireland in July 1954 was seen as a tragic watershed by his friends in traditional music circles. His highly publicized American Wake went on for several days, starting in Miltown Malbay, Co. Clare, where Cooley was presented with a new Paulo Soprani accordion, and finishing in Touhey's bar in Ennis before taking the road to Cobh in Seán Reid's Morris Minor, the car that had ferried Cooley and his cohorts all over Ireland during the 'hungry forties'.

Cooley's arrival in New York coincided with the close of the 'Golden Age' of Irish traditional music in America. This Golden Age was headlined in the 1920s by a trio of Sligo fiddlers – Michael Coleman, James Morrison and Paddy Killoran. Their recordings, which were key cultural remittances in Ireland, dictated the course of Irish traditional music in the middle decades of the twentieth century.[2] Eclipsed by the Great Depression and World War Two, Irish commercial recording made a brief recovery in the postwar years when fiddlers such as Hughie Gillespie from Donegal, the Cronin brothers from Kerry, and Clare flute player Frank Neylon made it on to the roster of small commercial labels. But the larger American commercial labels, driven by new markets and consumer tastes, had turned their attention away from ethnic recordings. While the careers of Irish–American idols such as Bing Crosby, Gene Kelly and Donald O'Connor were on the ascent – Crosby alone sold 500 million recordings and starred in more than one hundred films (Moloney, 'Irish–American Popular Music', pp.398–9) – the fortunes of their traditional elders were for the most part on the descent by the 1950s.

Although Irish traditional music may have been beyond the radar of popular and 'high art' cultures, it nonetheless proved remarkably resilient in the fast-moving currents of cultural change in America in the 1950s. Its adaptability was due, to some extent, to its own eclectic historiography. The hermetic purity and nationalist teleologies prescribed to Irish traditional music by revivalist organizations such as the Gaelic League and Comhaltas Ceoltóirí Éireann often ignore the fact that the music is the product of a highly nuanced and multilayered past. A *bricolâge* of *sean nós* songs, Anglo-Scottish ballads, Irish jigs, clan marches and harp tunes, English hornpipes, Scottish reels, Bohemian polkas, French galops and Polish mazurkas that coalesced over time, the traditional repertoire contains considerable residue gleaned from the music of various European cultures in the eighteenth and nineteenth centuries. In the twentieth century brass and reed band repertoires (from British and German military traditions), jazz and big band music all made inroads, however subtle, into the porous milieu of traditional music.[3] With the exception of *sean nós* songs (inaccessible to many musicians in Ireland and more inaccessible to their American cohorts), the musicological distance between Irish dance tunes, traditional ballads carried by immigrants, and the sentimental parlour songs and theatrical hits of Irish America was by no means impassable (Williams, 'Irish Song', pp.474–8).

What made Irish traditional music in America different was the sheer scale of the New World *habitus*. Immigrant music-makers encountered a vast topography of performance settings, from the intensely private to the overtly public and unfamiliar. On one end of the spectrum lay a niche marketplace and clever entrepreneurs who embraced the challenging individualism of the professional stage and forged a business relationship with Irish and Irish–American 'consumers'. On the other end of the spectrum were their anonymous contemporaries who eschewed the public *gesellschaft* to preserve the musical dialects of an older communal *gemeinschaft* in their own homes, sessions and parish clubs – the latter of which were key conduits for regional styles of music and traditional set dancing (Whelan, interview with author, 2007). Between these two extremes lay a heteroglossic middle ground of musicians, singers and dancers who moved indiscriminately between reels and jigs, waltzes and quick steps, nationalist ballads, Moore's melodies, John McCormack's arias, American folk songs and country and western ditties. Irish traditional musicians in the postwar years were to be found in all sectors of this ethnomusicological *habitus*.

The most isolated cohort of performers in America comprised staunch 'traditionalists' from close-knit rural communities in the west of Ireland who had arrived with rare, and often already marginalized, dialects of traditional dance music. Many simply felt ghettoized in the New World. Flute player Jack Coen, from Woodford in the Sliabh Aughty region of east Galway (home to a unique repertoire and style), found few outlets for his music in America. Settling in the Bronx in the late 1940s, he felt that his kind of music – with its slow, ethereal rhythms, archaic settings and tonal subtleties – was played by a diminishing number of musicians and appreciated by an even smaller coterie of listeners. He recalled that 'there were a lot of musicians around, but I never came into contact with them. And they weren't going around in the same circles that I was going around in at that time. I just never bumped into them, not for a long time' (interview with Moloney cited in Collins, 'From Sliabh Aughty to Ellis Island').

Other issues also hindered the integration of many immigrant players into an already receding milieu of old-style regional music. New York was strongly predisposed to the fiddle dialect of south Sligo, since the glory days of Coleman, Morrison and Killoran. The recorded music of this triumvirate enjoyed such status that other dialects from equally rich storehouses in Kerry, Clare, Galway, Roscommon and Donegal were often ignored or dismissed (McHale and Coen, interview with author).[4] This disproportionate representation of the Sligo style was buttressed by a thriving traffic in American records. The demand for American 78s in Ireland was so strong that vendors such as O'Byrne DeWitt could send salesman Jer O'Donovan, a native of west Cork, on twenty-one trips across the Atlantic with new product prior to World War Two – years before the establishment of routine passenger aviation (Ó Donnabháin, interview with author, 1997; Ó hAllmhuráin, *Pocket History*, pp.108–9).

Musicians seeking *céilithe* and *feiseanna* resembling those they had experienced in Ireland prior to emigrating found little common ground in the New World. The only offerings in New York in the

1950s were monthly *céilithe* organized by the Gaelic League and an annual *feis* sponsored by the United Irish Counties Association. As a member of New Jersey's Englewood Céilí Band, east Galway flute player Mike Rafferty played once a month for a Gaelic League céilí club, which helped him stay connected with a dance community that depended explicitly on Old World music to keep them active (interview with Moloney quoted in Collins 'From Sliabh Aughty to Ellis Island').

For musicians prepared to step beyond the bounds of traditional orthodoxy, other options beckoned. Accordionist Jerry Lynch from Kilfenora, Co. Clare, for example, was willing to don a tuxedo and share the stage as a 'side man' with unionized musicians yielding saxophones and trumpets. In this hybrid milieu, reels and jigs were played on the same bill as waltzes, quick steps, fox-trots, and jives. Lynch, a stalwart of the Kilfenora Céilí Band (winner of three All Ireland Céilí Band titles, 1954–6), was well aware of external influences on the traditional soundscape before he left Clare. Ennistymon, the nearest market town to his home in Clogher, had absorbed the influence of American jazz and big band music in the 1930s and 1940s – despite the best efforts of the local clergy to shepherd its flock away from the sinful moan of the saxophone. Lynch played beside jazz musicians Pat Madigan and Jimmy Leydon in the Kilfenora Céilí Band. Its *fleadh cheoil* successes aside, the Kilfenora was a typical dance-band that played for a mixed clientele of set dancers, céilí dancers and modern dancers in the 1950s. The exceptions were *fíor céilí* dancers – the 'real céilí' hardliners, most of whom belonged to the Gaelic League and who regarded set and old-time dancing as foreign aberrations. Talented hybrid musicians like Madigan and Leydon were capable of spanning several genres. They frequently played in jazz ensembles, especially for an upper-class clientele in Lisdoonvarna, Clare's historic spa town (Leydon, interview with author, 1988). Lynch arrived in the America having already heard a range of non-Irish music. What musicians missed in live settings, they heard on radio – either 'Athlone Radio' (as Radio Éireann was dubbed), the BBC or American Armed Forces Radio broadcast from Germany that first introduced big band music to European audiences (Gedutis, *See You at the Hall*, p.70). To assume that Irish traditional musicians arrived in America in the 1950s hermetically sealed in some musical other-world is both simplistic and untenable. They were keenly aware of the eclectic soundscape they had come from, and its many umbilical links with American music.

BOSTON AND NEW YORK

Despite the migration of New England's textile industries to the southern states in the postwar years, Irish female immigrants continued to find work in service and utility industries in Boston (Kostinen, 'Dealing with Deindustrialization', pp.501–4). Their male counterparts were the tradesmen and construction workers who worked on Mayor Hynes's urban renewal project that crisscrossed Boston with highways and tunnels in the 1950s.

Home to ensembles such as Dan Sullivan's Shamrock Band and O'Leary's Irish Minstrels, who had recorded during the Golden Age of the 1920s, Boston was also a hive of Irish musical activity in these years. The nerve centre of this scene was Dudley Square in Roxbury, one of the city's oldest centres of Irish settlement and a terminal for trains and buses travelling in and out of the city. It was also a nucleus of Irish and Canadian bars where Newfoundland, Cape Breton and Irish revellers convened on a nightly basis. From the end of World War Two until the 1960s dancers flocked every weekend to Roxbury's dance-halls – the Intercolonial, the Hibernian, the Dudley Street Opera House, Winslow Hall and the Rose Croix. The area was a hub of Irish social and cultural life, as well as a bridge between the old country and the new. Recalling the Saturday night scene in Dudley Square in the 1950s, accordionist Joe Derrane, who 'cut his teeth' playing professionally in the area, remembers that

> The Kerry people went to the Dudley Street Opera House. There was Winslow Hall, on the third floor – they all seemed to be on the third floor! Most of the people, about three hundred to three-fifty, were from the west of Ireland: Connemara, Mayo, Donegal. Across the street was Rose Croix Hall, mostly Scots and Canadians, and some Irish. There would be about five to six hundred people there. The Opera House fit about six hundred, the Hibernian, a thousand, and the Intercolonial Hall, where Johnny Powell's band played, there were about a thousand to fifteen hundred people there.[5] (cited in Geditus, *See You at the Hall*, pp.49–51)

Decked out in slick tuxedos and sporting ritzy orchestral monikers, Irish musicians played with all kinds of dance-bands during the glory days of Dudley Square. The more traditional end of the scene included the Tara Céilí Band, featuring fiddlers Johnny Cronin and Larry Reynolds, and the All-Star Céilí Band; the modern end of the market was served by the Emerald Isle Orchestra, the Diplomats, the Four

Provinces Orchestra and Johnny Powell's Band, featuring accordion greats Billy Caples and Joe Derrane. Although individual bandsmen may have favoured particular genres, most professional and semi-professional ensembles played a hybrid mix of traditional dance tunes and modern big band hits. Though the dance-hall was a key driving force in Boston's musical life, the city was also home to accomplished individual performers during this period (for instance, the Cronin brothers from Kerry, Frank Neylon and Joe Commane from Clare, Mike McHale from Roscommon, and Brendan Tonra from Mayo). When not playing on the big stage, many of these could be found playing for weddings and Irish county associations throughout New England, for kitchen rackets in South Boston, or listening to *sean nós* songs in Dorchester, the largest Gaeltacht community west of Carna.

Like their homologues in Boston, Irish music-makers in New York found themselves confronted with an array of choices, from the small sessions of regional stylists to the new professional vistas of the dance-hall, the radio station and the recording studio. Remnants of an older milieu also prevailed among the city's Irish–American community. In the 1950s, three decades after the demise of mainstream vaudeville, the McNulty Family was still keeping Irish–American vaudeville alive on the east coast (Moloney, 'Irish–American Popular Music', pp.399–400). Billed as the 'Royal Family of Irish Entertainers', Ann, Pete and Eileen McNulty were a mother, daughter and son troupe. Purveying sentimental songs like *A Mother's Love is a Blessing* and Percy French's *The Darling Girl from Clare*, they played and danced, and also performed skits and sketches. 'Ma' McNulty was an accomplished accordionist and impressed audiences with her many coloured accordions each in a different key. She created a successful stage career in a world dominated almost exclusively by male performers.

In New York, as in other immigrant cities, the dance-hall was a primary forum for Irish music in the 1950s. Key venues were the City Center Ballroom on the West Side and the Jaeger House on the Upper East Side. The standard formula of big band hits and traditional dance tunes prevailed in both. Popular bands who played at the City Center were Mickey Carton's Band and Brendan Ward's twelve-piece orchestra. Ward emigrated to the Unites States in 1955 to form an orchestra for the new ballroom owned by Kerry entrepreneur Bill Fuller, whose empire of halls and hotels stretched from Camden Town to San Francisco (Almeida, *Irish Immigrants in New York City*, p.124). Astutely aware of contemporary tastes, Ward doled out a mix of Tin Pan Alley hits, Strauss waltzes, tangos, cha-chas and rumbas to City

Center punters. His union-regulated forty-minute sets were inter-spersed with twenty-minute sets of reels, jigs and old-time waltzes, in what one music historian has termed 'watered-down' traditional music (Miller, 'Irish Traditional and Popular Music', p.493); this was usually provided by a small ensemble of accordion, drums and piano. A long-time regular of this Irish gig at the City Center was Paddy Noonan, who played piano accordion – a new and not always wel-come *arriviste* into the older fold of traditional instruments. For rev-ellers wishing to escape the bustle of Manhattan during the summer months, the smaller Irish houses on Rockaway Beach in Queens also offered traditional music and dancing (Keating, interview with author, 1998). For those with cars, upstate Irish villages such as East Durham and Leeds in the Catskill Mountains were popular haunts for musi-cians and dancers, particularly before low-cost summer flights on Aer Lingus lured immigrants home to Ireland on holidays (Ó Donnabháin, 'An Ceol Traidisiúnta sna Catskills,' pp.42–3).

Beyond the commercial domain of the dance-hall lay a diffuse milieu of traditional performers, some of them – such as Paddy Killoran and Mick Flynn – veterans of the Golden Age, others who had arrived recently and were determined to maintain their music. This coterie was particularly enthusiastic when members of the Tulla Céilí Band came to New York in 1956, and returned with the full band, then reigning All-Ireland champions, two years later. In March 1956, Dr Bill Loughnane and Paddy Canny were invited to play in New York for Saint Patrick's Day. Loughnane and Canny brought five sets of hurleys for the Clare GAA team in New York, as well as a batch of shamrock picked beside Kilbarron Lake in east Clare. On Saint Patrick's Day Loughnane threw in the ball at the opening of Gaelic Park in the Bronx and Canny gave a solo concert in Carnegie Hall. Their trip was followed by a tour of the full Tulla Céilí Band during Lent 1958. In Ireland Lent was a slump period for bands, as public dancing was discouraged by the Catholic clergy (Keane, *Tulla Céilí Band*, p.69). Accompanied by teenaged accordion champion Tony Loughnane, the Tulla played in New Jersey and New York, including a St Patrick's night concert at Carnegie Hall, where they shared the stage with the TV celebrity Pat Boone. The *Clare Champion* of 12 April 1958 reported:

> The band performed at dances in various parts of New York and got the unstinted appreciation of audiences. Capacity crowds were everywhere they went, and in many cases, only the most

efficient stewarding made it possible to get into and out of the halls, so great were the throngs to meet them ...

Dr Bill Loughnane made good use of the tape recorder, but unfortunately, he could record only a small part of the numerous messages the exiles wished to send home. He intends to play these recordings at various gatherings, so that those who have relatives in America can in many cases hear the voices of their loved ones. The band proved worthy ambassadors and helped to bind still closer the ties which held together the people here at home and the Irish in America. (Keane, *Tulla Céilí Band*, pp.79–80)

Not all of these 'worthy ambassadors' went back to Ireland with the band, however. Accordion player and composer Martin Mulhaire chose to settle in New York, where for the next forty years he worked as a professional musician, playing guitar in modern dance-bands and accordion in traditional ensembles throughout the tri-state area (Mulhaire, interview with author, 2001). Banjoist and flute player Séamus Cooley also remained in America, where he spent the next twenty-seven years playing with his brother Joe and fiddler Johnny McGreevy in various ensembles in Chicago (Vallely, *Companion to Irish Traditional Music*, p.88). Within a few years Tulla flute player Michael Preston would resign his 'secure' job with CIE, the Irish railway company, and follow his cohorts to New York (Preston, interviews with author, 1983, 2001).

The 1958 visit of the Tulla Céilí Band was a major boost to players who were marginalized by the commercial dance milieu, such as the New York Céilí Band that was formed in the mid-1950s. Although opportunities to play professionally were fairly minimal in the greater New York area, the band eschewed the unionized regulations and professional protocols of the orchestral arena and focused instead on preserving the older dialects of Sligo, Galway and Tipperary that were endemic among the band-members.[6] Its line-up included Andy McGann, Paddy Reynolds, Larry Redican, Lad O'Beirne, Jerry Wallace, Jack Coen, Felix Dolan and Paddy O'Brien. Attracted by the prospect of 'going home' to complete at the All-Ireland Fleadh Cheoil, which had begun in 1951 and which was very much a novelty for immigrant players, the New York Céilí Band decided to compete at the All-Ireland Fleadh in Boyle, Co. Roscommon in 1960. Although they won the overseas competition and three of their members were placed in the All-Ireland trio competition, they failed to take All-Ireland honours back to New York – apparently because they had played without a drummer (Dolan, interview with author, 2008). Ironically, the competition was won by the Tulla Céilí Band, who had inspired them in New York two years earlier.

Beyond the east coast industrial corridor and the automobile belt in the upper midwest, the two cities that witnessed the most consistent increases in their Irish music communities in the 1950s were Chicago and San Francisco – both of which had older Irish music clubs dating from the post-Famine years of the nineteenth century (McCullough, 'Irish Music in Chicago'; Ó hAllmhuráin, 'Old Age Pipers and New Age Punters', pp.108–30).

Ever since Chicago police captain Francis O'Neill (1846–1936) published his massive corpus of Irish music, Chicago has stood at the apex of the Irish traditional music world. During the 1930s Chicago musicians made recordings for Victor, Celtic and Columbia, among them Clare dancer Pat Roche, whose Harp and Shamrock Orchestra was the first Irish act recorded by the Decca label. Recorded at Chicago's Century of Progress World's Fair in 1934, his ensemble – which included Eleanor Neary, Joe Shannon and Johnny McGreevy, all teenagers at the time – was one of the first céilí band-like ensembles in America (Vallely, *Companion to Irish Traditional Music*, p.417). But after this flurry of recording activity it would be thirty years before Chicago-based musicians would again record Irish traditional music. During the 1940s Irish musicians in Chicago retreated into their own inner *gemeinschaft* of house parties, weddings and community dances.

New economic opportunities in the 1950s, however, brought a new influx of performers, among them Pat Cloonan, Jim Coyle, Terry 'Cuz' Teehan, Maidhc Dainín Ó Sé, Brendan Williams, Kevin Henry, as well as the Cooley and Cronin brothers, who spent time in New York and Boston before moving to the mid-west. The parents of choreographer Michael Flatley and composer Liz Carroll – both key ambassadors of Irish–American music and dance today – also emigrated to Chicago during this period. Forming céilí bands, hosting sessions and garnering new radio audiences through shows hosted by Pat Roche and P.J. Concannon, this new enclave raised the profile of Irish traditional music in the Windy City. Inspired by the formation of Comhaltas Ceoltóirí Éireann in Ireland in 1951, the Irish Musicians' Association of America was founded in Chicago in 1956, spearheaded by flute player Frank

Thornton. In less than ten years the IMAA had twenty-two chapters throughout the United States, though it survived less than a decade (Ibid., p.419).

In San Francisco the completion of the Golden Gate Bridge and the Bay Bridge in the late 1930s dramatically reduced the geographic isolation of the city. A mammoth influx of wartime workers shortly afterwards created enormous housing shortages. These pressures increased further after the war, when thousands of demobilized veterans returned home and wartime workers opted to remain in the Bay Area. In the resulting expansion, many Irish families, striving for upward social mobility, left inner-city communities for the East Bay, South San Francisco and the Outer Sunset, thus sundering established centres of Irish settlement that had endured for nearly a century. But even as settled Irish–American families were leaving the Mission District, newly arrived immigrants were still frequenting its Irish dance-halls, especially the Éire Óg club at the Irish–American hall on Valencia Street and the Knights of the Red Branch hall (referred to as the KRB) on Market Street. Set and céilí dancers met weekly at the KRB until it ceded its place to the new United Irish Cultural Center in 1974 (Hickey, 'Where Hallinan Met Her Knight', p.14). Dancers who wanted a more homely setting could retire to Bryce's basement on Church Street, as well as to Mrs Piggott's and Abbie Murphy's private homes, all of which had rooms set aside for dancing. Like their precursors in the prewar years, tea, coffee and soda bread were all part of the hospitality offered at these house-dances. Despite their loyalty to traditional dancing during their early years in exile, many immigrants were enticed by the showband scene that was sweeping through Ireland and its emigrant communities by the late 1950s. In San Francisco many flocked to John Whooley's Avalon Ballroom and Bill Fuller's Carousel Ballroom (later Bill Graham's Fillmore West).[7]

Traditional performers who arrived in the Bay Area in the 1950s included Kerry fiddler Seán O'Sullivan and accordionists Con Dennehy, Mick Lucey and Tadhg Reidy, the latter a pupil of the Sliabh Luachra master Pádraig O'Keeffe. However, the San Francisco Irish failed to produce recording celebrities like New York's Sligo fiddlers. The Knights of the Red Branch, seeking to redress this, purchased recording equipment in the mid-1950s; among the performers who benefitted was Donegal fiddler Danny O'Donnell. Born in the early 1900s, O'Donnell left Ireland in 1948 and moved to the Bay Area from New York in 1956. In San Francisco he helped to rejuvenate a coterie of Donegal fiddlers that included Dudley Byrne and Joe

Tammony. During his stay on the west coast, O'Donnell made some private acetate recordings; a surviving copy includes the well-known reels *The Music in the Glen, Farewell to Ireland* and *The Dawn* that highlight his superb mastery of different fingering positions (Mac Aoidh, *Between the Jigs and the Reels*, p.138).

THE MUSICAL LEGACY OF THE 1950S

For more than a century, the fortunes of Irish traditional music in America have depended on the receptivity of the host communities that patronize it and the media technologies that transmit it. Clearly, mainstream recording companies in America rejected the music during the postwar years – but the entrepreneurial drive of new immigrants and old investors soon came to its rescue.

By the late 1950s consumers turned their attention to long-playing records. The first recording of Irish music on LP was made by Alan Lomax in 1955. Released as part of the Columbia World Library, the music for this LP was collected by Lomax and Séamus Ennis in 1951 (Cohen, *Alan Lomax*, pp.180–1). Seizing a rare opportunity, Clare brothers James and John O'Neill (nine of whose siblings emigrated to the United States between 1945 and 1960) and Sligo fiddler Paddy Killoran founded Dublin Records in New York and charged headlong into an industry dominated by media moguls Victor, HMV and Columbia. Dublin Records found a tiny niche by American standards, yet a sizeable one by Irish standards. They recorded musicians who had garnered a reputation as All-Ireland champions in the 1950s and sold their records to Irish immigrants in a booming American market; in 1960 alone, they published twelve LPs. Their catalogue stressed céilí bands: the Kilfenora, the Tulla, Laichtín Naofa and Leitrim, though their celebrated 1959 release *All Ireland Champions – Violin* featuring Paddy Canny, P.J. Hayes, Peadar O'Loughlin and Bridie Lafferty is considered 'the' iconic disc of the period (Keville, 'Style Recorded', pp.33–6). In Boston, Justus O'Byrne DeWitt, whose family sponsored the first flat disc recordings of Irish music in America in 1916, started Copley Records in 1948 and issued classic recordings of Paddy Cronin, Frank Neylon, Jerry O'Brien, Joe Derrane and Johnny Powell, as well as the Irish tenor Connie Foley (Ní Fhuartháin, 'O'Byrne DeWitt and Copley').

While Irish traditional music may have lost its lustre for some Irish Americans who were busy crossing the Rubicon from Culchie to Yank in the 1950s, by the end of the decade it was still the primary *forté* of the immigrant. Soon, however, a new wave of non-Irish neophytes was ushered into the fold by the euphoria of the folk revival, which had its own Irish emissaries in the Clancy Brothers and Tommy Makem. Their career began in 1956 with the recording *The Rising of the Moon* on the Tradition label – followed in subsequent decades by some fifty-four other albums. More than any other ensemble, the Clancys introduced Irish music to mainstream American culture in the 1960s and cemented a reputation that has remained intact beside folk icons Pete Seeger and Woody Guthrie for almost half a century. Many 'folkies' introduced to Irish ballads by the Clancys went on to learn Irish dance music and have since become a key cohort in the eclectic tapestry of Irish music in America.

The heteroglossic history and the shifting topography of Irish traditional music in America in the 1950s might well suggest its dislocation and dilution. However, the decade proved as seminal in many respects as its Golden Age precursor in the 1920s. Beneath the glittering ballrooms, tuxedoed fiddlers and *geansaí*-clad balladeers lay a thriving nexus of ethnic composition. During the 1950s the Irish music community in America housed a coterie of folk composers, among them Ed Reevy, Martin Mulhaire, Paddy O'Brien, Larry Redican and Brendan Tonra, whose unique compositions continue to occupy the foreground of Irish traditional music today. These new repertoires – many of which have been published and are available worldwide – have been counterbalanced astutely by the dynamic teaching and advocacy of older music dialects from Clare, Galway and Kerry by druidic guardians such as Jack and Fr Charlie Coen, Mike Rafferty, Marty O'Keefe and Paddy Cronin. These exiled players preserved a canonical treasury of music from an older *habitus* that found a more discerning sanctuary in America than it did in many parts of Ireland during the past half-century. In this epistemological context, America proved to be the great preserver, rather than the great leveller, of Irish traditional music in the 1950s.

REFERENCES

Almeida, Linda Dowling. 'A Great Time to be in America: The Irish in Post-Second World War New York City', in Dermot Keogh, Finbarr O'Shea and Carmel Quinlan (eds), *Ireland in the 1950s: The Lost Decade*. Cork: Mercier Press, 2004, pp.206–20.
—— *Irish Immigrants in New York City, 1945–1995*. Bloomington, IN: Indiana University Press 2001.
Carolan, Nicholas. 'A Discography of Irish Traditional Music'. *Ceol,*

vol. 4, no. 2 (1984), p.45.

Cohen, Ronald D. *Alan Lomax: Selected Writings 1934–1997*. New York: Routledge, 2003

Collins, Tim. 'From Sliabh Aughty to Ellis Island: The East Clare/Southeast Galway Music Diaspora, and its Influence on Irish-American Music Culture'. Paper presented at the American Conference for Irish Studies, New York, 20 April 2007.

Delaney, Enda. 'The Vanishing Irish: The Exodus from Ireland in the 1950s', in Dermot Keogh, Finbarr O'Shea and Carmel Quinlan (eds), *Ireland in the 1950s: The Lost Decade*. Cork: Mercier Press, 2004, pp.80–6.

Fleischman, Aloys. 'Music in Nineteenth-Century Ireland', in Brian Boydell (ed.), *Four Centuries of Music in Ireland*. London: BBC Books, 1979, pp.39–44.

Gedutis, Susan. *See You at the Hall: Boston's Golden Era of Irish Music and Dance*. Boston, MA: Northeastern University Press, 2004.

Hickey, Anne. 'Where Hallinan Met Her Knight'. *Irish Herald/ New Irish Gael*, April 2000, p.14.

Keane, Chris. *The Tulla Céilí Band: A History and Tribute*. Shannon: McNamara, 1997.

Kenny, Kevin. *The American Irish: A History*. Harlow: Longman, 2000.

Keville, Claire. 'A Style Recorded – A Sense of Time and Place'. MA thesis, University of Limerick, 2000.

Kostinen, David. 'Dealing with Deindustrialization: Economics, Politics, and Policy during the Decline of the New England Textile Industry, 1920–1960'. *Journal of Economic History*, vol. 60, no. 2 (June 2000), pp.501–4.

Mac Aoidh, Caoimhín. *Between the Jigs and the Reels*. Manorhamilton: Drumlin Press, 1994.

McCullough, L.E. 'Irish Music in Chicago: An Ethnomusicological Study'. Ph.D. dissertation, University of Pittsburgh, 1978.

Miller, Rebecca. 'Irish Traditional and Popular Music in New York City: Identity and Change, 1930–1975', in Ronald H. Bayor and Timothy J. Meagher (eds), *The New York Irish*. Baltimore, MD: Johns Hopkins University Press, 1996, pp.481–507.

Moloney, Mick. 'Irish–American Popular Music', in J.J. Lee and Marion R. Casey (eds), *Making the Irish American: History and Heritage of the Irish in the United States*. New York: New York University Press, 2006, pp.381–405.

Ní Fhuartháin, Méabh. 'O'Byrne DeWitt and Copley: A Window on Irish Music Recording in the USA, 1900–1965'. MA thesis,

University College Cork, 1993.

Ó hAllmhuráin, Gearóid. *A Pocket History of Irish Traditional Music.* Dublin: O'Brien Press, 1998.

—— 'Old Age Pipers and New Age Punters: Irish Traditional Music and Musicians in San Francisco, 1850–2000', in Donald Jordan and Timothy J. O'Keefe (eds), *The Irish in the San Francisco Bay Area: Essays on Good Fortune.* San Francisco, CA: ILHS, 2005, pp.108–30.

Ó Donnabháin, Barra. 'An Ceol Traidisiúnta sna Catskills'. *Treoir, Iris Oifigiúil Chomhaltas Ceoltóirí Éireann*, vol. 34, no. 2 (2002), pp.42–3.

Richards, Rand. *Historic San Francisco: A Concise History and Guide.* San Francisco, CA: Heritage House Publishers, 1991.

Smith, Graeme. 'My Love is in America: Migration and Irish Music', in Patrick O'Sullivan (ed.), *The Irish World-Wide: History, Heritage, Identity*, vol. 3, *The Creative Migrant.* Leicester: Leicester University Press, 1994.

Vallely, Fintan (ed.). *The Companion to Irish Traditional Music.* Cork: Cork University Press, 1999.

Williams, William H.A. 'Irish Song in America', in Michael Glazier (ed.), *The Encyclopedia of the Irish in America.* South Bend, IN: University of Notre Dame Press, 1991, pp.474–8.

INTERVIEWS

Original recordings, transcripts or field notes of all interviews are in the possession of the author.
Michael Preston, Ennis, 29 August 1983.
Jimmy Ward, Miltown Malbay, 7 July 1986.
Jimmy Leydon, Ennistymon, 4 March 1988.
Mike McHale and Jack Coen, New York, 12 July 1996.
Barra Ó Donnabháin, New York, 5 February 1997.
Mary Keating, New York, 18 July 1998.
Marty O'Keefe, Rochester, NY, 20 February 1999.
Martin Mulhaire, New York, 14 June 2001.
Michael Preston, New York, 14 June 2001.
John O'Neill, New York, 19 April 2007.
Jack Whelan, Long Island, NY, 19 April 2007.
Felix Dolan, New York, 17 July 2008.
Barbara MacDonald Magone, San Francisco, 2 August 2008.

Playing 'Irish' Sport on Baseball's Hallowed Ground: The 1947 All-Ireland Gaelic Football Final

SARA BRADY

INTRODUCTION

On 14 September 1947, at the Polo Grounds in the Harlem section of New York City, Cavan beat Kerry 2–11 to 2–7 in an exciting contest commentated by the renowned Irish sports broadcaster Micheál ÓHehir, who successfully (and famously) bargained at the last minute for an extension to the pre-booked broadcast in order to finish out the match. Played in commemoration of the hundredth anniversary of the 1847 beginning to Irish famine emigration, the 1947 All-Ireland is not only a unique historical event in Irish history, but also a critical moment in postwar Irish America. The logistics of such a performance indicate a strong attachment to Ireland. The game, orchestrated and financed in part by a group of Irish–American power brokers in New York City that included John 'Kerry' O'Donnell, further evidences the assertion of a specifically Irish identity during a time in the United States that most scholars associate with assimilation. The 1947 All-Ireland transformed the performance space of the Polo Grounds – a baseball diamond better known for the 'American' prowess of Bobby Thompson and Willie Mays – into an 'Irish' place for a day. This chapter analyses the combination of factors contributing to the success of the event, including the tenure of New York's Irish-born mayor, Bill O'Dwyer, and investigates how this match, a previously under-researched historical event in Irish–American history, used the performance of sport to distinguish Irish ethnicity in late 1940s New York.

In 1976 the well-known sports commentator Micheál Ó Hehir described for RTÉ audiences the suspenseful end of the 1947 All-Ireland Gaelic football final. Despite booking in advance radio lines from 2 to 5 p.m. that hot Sunday afternoon at New York's Polo Grounds, Ó Hehir explained,

> between bishops and mayors ... being introduced to the teams, and being introduced to the crowds, things ran late ... and as we approached five minutes to five ... I began quite innocently saying if there's anybody along the way there listening in just give us five minutes more and I kept begging for this ... and whether it was that somebody along the way heard the appeal ... the five minutes was left on and the entire All-Ireland final from the Polo Grounds was heard here in Ireland. It was the first time that I felt that I was doing something special for ordinary people in Ireland ... I was the link between home and this game. It gave me kind of a feeling of importance that I hadn't really felt before and made me realize in some way that, well, I was ... part of the country if you like and the reaction of the people in Ireland to the efforts that particular day that did give me a feeling of being somewhat of an ambassador.
> (Ó Hehir, 'This Game Is Not Over Yet', RTÉ, 15 February 1976)

Ó Hehir's plea – coming at a moment when Cavan, the ultimate victors, were just one point ahead – made that September broadcast the most well known in his career. His description years later captures more than the excitement of the last few moments of the game: it marks the documentation of a unique performance in the history of sport in Ireland and in the United States. Specifically, the 1947 All-Ireland Gaelic football final represents a key event in Irish America and Irish New York in particular. Unlike the centuries-old New York Saint Patrick's Day parade, in which proverbial wisdom claims 'everyone is Irish for a day', during the 1947 All-Ireland a 'bit of ould sod was transplanted' (Daley, 'It Was a Great Day for the Irish', p.22) from Ireland. On 14 September 1947 an export of expressive culture, having travelled by ship and by plane, filled a particularly 'American' space – the Polo Grounds – making the stadium 'Irish' for a few hours.

'THE WISH OF MANY PEOPLE, TO VIEW AN ALL-IRELAND,
CAME TO PASS'

In his welcome speech at City Hall a few days before the game, the
Mayo native and New York Mayor Bill O'Dwyer touched on the cultural gravity of such an export:

> When the Dodgers win the National League ... if we were to sug-
> gest playing the World Baseball series outside Brooklyn and tak-
> ing it to Ireland or any other country I would not accept respon-
> sibility for the peace of the city. Well, that's parallel to what the
> GAA are doing in playing this great game in New York, and New
> York should be proud to welcome the generous offering of the
> best Ireland has in sport to this country.
>
>   (Cogley, '1947: History is Made in New York', p.122)

The idea of bringing the All-Ireland to the US had been proposed during
Gaelic Athletic Association (GAA) Central Council meetings several
times before. Such gestures were 'regarded as a more or less formal tribute to the work of the exiles', and not much had been made of them in
the past (ibid.). But the proposition to organize an American All-Ireland
made in the spring of 1947 by the Reverend Michael Canon Hamilton,
who represented New York at the Central Council, was indeed serious.

What could have inspired such an enormous logistical, economic,
political and cultural undertaking? One of the motivations for an
American All-Ireland was a perceived diminishment of an
Irish–American presence in the US and New York. After decades of
steady emigration from Ireland to the United States, a drastic decrease
occurred between the 1920s and 1930s. During the former decade,
more than 211,234 Irish came to the US; in the 1930s the net flow
amounted to only 10,973 (*Yearbook of Immigration Statistics*, p.13).
Since the onset of the Great Depression, with Irish immigration practically halted, attendance at Gaelic games in New York had plummeted,
and control over the Bronx-based headquarters of the New York Gaelic
Athletic Association, Innisfail Park (now Gaelic Park), had to be relin-
quished to its lessor, the City of New York. John Byrne writes the history of the New York GAA during the pre- and post-World War Two era
with hints of drama: 'There had been no immigration for a decade and
hence no new athletic material. The Second World War was draining off
the younger Gaels and the games were at a low ebb. However, even during these trying years the championship competitions continued'
(Byrne, 'New York G.A.A.', p.11).

The sense that the games would be 'lost' permeated the mindset of GAA enthusiasts in the city. Near the end of the war, in 1945, John 'Kerry' O'Donnell became the new long-term landlord at Innisfail and a key player in the New York All-Ireland project: 'the GAA again had a park solely for its own use. Everyone was working and immediately things were looking up' (ibid.). As the 1940s wore on, the 'Irish situation' continued to improve: in contrast to the dearth of new Irish over the 1930s, immigration doubled over the next ten-year period to 19,789 (*Yearbook of Immigration Statistics*, p.13). It was the beginning of a 'great new era' for the New York GAA despite the 'nucleus of the GAA' being made up of 'American-born Gaels' (Byrne, 'New York G.A.A.', p.11).

Wary of such optimism, the association 'needed some big event to re-arouse interest in it' (ibid.). Canon Hamilton made his intentions clear at the Easter 1947 Central Council meeting. His speech appealed, by 'recall[ing] the horrors of the Famine' (Comerford, 'Some Unusual Facts', p.135), to the emotional connection between Ireland and the United States: 'It would be great,' he reasoned, 'if the descendants of these unfortunate Irish, who were kith and kin, could see an All-Ireland Football Final in America during 1947 which would be around the one hundredth anniversary of their forefathers in America' (ibid.). Hamilton's initial formal plea was unsuccessful, however, and the 'matter was put back and Congress adjourned until after a match at Croke Park' (Cogley, '1947', p.122). The GAA had, and arguably still has, a rocky relationship with the New York board. Despite the reality that emigration to the US had allowed the Gaelic games a parallel development on both sides of the Atlantic since the founding of the GAA in 1884, the Dublin Central Council maintained the GAA priorities of keeping the Gaelic games 'Irish' and resisting affirmation of GAA activity in the Irish diaspora.

However, a subsequent effort to pass the motion to hold the football final abroad was more successful. At a GAA meeting weeks after Canon Hamilton's initial plea, according to *Irish Independent* journalist Mitchell Cogley, 'a Clare delegate, seconding the motion, proceeded to wring the withers of all present by reading a letter in which the pleas of a New York exile were so heart-rending that only the hardest of hearts went untouched and the motion was passed by a substantial majority' (ibid.). The letter, pleading that first-, second- and third-generation Irish Americans have the chance to witness an All-Ireland, was later revealed to be fake, written by the delegate who read it out (GAA, '1947-Final in the Polo Grounds'). There was an overall feeling that the endeavour might not actually happen. Cogley recalls, 'What a thoroughly unlikely event this was!' (Cogley, '1947', p.122). GAA historian Marcus de Búrca explains that to many 'the idea of playing what had become the biggest national sports event of the year outside the country bordered on the unthinkable' (GAA, '1947-Final in the Polo Grounds'). The Central Council considered the games played abroad to be of a substandard quality. Even though the proposal grew out of a desire to support waning Irish sports in the United States, some 'GAA members with no [American] connections were naturally unenthusiastic [and] doubted if Gaelic games there merited support from home' (ibid.). Alternative arguments were made for the deep desire for 'exiles' to be able to see an All-Ireland and the 'possible effects on the average Gaelic spectator, who would now be deprived of the customary climax to his seasonal championship fare' (ibid.). Cogley adds: 'there was much dissatisfaction that the Gaels at home were to be deprived of what promised to be a great final' ('1947' p.122). However, due to the efforts of mostly men on both sides of the Atlantic, '[t]he wish of many people, to view an All-Ireland, came to pass' (Byrne, 'New York GAA', p.11).[1]

SOME BY AIR, SOME BY SEA

Once the Central Council confirmed the decision to hold the 1947 football final in New York, teams rallied for the chance to participate. 'With such a goal, there was no way Kerry could be stopped' beating Cork and Meath while 'emergent Cavan were on the march and came out of Ulster, dethroning Antrim' and defeating Roscommon in the semi-final (Cogley, '1947', p.122). GAA general-secretary Paddy O'Keeffe, whose efforts would in the end prove the most crucial of those involved, travelled to New York months in advance to begin preparations for the event. In early September 1947 the Cavan and Kerry Gaelic football teams, accompanied by managers, officials and journalists, travelled by boat and by plane to New York to play what would be the only All-Ireland football final played on non-Irish soil. Passengers on the *Mauretania*, which arrived in New York on 8 September from Southampton via Cobh, included fourteen players (half from Cavan, half from Kerry) and eleven GAA officials ('14 Players Here for Gaelic Final', *New York Times*, 9 September 1947, p.45). Frank Durkan, who happened to emigrate on the same ship, recalled the excitement felt throughout the week-long crossing; 'being on that particular boat was a huge source of pride for a young Irish immigrant' (interview with author, 7 May 2003, New York).

Although some from each team flew and some sailed, more Cavan players ended up on the 22-hour air journey, arriving sooner (and better rested) than most of the Kerry contingent. On the TWA Skymaster were players, GAA administrators, RTÉ's Micheál Ó Hehir, Mitchell Cogley and Anna Kelly of the *Irish Press*. Cogley remembers being 'more than mildly surprised to find her a traveling companion on this assignment for she really didn't know the difference between a full forward and a left hook' (Cogley, '1947' p.122). In a condescending tone that affirms the decidedly masculine achievement of the 1947 project, Cogley's contribution to the 1976 commemorative history of the New York GAA assured readers that it 'transpired of course that her visit was socio-political, and only coincidental with major business' (ibid.). Kelly's presence, however, is a refreshing reminder of the ultimate cross-gender popularity of the Gaelic games, despite the century-old desire of the GAA to fix Irish manhood to Irish sport.[2]

Patriarchy, as it turns out, played a crucial role in the staging of the 1947 All-Ireland. Several events centred around the male-dominated political and religious machine of Irish New York occurred around the match, organized in large part by Mayor O'Dwyer's office and later John 'Kerry' O'Donnell, including a mayor's welcome at City Hall, where the New York police band 'thundered out' *It's a Great Day for the Irish* (Cogley, '1947', p.122). After O'Dwyer's reception a 'cavalcade of thirty cars, accompanied by motor cycle police with sirens blaring' made their way 'through streets lined with cheering thousands from City Hall to the Roosevelt Hotel for the official banquet' attended by 1,500 (de Búrca, *GAA: A History*, p.182). On the morning of the match, a high mass was held at St Patrick's Cathedral, after which Mayor O'Dwyer and key GAA figures were given an audience with Cardinal Spellman of New York and received his blessing. The teams, delegates and fans then headed for the upper reaches of Manhattan: the home of the New York Giants baseball team, the Polo Grounds.

BASEBALL'S HALLOWED GROUND

The unusually named Polo Grounds was famous for its unique horseshoe shape and short foul-line distances. The site was originally located near the north-east corner of Central Park at the end of the nineteenth century, the only era during which the grounds were actually used for polo. During the 1880s the bleachers were known as 'Burkeville', after baseball star Eddie Burke (Bensberg, 'Eddie Burke's Death', p.6), and had a reputation for its Irish immigrant fans (Rader, *Baseball*, p.41) and for gambling (Coffey, *27 Men Out*, p.40). In 1889 the grounds relocated to Coogan's Hollow at 155th Street and 8th Avenue. The Hollow was below Coogan's Bluff, 'a massive edifice ... tucked in between the Harlem River and a lofty outcropping of mica schist' (Thornley, *Land of the Giants*, p.3). A 1911 fire necessitated rebuilding, and in 1923 further renovation expanded seating capacity to 56,000.

The Polo Grounds became the site of many key moments in baseball. It provided a home for the New York Giants until they moved to San Francisco in the late 1950s, and hosted two Negro League World Series in 1946 and 1947. Babe Ruth hit his first out-of-the-park home run at the Polo Grounds in 1920, and in 1951 the famous 'miracle of Coogan's Bluff' happened when New York Giant Bobby Thomson hit a homer (the 'shot heard 'round the world') that secured the pennant play-off game against the Brooklyn Dodgers. It was there, too, that Willie Mays made his legendary catch during the eighth inning of the first game of the 1954 World Series. The Polo Grounds was also home to the expansion team New York Mets for a few years in the early 1960s before the completion of Shea Stadium. Fans either loved or hated the Polo Grounds. Though it was popular because it was accessible by public transport, many fans disliked the fact that they often had to peer around obstructing pillars to watch a game. Others loved the free view found from above looking down over the field. The Polo Grounds more successfully inspired future stadium design than it boasted innovation itself. Still, for decades – before the Giants played their last game in 1957 and before demolition in 1964 to make room for apartment buildings – it remained a cornerstone of New York baseball, as well as of occasional other events including college and professional football (hosting the New York Giants and Jets), soccer, boxing, and even rodeo, opera and religious rallies. It was, in short, a key venue in New York's public life.

CAVAN ACHIEVES THE 'SEEMINGLY IMPOSSIBLE' (QUINLAN,
'CAVAN'S GREAT VICTORY', *IRISH PRESS*, 15 SEPTEMBER 1947)

'On the day of the match,' Judge James J. Comerford wrote, 'The Polo Grounds looked like a replica of Croke Park in Dublin. The GAA President, Dan O'Rourke of Roscommon, smiled the smile of satisfaction as he sat in the Main Box with all the GAA Officials of both countries and with the American dignitaries of Church and State' ('Some Unusual Facts', p.135). Wedger Meagher reported in the *Daily Mirror* that 'The scene at the Polo Grounds was the realization of an Irishman's Dream with the teams led on to the field by a Police Band and massed Pipers, marching round the pitch while the crowd cheered' ('Donoghue the Babe Ruth of Gaelic Football', *Irish Press*, 16 September 1947). Mayor O'Dwyer, who 'could have run for re-election' (Daley, 'Great Day for the Irish', *New York Times*, p.22) that day, was set to throw in the first ball ('50,000 Will Watch Irish Final Today', *New York Times*, p.S3). In the stands were 34,941 spectators – an impressive number, but fewer than expected, and a figure that later reports would subsequently exaggerate to 50,000.[3]

Arthur Daley explained in the *New York Times* the unusual ritual of playing both the Irish and American national anthems before the game: this 'unexpected thrill … more than ever happens before a baseball game', Daley wrote, describing how the 'assembled Celts, with song in their hearts to start with, began to hum the melody and then the rich, full tune leaped forth from their throats in pulse-stirring fashion' ('Great Day', p.22). The 'Star-Spangled Banner' merely 'rang loud and clear' according to Daley. The Polo Grounds, it seems, shed a bit of its purely 'American' associations around baseball and football, taking on 'Irish' feel for the day through the energies generated by the performance of sport as well as song and spectatorship by fans in the bleachers.

The weather was distinctly *not* Irish, however. In blistering heat, Kerry opened with a lead on the bone-dry pitch. Kerry was the favourite; they were reigning champions and had secured the most All-Irelands to date. Cavan had only won two championships in its history, the last in 1935, and was the decided underdog. 'The Kerrymen started out as though they were going to blow Cavan right off the field' (Daley, 'Great Day', p.22). In the first half the score was 10–2 to Kerry, and, to paraphrase 'Casey at the Bat', it looked extremely rocky for Cavan – an allusion that may have been in the mind of a later versifier who composed a poem titled 'The Polo Grounds':

> We waited with fast beating hearts while Kerry did attack
> And we applauded bold Brian Reilly when he set the leather back
> But Kerry kept the pressure up and we were feeling blue
> When at half time the Kingdom were leading 10 to 2.
> (Cavan P&B Association, '150th Anniversary Program')

Perseverance seemed to pay off: by the second half Cavan was in the lead, with Paddy Donohue, 'the Babe Ruth of Gaelic football', showing his skill with eight points – inspiring Arthur Daley to describe him as 'the Dead-Eye Dick with his kicking' ('Great Day', p.22). Louis Effrat likened Cavan's passing techniques to basketball, and they worked, leaving Kerry to 'storm ... to the attack in a desperate closing effort, which was futile' (Effrat, 'Donohue's 8 Points Pace 17–13 Victory', *New York Times*, p.22).

Although it seems natural for US sports writers to make comparisons to more familiar games – the *New York Times*, for instance, described the game as 'Ireland's counterpart of our world series' ('50,000 Will Watch Irish Final Today') – the press seemed astonished by what they saw as the violence of the game and the subsequent fairplay attitude once it was over. 'The busiest man on the field,' according to Daley, 'was Dr Thomas G. Dougherty ... the official physician'. Daley found 'more violence' in the game 'than you'd find in a game between Army and Notre Dame', despite the fact 'that Gaelic football is what would technically be described as a non-contact sport' ('Great Day', p.22). Effrat called the game 'fast and rough', describing Gaelic football as a sport that 'might be termed legalized homicide'. Noting the 'furious action' of the match, Effrat continued:

> Apparently on the theory that anything – or nearly everything – goes, the gladiators ripped into each other at every turn, resulting in frequent spills, harder, it appeared than those witnessed in American football contests. Even the fans who were unfamiliar with the sport were thrilled by the speed, stamina and finesse of the visiting athletes. (Effrat, 'Donohue's 8 Points', p.22)

Equally surprising, however, to Effrat, was the fact that 'no one lost his temper, and at the finish, there was plenty of handshaking'. Daley writes, 'Hibernians who'd just spent sixty minutes knocking the bejabbers out of each other, rushed over, not to throw one final punch, but to shake hands in congratulation, magnificent gestures of sportsmanship.' His compliment, however, takes on a slightly more insidious tone when he reveals his expectations: 'Actually there wasn't one punch tossed all afternoon, an extraordinary circumstance when you consider that thirty Irishmen on the same playing field generally are expected to get involved in some sort of Donnybrook' ('Great Day', p.22).

The commentary of these journalists can be taken either as the observations of curious spectators more familiar with the official and unofficial rules of other, 'American' sports; or as offensive stereotyping. Interestingly, Daley's distinction between the 'normal' and 'Irish' crowds reinforces the idea that for a day the psychic space of the Polo

Grounds took on some 'Irishness': 'At the end the Irish bagpipers struck up "Wearing of the Green". And the crowd milled about the field, uninterested in heading for the exits as normal sports crowds do, but talking excitedly in lilting tones about the great game they had watched' (ibid.). Daley conveys the sense of an Irish crowd having the *craic* – having that kind of fun known only to the Irish – in a city known in this period for being a melting pot, a site within which immigrants tended more toward assimilation than distinction.

EXPORTS AND PROFIT

Although it can be argued that the game infused a sense of the Irish taking over a highly American and a very New York-specific perform-ance space for a day, it is interesting to note the extent to which the original impetus for the match – the commemoration of the Great Famine – was downplayed. Throughout the publicity and coverage of the event, references to the Famine remain vague, generalized and underemphasized. Instead, the idea of export and profit as benefits of the project seem to outweigh any Famine memorial.

An image that remained with James Comerford from the day GAA secretary Paddy O'Keeffe and others boarded the ship bound for the return trip to Ireland after the final was that of O'Keeffe proudly walking

> up the gang plank. He carried a very large suit case in each hand. Dollar Bills, packed tightly, filled each suit case – to the brim. Behind Paddy walked other GAA Officials. Each man also car-ried a large suitcase also packed with Dollar Bills. In the cold and unsentimental language of the Science of Economics, Ireland had exported one of her greatest treasures and her most cherished sporting event – the All-Ireland Final – to America and in return had received back plain and raw Dollar Bills.
>
> (Comerford, 'Some Unusual Facts', p.135)

In 1947 the image of bags stuffed with dollar bills headed for Ireland had particular significance. After World War Two, during which Ireland remained neutral, the US aid that seemed to flow to so many countries largely avoided Ireland; 'Dollar Bills from the United States,' therefore, 'were badly needed' (ibid.). The Irish press emphasized the profits made from the game; in some ways such profits alleviated memories of much earlier disastrous 'American Invasion' conducted by the GAA in 1888, when private funds had to pay for Irish players' passage back home after bad weather and poor attendances led to GAA debt. Overall, 'the venture had succeeded in its two main objects. It attracted wide publicity in the United States and led to a revival of interest and participation in Gaelic games there'. Further, the project yielded a profit of more than £10,000, 'which enabled the central council to make a grant of £2,000 towards the promotion of the games in the United States' (de Búrca, *GAA*, p.182). But in 1947, with the war over, economic hope brewing and with the trip itself capable of being understood as somehow a mark of dissension from de Valera's insular policies, as well as of pride in the potential of Irish culture-as-export, going home with money in suitcases gave the GAA a boost – albeit a boost that would never to be topped, nor even replicated. Although the trip would be lauded by the future historian David Guiney in 1976, de Búrca's GAA history describes it as 'a unique experience that was not to be repeated', a review which emphasizes the authority of Gaelic games based in Ireland (ibid., p.206).

The Irish at home awaited the return of those who travelled, having listened to the famous Ó Hehir commentary the evening of the match. Both teams arrived home to large-scale homecoming events. In addition to receptions at Dublin's Mansion House and a welcome from Irish President Sean T. O'Kelly at Áras an Uachtaráin, players and GAA administrators found warm welcomes in their respective home towns. 'On the outskirts of Cavan town [the team was] met by thousands of cheering people and 18 bands and escorted through gaily decorated streets to the centre of town' ('Cavan's Triumphal Homecoming', *Irish Independent*, 6 October 1947). The Kerry team were also welcomed by big crowds and treated to 'a banquet and *ceilidhe*' in Killarney (ibid.).

Back in the United States, what followed was a heyday for Gaelic Park fostered by economic prosperity and increased immigration (48,362 for the years 1951–60) that lasted through the mid-1960s (*Yearbook of Immigration Statistics*, p.13). Boosted with the enthusiasm generated by having such an important event held on US soil, '[t]he cream of the crop of hurlers and footballers from Ireland were taking their places on their county teams in New York' (Byrne, 'New York GAA', p.12). By 1963 the New York teams had travelled to Ireland to play; in 1964 the Tipperary and Kilkenny hurling teams played in Gaelic Park for the New York GAA's Golden Jubilee. During the same year New York played in San Francisco, Auckland, Melbourne and Sydney, finishing their tour in Birr, County Offaly.

Later that year New York defeated Dublin at Gaelic Park, 2–12 to 1–13, a win that would cause a stir in Ireland: 'Over the years it had been traditional of home GAA officials to extol New York teams in defeat and create a controversy if New York won' (ibid., p.14). Such reactions, like de Búrca's dismissal of the historic importance of the New York All-Ireland final, raise interesting implications about the need for the Irish GAA to remain dominant over the nearly simultaneously founded United States GAA, as well as other clubs around the world.

Most important to note, however, is the moment of 'Irish America', and specifically 'Irish New York' captured on 14 September 1947. On that day Bill O'Dwyer was in the middle of his first term as mayor. Having emigrated from Bohola, Co. Mayo, in 1910, O'Dwyer symbolized the once more powerful rule over the Democratic party by the Irish. His re-election in 1949 was significant for the Irish, whose grip on the party waned by mid-century, and his professional demise after a police scandal and subsequent resignation in some ways marked the end of Irish power in the city, which by 1961 was indeed lost. (Alameida, *Irish Immigrants*, p.41). (The Irish, once the largest 'minority' in the city, and famous for their Tammany Hall tactics of offering practical help for the city's other often non-English speaking populations, eventually became just one of more than one hundred ethnicities in the greater New York City area [McNickle, 'When New York was Irish', p.338]).

Fifty years after the only All-Ireland to be held outside of the country, the New York GAA, in conjunction with the GAA's Central Council in Dublin, organized a commemorative game for the anniversary. Held in 1997 at Downing Stadium on Randall's Island in New York's East River before for a crowd of 14,000, this match was a disappointing replay of the 1947. However, instead of just radio transmission, fans were treated to live RTÉ television coverage. Predictably, 'Kerry gained some revenge for their 1947 defeat with a comfortable victory' (GAA, '1947'). The actual game, however, was merely a 'normal round of the National Football League' (ibid.) only played in honour of the Polo Grounds match. The smaller scale of the replay and its relative lack of press coverage and notoriety not only indicates the very different associations that a transatlantic cultural export had in a contemporary, globalized world, but also the significantly different place the Irish occupy, for better or worse, in late twentieth-century New York City.

REFERENCES

Almeida, Linda Dowling. *Irish Immigrants in New York City, 1945–1995*. Bloomington, IN: Indiana University Press, 2001.

Bensberg, Harvey A. 'Eddie Burke's Death'. *Sporting Life*, 14 December 1907.

Byrne, John. 'The New York G.A.A., 1914–1976', in David Guiney (ed.), *The New York Irish*. Dublin: Gaelic Press, 1976, pp.6–24.

Cavan Gaelic Football and Social Club of New York. 'The Polo Grounds'. 29th Annual Dinner Dance program, 14 December 1996. Archives of Irish America, New York University, AIA3, Series A, box 1.

Cavan Protective and Benevolent Association, Inc. 'The Polo Grounds'. 150th Anniversary program. Archives of Irish America, New York University, AIA3.

Coffey, Michael. *27 Men Out: Baseball's Perfect Games*. New York: Simon & Schuster, 2004.

Cogley, Mitchell. '1947: History is Made in New York', in David Guiney (ed.), *The New York Irish*. Dublin: Gaelic Press, 1976, pp.122–4.

Comerford, James J. 'Some Unusual Facts about Past Gaelic Games in America', in David Guiney (ed.), *The New York Irish*. Dublin: Gaelic Press, 1976, pp.131–5.

Daley, Arthur. 'It was a Great Day for the Irish'. *New York Times*, 15 September 1947, p.22.

De Búrca, Marcus. *The GAA: A History*. Dublin: Gill & Macmillan, 2000; first published 1980.

Effrat, Louis. 'Donohue's 8 Points Pace 17–13 Victory'. *New York Times*, 15 September 1947.

GAA. '1947-Final in the Polo Grounds'. Cumann Lúthchleas Gael official website, www.gaa.ie/page/1947_final_in_the_polo grounds. html (accessed 23 August 2007).

Guiney, David (ed.). *The New York Irish*. Dublin: Gaelic Press, 1976.

McNickle, Chris. 'When New York was Irish, and After', in Ronald H. Bayor and Timothy J. Meagher (eds), *The New York Irish*. Baltimore, MD: Johns Hopkins University Press, pp.337–56.

Ó Hehir, Micheál. 'This Game Is Not Over Yet'. RTÉ Libraries and Archives, 15 February 1976. http://www.rte.ie/laweb/ll/ll_t07g.html (accessed 15 February 2008).

Quinlan, A.P. 'Cavan's Great Victory Over Kerry'. *Irish Press*, 15 September 1947.

Rader, Benjamin G. *Baseball: A History of America's Game.* Champaign, IL: University of Illinois Press, 2002.

Robinson, Ray. *The Home Run Heard 'Round the World: The Dramatic Story of the 1951 Giants–Dodgers Pennant Race.* New York: Harper Collins, 1991.

Thornley, Stewart. *Land of the Giants: New York's Polo Grounds.* Philadelphia: Temple University Press, 2000.

United States Citizenship and Immigration Service (USCIS). *Yearbook of Immigration Statistics, 2003.* Washington, DC: US Government Printing Office, 2004.

'14 Players Here for Gaelic Final'. *New York Times*, 9 September 1947, p.45.

CHAPTER THREE

'The Irish Movement in this Country is Now Moribund': The Anti-Partition Campaign of 1948–51 in the United States

TROY D. DAVIS

In the aftermath of World War One, Irish–American agitation against a continued Anglo-American alliance in peacetime was intense. Millions of Irish Americans, responding to Irish republican propaganda, mobilized in support of the nationalist cause in the 1919–21 Irish War of Independence. Ultimately, their campaign cooperated with the larger isolationist movement in America and helped to scuttle President Woodrow Wilson's internationalist foreign policy, which depended for its success upon close cooperation between the United States and the United Kingdom. As the Second World War came to an end in 1945, it was a matter of near certainty among American and British diplomatic observers in Ireland that leading Irish political figures, especially Eamon de Valera, had plans to imitate the nationalist successes of a quarter-century earlier by launching a postwar campaign against Irish partition, which would include an American component. Some of those diplomatic observers, basing their reactions on the earlier post-World War One experience, feared that such a campaign might do real and lasting damage to Anglo-American relations. David Gray, US minister to Ireland during World War Two, was foremost among the alarmists. Other American and British foreign policy-makers, more familiar with postwar conditions in the United States itself, were less concerned about the potential impact of such an anti-partition campaign. They believed Irish Americans of the late 1940s were much less interested in conditions in Ireland than their counterparts of the late 1910s and early 1920s had been. A survey of visits to the United States by politicians – both nationalist and unionist – from Ireland and Northern Ireland during the anti-partition campaign of 1948–51 indicates that the latter group of policy-makers was essentially correct. Deep-seated social and political changes that had taken place in the United States between the end of World War One and the end of World War Two made the postwar Irish–American community much less receptive to Irish nationalist appeals than their counterparts of a generation earlier.

In the summer of 1945, when World War Two ended, the diplomatic relationship between the US and Ireland was as strained as it had ever been in the quarter-century of the smaller state's existence. The United States, of course, was one of the three main Allied powers in the conflict, while Ireland, under the leadership of Taoiseach and Minister for External Affairs Eamon de Valera, followed a policy of neutrality. Relations between belligerents and neutrals in time of war are almost always delicate, but the fact that Ireland had long had a difficult relationship with the United Kingdom, the United States' closest World War Two ally, made Irish–American relations especially so. The thorniest issue in Anglo-Irish affairs during the war, as it had been since the early 1920s, was the partition of the island of Ireland into two political entities: the six-county province of Northern Ireland, a part of the United Kingdom; and the twenty-six-county state of Ireland. The Irish government's dissatisfaction over partition gave its relations with the Allied side in World War Two a particular edge when specific points of contention arose, such as Irish resistance to British demands for naval bases in the Twenty-Six Counties early in the conflict and Dublin's protest against the stationing of US servicemen in Northern Ireland beginning in early 1942.

The predictable strains arising from the two nations' different responses to the war are only part of the story. A much more specific factor lay behind many of the complications in the relationship between the two countries as it stood in 1945: namely, the role that David Gray played as wartime American minister to Dublin. Gray brought a decidedly undiplomatic spirit to his position as the head of the US Legation in Ireland, regularly seeking to undermine the international standing of de Valera and his government. Most notably, he helped create the myth that the German Legation and the Japanese consulate in Dublin were spy nests that endangered Allied military plans in Europe; formally requested that the Irish government take the unneutral step of shutting down those missions and expelling the

Axis representatives working there; and then made sure that the American press gave wide publicity to the Irish refusal to accede to the request (Dwyer, *Strained Relations*, pp.118–27, 134–37; Dwyer, *Irish Neutrality and the USA*, pp.190–5).

Gray took this antagonistic approach to his job during World War Two due largely to his understanding of Irish and American history in the aftermath of World War One. In Gray's view of that history, Woodrow Wilson's internationalist plans for securing a lasting peace following the war, which depended in large part on the creation of a successful League of Nations, had been upset by a coalition of Irish-American isolationists in the wake of the Anglo-Irish War. Another ingredient in Gray's understanding of the breakdown was the central place of Eamon de Valera, whom Gray believed had played a crucial role in converting most Irish Americans to isolationism and had thus destroyed Wilson's grand design for a stable world. Without too much exaggeration, it might be said that Gray believed World War Two had, to a large degree, been the fault of Eamon de Valera. The minister therefore did everything in his power to discredit de Valera in the eyes of Irish Americans and other Americans during the global conflict that ended in 1945 (Dwyer, *Irish Neutrality and the USA*, pp.162–8).

Specifically, Gray was convinced that the taoiseach had plans to launch an anti-partition campaign in the United States after the war. It was in order to head off this threat to the postwar order that Gray had sought so single-mindedly during the war to undermine the image of Ireland and its leader in the United States, especially among Irish Americans. As events unfolded in the later 1940s and early 1950s, Gray's predicted anti-partition campaign would come to pass. His fear that the campaign might pose a serious threat to the Anglo-American relationship proved misplaced, however, as the American minister's belief that de Valera might succeed in working up Irish–American hostility to the 'special relationship' between the United States and the United Kingdom turned out to be grossly mistaken.

The campaign in the US did not begin immediately after the war, as Gray had anticipated. There was in America between 1945 and 1948 some anti-partition activity, but it was low-key in nature and received only scant publicity. It consisted largely of petitions by such groups as the American Association for the Recognition of the Irish Republic (an organization that de Valera had formed during his 1919–20 US tour) and the American League for an Undivided Ireland. The petitions were generally addressed to the State

Department or White House, and called on the US government to promote Irish unification. The petitions always received the State Department's standard response to such requests: while US officials appreciated the petitioners' views on the matter, the 'altering of political boundaries between Ireland [Éire] and Northern Ireland, which is part of the United Kingdom, is not a matter in which this Government might properly intervene' (John J. Reilly to James F. Byrnes, 8 August 1945; Alger Hiss to Reilly, 18 September 1945). For the most part, officers of the State Department did not believe such communications reflected any widespread sentiment. As John D. Hickerson of the department's European Division informed Gray in October 1945, when reporting an increase in the number of letters the department was receiving concerning partition, the general feeling among officials was that the domestic pressures previously associated with the Irish question would 'never be as heavy as in the past' (Hickerson to Gray, 30 October 1945).

During the 1945–8 period as well, anti-partition activities in the United States did not receive the active encouragement of the Irish government. What support such activities did get in Ireland generally came from more radical nationalist organizations, such as the Irish Anti-Partition League, a group founded by nationalists in Northern Ireland in late 1945. For example, Denis Ireland, a Northerner who travelled to the US in the spring of 1947 in an attempt to garner Irish Americans' support for the anti-partitionist cause, was a member of the League. The group also played an active role in an Irish Race Convention held in New York in September 1947, while the Irish Legation in Washington kept the Convention and its proceedings at arm's length (US Legation in Dublin to Secretary of State, 16 June 1947; Chancery of British Embassy in Washington to Foreign Office, 26 December 1947).

In 1948 the situation changed and the more active anti-partition campaign long foreseen by Gray – complete with the Irish government's official involvement – was inaugurated. (In the summer of 1947, Gray had been replaced as minister to Ireland by George Garrett.) The onset of the campaign was triggered by events in Irish politics, particularly the general election of February 1948, in which de Valera's Fianna Fáil party was driven from power for the first time since 1932. The Fianna Fáil government was replaced by the first interparty government of 1948–51, a coalition of five disparate parties held together primarily by their desire to oust de Valera from office. De Valera, thus, traded the position of taoiseach for that of leader of the opposition. The new taoiseach was Fine Gael's John A. Costello, and de Valera's successor as Minister for External Affairs was Seán MacBride, the leader of the new Clann na Poblachta party, which hoped to replace Fianna Fáil as the premier party of constitutional republicanism in Ireland. The political dynamics of this change in government had the effect of reigniting the partition question as a live issue in Irish affairs. On the one hand, the achievement of unification was the Clann na Poblachta party's *raison d'être*, and MacBride was therefore determined to raise the issue. Just as important, Fianna Fáil – with its leadership of constitutional republicanism at risk – responded to the challenge by calling for an end to partition more forcefully than it had done in many years. As Lord Rugby, the British Representative in Ireland, put it, 'each party must now outdo its rivals in a passionate crusade for Irish unity' (Bowman, *De Valera and the Ulster Question*, pp.267–9).

It was de Valera, now out of office, who fired the first salvo of the anti-partition campaign in the United States when he travelled to that country to spread the unification message in March 1948, just a month after his party's defeat in the general election. At least two factors made such a move politically attractive to the Fianna Fáil leader. First, de Valera was by far the best-known Irish political figure in the United States, having toured the country extensively during the interwar years. Second, his sixteen years as Minister for External Affairs convinced many Irish voters that he knew better than any other Irish leader how to deal with the rest of the world. The effect of the US trip on the thinking of the Irish electorate was almost certainly the most important motivation behind de Valera's decision to launch the campaign, as his rhetoric during the US visit was served up primarily for home consumption in Ireland. As an American diplomat put it in a report to Secretary of State George C. Marshall, de Valera was above all a politician, and his campaign abroad was merely 'the best way to practice his trade' at the time (ibid., p.274).

As de Valera's tour of the United States proceeded, this assessment of the political motives behind the visit was borne out, as was John D. Hickerson's earlier assertion that American interest in Irish affairs would never be as heavy as in the past. The tour opened in New York City on March 9 with a parade for the Irish leader from the Battery to City Hall. Sir Frank Evans, the British consul-general in New York, reported to Lord Inverchapel, the British ambassador to Washington, that the atmosphere of the parade was enthusiastic but seemed to lack the warmth shown to many other foreign visitors after

World War Two. In his review of US press coverage of the event, Evans noted that most American reporters who interviewed de Valera seemed at least as interested in Ireland's wartime neutrality – and its possible neutrality in the future – as they were in partition. Evans concluded that it seemed clear, based on de Valera's reception, that the mass of Americans were no longer very interested in Irish affairs and that only a small number of 'fanatical' Irish Americans continued to believe Britain was still hostile to Ireland. At any rate, he concluded, it seemed that the Irish were no longer in a position, as they had been in 1920, to work up hostility to the United Kingdom over Irish domestic affairs. Thus, it seemed very unlikely that de Valera's tour would have any meaningful impact on the degree of Irish–American influence in the United States (Evans to Inverchapel, 11 March 1948).

The Fianna Fáil leader's anti-partition rhetoric became more heated as his tour continued; but, in keeping with the political strategy behind the tour, his statements received more press coverage in Ireland than they did in America itself. Nor did the ratcheting up of de Valera's verbal onslaughts against the border seem to do much to alter the relative lack of interest in the issue among Irish Americans. Commenting on the tour to the Commonwealth Relations Office near the end of March, for example, Lord Rugby (who during the war had shared Gray's alarm over anti-partitionism's potential to disrupt Anglo-American relations) wrote that, while he would never suggest that an Irishman could forget, it did appear that Irish Americans at least were 'slightly less frenzied' than they had been in the past (Rugby to Machtig, 30 March 1948). Lord Inverchapel agreed. In two reports to British Foreign Minister Ernest Bevin regarding the tour, which ended on April 9, the ambassador concluded that aside from a few Irish–American groups, Irish politics had ceased to be much of an issue in the United States. Certainly, Inverchapel was satisfied that the visit would have no meaningful effect on official American policy. Though de Valera had met with both President Harry Truman and Secretary of State Marshall near the beginning of the tour, de Valera himself had publicly described his talk with Truman as nothing more than a 'friendly chat', while Marshall told reporters after his conversation with the former taoiseach that they had discussed no political questions (Inverchapel to Bevin, 9 April, 16 April 1948). Even David Gray, who had retired from his diplomatic career, shared the sanguine British assessment. Writing to Rugby two weeks after de Valera's 1948 trip ended, Gray noted with satisfaction that his old nemesis had not created the anti-British maelstrom Gray had feared. 'You know what an alarmist I have been about Irish influence in this country in creating opposition to yours,' the former minister wrote. 'Well I now believe it is negligible and will remain so while Britain follows the line she is pursuing towards us and the rest of Europe' (Gray to Rugby, 21 April 1948). De Valera's plans for World War Two seemed to be coming to naught – due, no doubt, in large part to Gray's own diplomatic prowess during World War Two.

The fact that the Fianna Fáil chief's American tour received much more press coverage in Ireland than it did in America did not escape the notice of the new Irish government. As Norman Archer, secretary of the British Representative's Office in Dublin, reported to another British diplomat two weeks into the tour, the most noteworthy effect de Valera's increasingly strong pronouncements against partition had on politics in Ireland was to force the interparty government to say more about the issue than it likely had any desire to say (Norman Archer to Ben Cockram, 23 March 1948). Predictably, that political dynamic led members of the coalition government itself to become involved in the anti-partition campaign, including its American dimension. Not surprisingly, the government minister who took the most active role in the campaign was Seán MacBride. As minister for external affairs, both the border and Irish–American relations fell under MacBride's purview, and as leader of Clann na Poblachta, his nationalist ideology was more pronounced than that of his government colleagues. In a demonstration of the political impact of de Valera's American tour, MacBride made his first major statement on how the partition question might relate to his government's policies *vis-à-vis* the United States on 10 March 1948, just the second day of his political rival's trip. In particular, MacBride commented on how the division of Ireland might affect the Dublin government's response to the Marshall Plan. Speaking with what he claimed to be full government authority, MacBride said he found it difficult to be enthusiastic about any plan for European economic recovery that did not treat Ireland as a single economic entity. That pronouncement led the State Department to instruct George Garrett, Gray's successor as American minister to Dublin, to advise MacBride that Washington disapproved of such attempts to link the Marshall Plan, which the department was then attempting to shepherd through Congress, with 'Ireland's purely domestic political problem of partition' (Davis, *Dublin's American Policy*, pp.122–3).

Such criticisms from American officialdom point up what was

clearly a political advantage for de Valera during the anti-partition campaign. Safely out of power between 1948 and 1951, de Valera enjoyed relatively more freedom than did his opponents in government. He was able, during his stay in the US, to impress Irish voters by making strong statements on the issue of the border without having to take responsibility for his nation's foreign policy. Though de Valera's successors in government did not have that luxury, the leaders of the interparty ministry did undertake their own missions to America in order to demonstrate to the Irish electorate that they were equally committed to working for a united Ireland. Thus, Seán MacBride made three trips to the United States during the coalition's tenure in office, and Taoiseach John A. Costello made one, MacBride's visits occurring in May–June 1948, April–May 1949, and March–April 1951; and Costello's in August 1948. In each instance, the two ministers actively presented the anti-partition case in public addresses and press conferences, but for the most part they were more circumspect than de Valera had been in his pronouncements.

Perhaps because of this comparative caution on the part of Costello and MacBride – plus the fact that de Valera was always something of a *bête noire* in the eyes of the British establishment – none of their forays to America received anything like the scrutiny from British officials that de Valera's trip did. Nor did any of their trips lead to any revision of the general British opinion that postwar Irish–American interest in Ireland's political affairs was close to extinction. For example, the British Embassy in Washington, in a report to the Foreign Office on MacBride's tour of 8 April–2 May 1949, noted that not one Boston newspaper provided any editorial comment on MacBride's appearance in that heavily Irish–American city. Embassy staff also reported that in the other cities he visited, including Washington DC, Chicago, Los Angeles, San Francisco and New York, the Minister for External Affairs was met by unenthusiastic Irish–American audiences and hostile press questioning over Ireland's plans not to join the anti-communist alliance created by the North Atlantic Treaty, which was signed just a few days before MacBride's arrival. The report concluded with the typically dismissive British judgment that 'The attitude of Southern Ireland [sic] during the war, taken in conjunction with their present inability to face up to political realities, form a background against which it would be almost impossible to resurrect any widespread feeling or sympathy in this country for the Southern Irish [sic] cause.' The North American Department of the Foreign Office found this analysis of the situation 'reassuring' (British Embassy Washington to Foreign Office, 6 June 1949; North American Dept of Foreign Office to Chancery, 17 June 1949).

The conviction on the part of British diplomats and policy-makers that few Irish Americans maintained any burning interest in Irish political issues finally led the British to encourage the most intriguing visit by a politician from the island of Ireland to the United States during the entire anti-partition campaign of 1948–51: that of Northern Ireland Prime Minister Sir Basil Brooke, who spent more than a month in the US in April and May 1950. British officials explicitly referred to this visit by a leading unionist figure as an 'experiment' designed to test the depth of Irish–American support for the nationalist position in the partition controversy.

The history behind the British decision to encourage Brooke's visit to the US provides an instructive look at the evolution of the United Kingdom's strategy for dealing with the partition controversy in America. Before de Valera's 1948 American visit, partition was not a live issue in the United States, and the official British attitude was that it was in the interest of Northern Ireland and the United Kingdom as a whole to keep it that way by 'letting sleeping dogs lie'. That was the Foreign Office's advice to Prime Minister Brooke, for example, in June 1946, when the Ulsterman proposed that Northern Ireland's agent in London be sent to the US to publicize the fact that his province was politically separate from the rest of Ireland and had *not* been neutral during World War Two. Foreign Office officials explained to the prime minister on that occasion that such a mission would almost certainly do more harm than good, as it might revive American involvement in Irish affairs. The British Embassy in Washington, for example, considered that it was 'sheer wishful thinking on the part of the Northern Ireland government to imagine that they would do their cause in the United States any good by accentuating the political fact of partition'. Doing so would merely make the issue a topic of debate, so any propaganda campaign by the Northern Ireland government itself would be 'disastrous'. In the face of such strong objections, Brooke abandoned his 1946 proposal (Evans to Nevile Butler, 22 June 1946; Butler to Evans, 31 July 1946; Chancery, British Embassy Washington, to North American Department, Foreign Office, 23 September 1946).

Three years after its rejection of the prime minister's original suggestion, however, the Foreign Office encouraged a publicity campaign in the United States by Sir Basil himself. In June 1949 Brooke reported to the British home secretary that the Ulster–Irish Society of New York had invited him to be its guest of honour at the organization's annual banquet in the spring of 1950. Brooke and his colleagues in the Northern Ireland cabinet were unanimous in their opinion that the premier should accept the invitation. Because such a visit to the United States might affect Anglo-American relations, the Home Office asked the Foreign Office for Foreign Minister Bevin's reaction to the proposed visit. The Foreign Office's response to this proposed trip was markedly different than its reaction to Brooke's 1946 suggestion. On this occasion the North American department of the office reported to Sir Oliver Franks, Lord Inverchapel's successor as UK ambassador in Washington, that 'as a result of the noisy propaganda of the many American–Irish societies which represent, if anything, the view of the Irish Republican Government [Ireland formally became a republic in April 1949], the Northern Irish case has largely gone by default' (Broad to Franks, 7 May 1949). The department, therefore, believed that Brooke should be encouraged to speak at the banquet and, if possible, at other American venues. Ambassador Franks, again in contrast to Lord Inverchapel's position in 1946, agreed with the recommendation, as did Foreign Minister Bevin, and the Foreign Office's views on the matter were forwarded to the Home Office on July 7 (Kinna to Nunn, 7 July 1949).

Clearly, the Foreign Office's about-face on the wisdom of publicizing the unionist position on partition in the United States represents a major shift in official British thinking on the question between 1946 and 1949. By June 1949, when Prime Minister Brooke expressed his interest in travelling to New York, the anti-partition campaign had been in operation in the United States for more than a year, and Irish nationalist politicians had made four relatively high-profile visits to the United States. In each instance, British officials were convinced that such agitation in the United States had failed to strike a chord with most Irish Americans. Thus, as the Washington Embassy reported to the Foreign Office in December 1949, the Embassy still believed that Irish Americans who were interested in partition had failed to gather any real momentum behind their cause, and they thought it unlikely that anti-partitionists' reaction to a trip by Prime Minister Brooke could be 'mobilized into an effective movement' (Chancery, British Embassy Washington, to North American Department, Foreign Office, 15 December 1949).

This confidence was borne out by Sir Basil's visit and the Irish-American responses to it. To be sure, Brooke's tour did generate protests in some quarters. In New York, for example, Mayor William O'Dwyer announced to a Saint Patrick's Day gathering a few weeks before the prime minister's arrival in America that Brooke would be welcomed to City Hall over O'Dwyer's dead body (qtd in Franks to Bevin, 2 June 1950). Such protests, however, were not common. Only a handful of demonstrators met Brooke's plane when he began his visit to America with a brief lay-over in New York on 6 April 1950, and none at all were on hand when he flew on to Washington later that day. In Washington between April 7 and 11, Brooke attended a number of social and ceremonial functions, including a conversation with Secretary of State Dean Acheson, an informal press conference with journalists at the British Embassy (during which Ambassador Franks was pleased by the vagueness with which the prime minister answered the reporters' questions), and commemorations of the US military presence in Northern Ireland during World War Two. The stay in the capital concluded with Brooke's address to a sparsely attended meeting of the National Press Club (Franks to Bevin, 2 June 1950).

Following the events in Washington, Brooke returned to New York for a week-long visit, which Major C.B. Ormerod, the British Information Service (BIS) representative there considered an 'outstanding success' despite the initial forebodings raised by Mayor O'Dwyer's remarks. At a luncheon arranged by BIS the premier presented the unionist view of Northern Ireland's historical position to a group of carefully selected journalists, and afterwards, an NBC correspondent asked him to give a radio address for that network the following weekend. At the Ulster–Irish Society dinner that had originally occasioned the prime minister's visit to the US, Sir Basil spoke extemporaneously and received a standing ovation. Although approximately a thousand demonstrators turned out to protest against Brooke's appearance, Ormerod noted that not a single New York newspaper printed a picture of the demonstrators, a fact that he characterized as 'unprecedented'. Besides these public appearances, Sir Basil was also invited to a number of private functions in New York, where he met influential journalists and political figures; for instance, the newspaper columnist Dorothy Thompson held a small party for the premier, which her well-known colleague George Sokolsky also attended. Bernard Baruch, the noted American financier and statesman, later 'damned the Mayor most heartily' – sentiments that Thompson would also express in her column (C.B. Ormerod to Controller, BIS, 21 April 1950).

Following the New York leg of his journey, Brooke spent three days in Philadelphia, where he addressed a number of civic and academic audiences, and after a private trip to see friends in North Carolina between April 22 and May 2, he went on to Chicago, the last stop of his American visit. There, in contrast to the prime minister's experience in New York, Irish–American mayor Martin Kennelly received Brooke at City Hall; he was also entertained by Robert McCormick, the publisher of the *Chicago Tribune*. Though McCormick had a past reputation as being anti-British, his friendliness on this occasion was underlined by what Ambassador Franks called a 'remarkable' editorial in the *Tribune* condemning the bad manners of 'professional Irishmen' like Mayor O'Dwyer. As in Philadelphia, Brooke spoke before a number of civic organizations in Chicago. He then spent the final weekend of his stay in America in Springfield, Illinois, as the guest of Governor Adlai Stevenson. According to Ambassador Franks, Brooke was not the target of any demonstrations at all in Chicago, a surprising fact considering the heavy Irish–American presence in that city. The Northern premier ended his month-long stay in the US on May 8, when he left Illinois for further touring in Canada (Franks to Bevin, 2 June 1950).

The official British response to Brooke's American tour was overwhelmingly positive, as Ambassador Franks's report of 2 June 1950 to Foreign Secretary Bevin on the trip makes quite clear. 'Considered in retrospect,' Franks wrote,

> I think the Prime Minister's visit shows a clear balance on the profit side and has proved a most interesting experiment in testing out, and in showing the shallowness of, the Irish movement in the United States today ...
>
> In the two or three weeks since Sir Basil Brooke left the United States, there has been nothing to suggest that the after-effects of his visit will be to promote a general revival of interest in the partition question. In my opinion the fact that he should have been able to carry out a successful visit to such cities as New York and Chicago, without meeting with any significant opposition, is ample proof that the Irish movement in this country is now moribund. (Ibid.)

Clearly, Franks's assessment of Brooke's stay in America reflects a certain bias on the partition question, but it also seems to be a reasonably accurate evaluation, based on Brooke's actual experiences in the US. Long predisposed to believe that they had little to fear from anti-partitionist activity in America, British officials now had what seemed to be fairly hard evidence that their judgment was correct.

What finally brought the campaign to a decisive end was yet another change in the electoral fortunes of Eamon de Valera. Just as de Valera's loss of power in February 1948 had led to the inauguration of the campaign, his return to power led to its conclusion. De Valera became taoiseach again following the Irish general election of May 1951. One of the most noteworthy results of that election was a considerable decline in support for MacBride's Clann na Poblachta party, which saw its representation in the Dáil go from 10 seats to 2. Thus, one of de Valera's major political objectives in kicking off the campaign – to defend Fianna Fáil from MacBride's upstart republican party – had been achieved.

Once safely back in office, de Valera and his Fianna Fáil colleagues allowed the anti-partition campaign to dissolve. John Bowman has aptly characterized the 1948–51 period as a 'distinct phase in the history of partition', during which propaganda had been tried and found to be of limited efficacy (Bowman, *De Valera and the Ulster Question*, p.275). De Valera himself admitted as much to the Dáil in July 1951, when he acknowledged that he had no solution to partition; he was also quick to point out, however, that none of his opponents had any solution, either (*Dáil Eireann Parliamentary Debates, Official Report*, vol. 122, 19 July 1951, col. 2024). The Fianna Fáil chief was able to avoid any political embarrassment over this admission because all of Ireland's major political parties, including those of the first interparty government, had participated in the anti-partition campaign. Thus, de Valera himself could not be singled out for blame now that the campaign had failed. As for the vestiges of anti-partitionism among those Irish Americans who did take an interest in the issue, by October 1951, British officials were dismissing the cause as one generally considered a 'bore or a joke' in the United States (Notes on Interdepartmental Meeting at the Home Office, 25 October 1951).

The anti-partition campaign of 1948–51 failed to garner meaningful Irish–American support for two major reasons. First, a foreign policy consensus existed in the United States during the immediate postwar period. Most Americans of that era, including Irish Americans, rejected the isolationism that had characterized US policy between World Wars One and Two, and indeed believed that American isolationism had helped contribute to the outbreak of World War Two. The onset of the Cold War reinforced this acceptance of an expanded world role for the United States, as most Americans saw Soviet actions after World War Two as a threat to peace. They therefore accepted such internationalist initiatives as the Truman Doctrine, the Marshall Plan, and the creation of NATO as means by which the US could, and should, lead the anti-communist West in an effort to 'contain' the expansion of Soviet-style communism. In all of these Cold War initiatives, Britain was a chief ally of the United States, just as it had been during the Second World War. Thus anti-partitionist efforts to pressure the US government into supporting Ireland – which had been neutral in World War Two and which refused to join the NATO alliance in 1949 – in its territorial dispute with the United Kingdom were destined to fail. The few Irish Americans who took the anti-partition campaign seriously therefore had no political partners to support their position, as Irish–American opponents of the League of Nations had had in 1919–21.

The second explanation for the campaign's failure to attract widespread support in the US relates to changes that took place in the Irish–American community's sense of itself and its interests between the aftermath of World War One and the early Cold War era. Several historians of Irish America, including Thomas Brown, Lawrence McCaffrey, Francis Carroll and Joseph P. O'Grady, have argued that the earlier generation of Irish Americans had taken such an intense interest in political affairs in Ireland for reasons related to their own lives in the United States. Specifically, they had pinned their hopes for greater prestige and respect in America on the achievement of Irish independence, reasoning that, if the Irish in Ireland gained self-government, then the lot of the Irish in America would improve as well. The Irish would no longer be servile subjects of the British Empire, but citizens of a free and sovereign nation, and the status of their cousins in America would rise accordingly. The achievement of practical independence for twenty-six of Ireland's thirty-two counties in 1921 seemed, to most Irish Americans, to be the culmination of their fight for acceptance in American society. The failure of the post-World War Two anti-partition campaign to attract widespread support in the Irish–American community suggests that by the late 1940s and early 1950s a large degree of political assimilation had taken place among most members of that community (Davis, *Dublin's American Policy*, pp.89–94).

It should be noted, however, that there are other forms of assimilation than purely political assimilation. This analysis of the anti-partition campaign should not be taken as an indication that postwar

Irish America had been assimilated in every sense of the word. Nor should the campaign's lacklustre reception in the US be taken as evidence that Irish Americans of the early Cold War era no longer had any sense of an Irish–American identity that set them apart from their countrymen. The American and British diplomats and policy-makers were not particularly interested in such abstract notions as 'identity' or 'assimilation'. Their only concern was with anti-partitionism's potential to disrupt Anglo-American relations; once they were satisfied that the campaign's potential was limited in that regard, their interest in the nature of postwar Irish America essentially ceased.

REFERENCES

Bowman, John. *De Valera and the Ulster Question, 1917–1973*. Oxford: Clarendon Press, 1982.

Carroll, Joseph T. *Ireland in the War Years, 1939–1945*. Newton Abbot, Devon: David & Charles, 1975.

Dáil Eireann. *Parliamentary Debates, Official Report*. Vol. 122. Dublin: Stationery Office, 1951.

Davis, Troy D. *Dublin's American Policy: Irish–American Diplomatic Relations, 1945–1952*. Washington, DC: Catholic University of America Press, 1998.

Dwyer, T. Ryle. *Irish Neutrality and the USA, 1939–47*. Dublin: Gill & Macmillan, 1977.

Strained Relations: Ireland at Peace and the USA at War, 1941–45. Dublin: Gill & Macmillan, 1988.

Fisk, Robert. *In Time of War: Ireland, Ulster, and the Price of Neutrality, 1939–45*. Philadelphia: University of Pennsylvania Press, 1983.

ARCHIVAL SOURCES

DF   Decimal Files
DO   Records of the Dominions Office
FO   Records of the Foreign Office
NAK   National Archive in Kew, Richmond, Surrey
NAW   National Archives, Washington, DC

John J. Reilly, American Association for the Recognition of the Irish Republic, to James F. Byrnes, Secretary of State, 8 August 1945; Alger Hiss, State Department, to Reilly, 18 September 1945, State Department Decimal File 841D.00, NAW.

John D. Hickerson to David Gray, 30 October 1945, DF 711.41D27, NAW.

Evans to Nevile Butler, Foreign Office, 22 June 1946; Butler to Evans, 31 July 1946; Chancery, British Embassy Washington, to North American Department, Foreign Office, 23 September 1946, FO 371/51741, NAK.

Dispatch, 'Intensified Press Campaign to Keep "Partition" Before the Public', US Legation in Dublin to Secretary of State, 16 June 1947, DF 841D.00, NAW.

Dispatch, Chancery of British Embassy in Washington to Foreign Office, 26 December 1947, Foreign Office Group 371, File 68045E, NAK.

Secret Letter, Evans, British Consulate-General New York, to Lord Inverchapel, British Embassy Washington, 11 March 1948, DO Group 35, File 3928, NAK.

Confidential Letter, Norman Archer to Ben Cockram, United Kingdom Delegation to the United Nations, 23 March 1948, DO 35/3928, NAK.

Secret Dispatch, Lord Rugby to Sir Eric Machtig, Commonwealth Relations Office, 30 March 1948, DO 35/3928, NAK.

Confidential Dispatch, Inverchapel to Ernest Bevin, 9 April 1948, DO 35/3928, NAK; Confidential Dispatch, Inverchapel to Bevin, 16 April 1948, FO 371/68045E, NAK.

Gray to Rugby, 21 April 1948, FO 371/68045E, NAK.

Confidential Dispatch, Chancery of British Embassy Washington to Foreign Office, 6 June 1949; North American Department of Foreign Office to Chancery, 17 June 1949, FO 371/74190, NAK.

Sir Basil Brooke to Home Secretary, 23 June 1949; J.J. Nunn, Home Office, to P.F. Kinna, Foreign Office, 1 July 1949; Philip Broad, Foreign Office, to Sir Oliver Franks, 5 July 1949; Memorandum, R.A. Beaumont, Foreign Office, to Ernest Bevin, 5 July 1949; Kinna to Nunn, 7 July 1949, FO 371/74190, NAK.

Confidential Letter, Chancery, British Embassy Washington, to North American Department, Foreign Office, 15 December 1949, NAK.

Confidential Political Report, Major C.B. Ormerod, New York Office, British Information Service, to Controller, B.I.S., 21 April 1950, FO 371/81648, NAK.

Confidential Letter, Franks to Bevin, 2 June 1950, FO 371/81648, NAK.

Notes on Interdepartmental Meeting at the Home Office, 25 October 1951, DO 35/3922, NAK.

PART TWO
RESPONSES TO SOCIAL CHANGE

'Hibernians on the March': Irish–American Ethnicity and the Cold War[1]

MATTHEW J. O'BRIEN

Although Irish America occupies a central place within the Irish diaspora, its relationship with Ireland itself is a complicated one. For many American academics, Irish–American ethnicity is merely a superficial ascription and Irish heritage is an option rather than an origin. In the end, social-scientific adherents of the 'ethnic fade' thesis have concluded that the passage of time dilutes the accuracy, or even sincerity, of traditional identification.[2] But dismissing Irish Americans on the basis of insufficient 'authenticity' misconstrues the essence of ethnicity itself, which is not based on resisting assimilation, but assisting the integration of past traditions with contemporary influences. By understanding the way in which successive generations reinterpret the ethnic past in light of the present, we are afforded a Janus-faced view of Irish heritage.

This double-insight proves especially important in understanding the popular redefinition of Irish–American ethnicity during the late 1940s and 1950s. As American energies passed almost immediately from the Second World War to the Cold War, American thinkers and leaders took up a paradoxical quest: fashioning a national ideology for a people stubbornly proud of their pragmatism. Standing in contrast to the racial and ideological conformity imposed by the National Socialists and Bolsheviks, the result was an emotive celebration of tolerance and integration, summarized in the patriotic identification of the United States as 'a nation of the immigrants'.[3]

This national movement held particular importance for Irish–American Catholics. As expatriate commitment to Irish nationalism ebbed, Americans of Irish–Catholic descent instead celebrated

their immigrant appreciation of America and prior service as champions of religious pluralism. While Irish anti-communism rested firmly
in the hands of the clerical authorities, the Irish–American laity took
the lead in the US, arguing for a more pluralistic faith that champi-
oned the respective rights of all religions in their collective battle
against atheistic Bolshevism. These years, and this new cause, were
especially important for the pre-eminent Irish–Catholic organization
at the time: the Ancient Order of Hibernians (AOH). During the late
1940s and early 1950s a new generation of Hibernian leadership
exchanged a parochial purpose for a civic mission. In the process the
AOH not only redefined their own institutional identity, but also
helped to change the religious self-conception of their adopted nation
as a whole.

THE EARLY ROOTS OF THE HIBERNIANS IN THE UNITED STATES

The roots of the Ancient Order of Hibernians go back nearly 180
years, to their role in providing Irish–Catholic immigrants with spiritual assurance, material assistance and even physical defence. The first
North American chapters appeared during the 1830s as an offshoot of
the Irish AOH, clinging to a defensive outlook that gained strength
with the upsurge in Irish sectarianism during the early nineteenth century (O'Dea, *History of the Ancient Order of Hibernians*).[4] Greeted
with nativist mobs upon their arrival in cities such as Boston, New
York and Philadelphia, the Hibernian commitment to self-defence
became even more central in the United States.

As overt nativism died down during the mid-nineteenth century,
the AOH turned from physical defence to upward mobility. The
growing organization shed its secretive tone to take a more respectable
role as a mutual-aid society for Irish–Catholic immigrants and their
families. In 1851 the AOH began to advertise in Irish–American ethnic newspapers, announcing public meetings, and two years later the
organization sought official incorporation from the County of New
York as 'a society for benevolent and charitable purposes' (ibid,
pp.14–15, 17). As they grew, the AOH seems to have swallowed up
smaller groups including the Hibernian Universal Benevolent Society,
the Hibernian Benevolent Burial Society and the Independent Sons of
Erin, with a new emphasis on self-reliance rather than self-defence
proclaimed to public audiences by signs that declared: 'We relieve our
sick and bury our dead' (Ridge, *Erin's Sons in America*, p.29). When
the storm of controversy over the Molly Maguires broke out in the

1870s, Hibernian leaders disavowed the secretive group and indignantly protested that their true mission was to 'promote friendship, unity, and true Christian charity among its members, by ... the maintaining of the aged, sick, blind, and infirm members, and for no other purposes what ever' ([New York] *Irish–American*, 26 February 1876, ibid., p.40).

The events of the early twentieth century, however, seemed to deprive the Hibernians of their purpose and by the eve of the Second World War the organization was on the brink of collapse. Not only had the Great Depression curtailed the Irish immigrant flow to the United States, robbing the AOH of new members, but economic desperation in North America had also culled current members from the ranks, as members dropped out and entire chapters folded. Even the national programmes for recovery seemed to hasten the demise of the AOH, as the new federal social security provisions rendered Hibernians' mutual aid programmes redundant.

The presidential addresses delivered at national conventions in cities such as Providence, Buffalo, and St Paul repeated the same disheartening theme of failed recruitment programmes and accumulating back-dues. The prognosis given by National President Michael Donohoe at the Fifty-Fifth National Convention in 1927 was grim:

> Never before were such liberal inducements held out for organizing work as those offered by our National Board in July 1925 and again in August 1926. In fact, some were fearful lest the amount of bonuses to be paid would impair our treasury and yet the results have been disappointing. The best we can claim for the bonus plan is its economy ... Every fraternal organization is finding it difficult to maintain – much less increase – its numerical strength. (*Proceedings of the Ancient Order of Hibernians 55th National Convention*, pp.27, 53)

Further evidence came from the flagging circulation of the organization's membership publication, the *National Hibernian*. AOH membership, measured by the self-reported circulation statistics of the organization's newspaper fell steadily after the First World War. Membership reports in 1927 showed a decrease of more than 10 per cent during the 1926 calendar year, with the loss of 3,600 members and the suspension of 2,500 in Pennsylvania and Massachusetts alone (Ayers & Sons, *Directory of Newspapers and Periodicals*).

The economic collapse of the Great Depression, with its particularly drastic effect on Irish–American networks, produced a free fall in

Hibernian membership. The circulation of the *National Hibernian* fell from 89,000 in 1929 to 48,090 three years later, at which point the paper scaled back to a bi-monthly publication schedule. This decline continued through the early 1930s as the chronic effect of the Depression took hold, and by 1935 the *National Hibernian* admitted that its readership had fallen to only 35,800 – about one-third of the level in 1929 (ibid.). The effect was particularly acute on the state level, as membership fell by more than three-quarters in fifteen states, including most of the Midwest. Despite an increasingly lenient treatment of chapters owing back dues, total membership continued to plummet until only an estimated 20,000 members were left on the eve of the Second World War. Franklin Roosevelt's social security programme rendered the Hibernians mutual-aid provisions obsolete, and the organization seemed to be destined for extinction.[5]

IRISH–AMERICAN ETHNICITY AND POSTWAR AMERICAN IDENTITY

The Second World War had a particularly beneficial effect on American popular conceptions of Irish ethnicity. Irish Americans enjoyed the widespread praise given to prominent members of their community such as Audie Murphy, the most highly decorated veteran of the conflict. At the same time, due to earlier work by Irish Americans as champions of an ethnic nationalism that would soon replace the previous, more Anglocentric model of American national self-identity, the general trend toward celebration of immigrant heritage offered an even more important endorsement of Irish America.

This popular appreciation is most clearly illustrated in the various depictions of Irish Americans as 'representative Americans' in scientific studies and history textbooks in the years immediately following the Second World War. For Milton Barron, a leading expert in the burgeoning field of American immigration and assimilation, the timing of the Irish arrival in the United States best explained this ethnic leadership. Barron described Americans of Irish descent as 'historically "mean" and culturally and demographically "median"'. The introductory role played by Irish Americans in the adaptation of numerous ethnic groups in the United States, previously criticized as interfering or cabalistic, now seemed much more benevolent and charitable given Barron's emphasis on Irish–American 'intermediacy' (Barron, 'Intermediacy: Conceptualization of Irish Status in America', p.257). Postwar accounts of American immigration history also identified the Irish as quintessentially American. A textbook edited by Francis

Brown and Joseph Roucek, *One America: The History, Contributions, and Present Problems of Our Racial and National Minorities* (1945), prominently featured the contributions of Irish–American soldiers during the Second World War in its discussion of the Irish in the United States. A.J. Reilly's summary of Irish Americans put to rest nativist charges of political conspiracy through his description of the 'decline in political influence and importance of Irish Americans' (Reilly, 'Irish Americans', p.48). But Reilly still identified them as the archetypal patriotic immigrants:

> A sense of finality attended their departure from their native land. They entered the United States as permanent citizens and spent themselves with incomparable prodigality in the service of the land they adopted as their own ...Their interest in the land of their forefathers is largely sentimental and entirely secondary to their primary interest, the United States of America, to which they have given much and received much in return. (Ibid., pp.50–1)

There was, however, some resistance to the growing status and influence attributed to Irish–American Catholics in postwar America. Louis Adamic, an American left-wing social reformer, also devoted considerable space to the Irish in his work on immigration and American society, *A Nation of Nations*. But Adamic departed from its generally appreciative tone of immigrants when he arrived at the Irish in the United States. With a critique based on a series of 1944 articles by Paul Blanshard published in the *Christian Century*, his critique of Irish ethnicity took a sectarian air as he insisted that authoritarian tendencies of Irish–American clerics placed them and their followers on the wrong side of the fight between democracy and totalitarianism. In an ironic foreshadowing of Senator Joseph McCarthy's later allegations, Adamic worried aloud about the influence of 'hundreds of Catholics' in the State Department, especially since 'most of these are Irish Catholics'. He also noted the Irish backgrounds of 'nearly all the bishops and priests and laymen Fey cites as heading the various Catholic projects and movements' (Adamic, *Nation of Nations*, p.340).[6]

THE COLD WAR AND THE REBIRTH OF THE AOH

Despite Adamic's protests, the widespread acclamation of Irish–American patriotism during the war and afterwards offered new opportunities for Americans of Irish descent. The AOH response to these changed political circumstances represented a marked departure from the previous mission of the organization. Loyally Catholic, the Hibernian organization enjoyed proven credentials in the fight against communism, and the leaders of the AOH soon resumed an intense campaign against American communists and supposed fellow-travellers. Within a year of the Japanese surrender, the national AOH convention passed a resolution that vowed to protect the United States from the 'Red termites of American communism' by 'removing every red Fascist and communist fellow traveler from all government agencies, all schools, and all labor unions in the United States of America' (*Irish World*, 3 August 1946, p.4). Postwar priorities even took precedence over the traditional references to Irish heritage, as the first resolution from the 1946 national conference identified the organization as 'intensely loyal to the rights of God and church and country [and] uncompromisingly loyal to the Constitution, Laws, and Government of the United States of America' before it mentioned 'the welfare of the Irish Race' and 'Hibernian ideals' (ibid.).

Although the vehemence of such statements might seem surprising, the postwar campaign to revive the AOH went beyond red-baiting. By the late 1940s several important leaders within the AOH seemed to have understood the need to redefine their institution within the more confident pluralism of postwar America. While Irish–American newspapers returned to the vitriolic isolationism of the late 1930s, the postwar leadership of the AOH embraced a new prospect of Irish–American civic leadership as a revitalizing force for the institution.

As their name would suggest, postwar accounts of the Ancient Order of Hibernians continued to refer to the centuries-old AOH legacy that extended back to medieval Ireland. Alongside these well-worn clauses, however, appeared a new call to action. These articles, columns and features not only focused on Irish–American interests (to the near exclusion of Irish events), but also consciously discarded the provincial isolationism of the 1930s for a more dynamic spirit that confidently asserted the natural role of Irish–American leadership within a pluralistic postwar America.

The key element to this redefinition of the AOH was through a new postwar recruiting campaign. As National Secretary Thomas Rogers observed in 1947, the AOH was changing, with more than three-quarters of the membership 'Americans of Irish descent' (rather than immigrants). But this was no mere demographic condition, as

Rogers declared the centrality of an indigenous American ideology as well: 'The Ancient Order of Hibernians is an American organization, dedicated to the support and protection of American institutions and the American way of life. Its officers are mostly composed of native Americans' (*Hibernian Digest*, January/February 1947, p.1).

The new recruitment programme involved two separate literary approaches. The first came in the pages of a new bi-monthly publication for AOH members, the *Hibernian Digest*. The inaugural issue noted the obvious problem of declining membership, from the four-year hiatus in organization and recruiting during the Second World War. Yet the publication's tone soon presented a new imperative for increasing membership with the assertion that 'the Irish American stands today as this nation's foremost advocate of tolerance between all peoples and creeds' (ibid.).

Hibernian recruiters found this new theme a successful one. The *Hibernian Digest* announced increasing enrolment, and at the same time it took care to further articulate the Irish–Catholic contribution to fostering American pluralism. It regularly carried news of the formation of new chapters of the AOH throughout the late 1940s, culminating in the declaration of a record class of new members initiated in May 1951 (*Hibernian Digest*, May/June 1950, p.1). Writers and editors issued regular explanations that portrayed Irish Catholicism within the light of American pluralism. In December 1947 the *Digest* published an article endorsing the Freedom Train, followed by a declaration that 'the bigot, the anti-Catholic, the anti-Semite, the anti-Protestant, the anti-Hindu, the anti-Moslem, all those who deny the spirit of Christ are to blame for the confusion' (p.5). Another editorial told readers, 'Don't Poison Yourself', announcing the emergence of 'American Brotherhood Week' to combat the 'evils of intolerance, racial and religious' through the words of 'the distinguished Yale writer and critic, Dr Henry Seidel Canby'. Later the *Digest* quoted George Reilly's acclamation of the Hibernians 'as defenders of our free institutions and opponents of bigotry in all its insidious forms'. Increasing membership, however, was essential, and for that the AOH must '[sign] up qualified community leaders throughout the community' (*Hibernian Digest*, October 1949, p.1).

In fact, there were even several remarkable instances when the editors of the *Digest* called for readers to remain considerate of the fears and anxieties of their former adversaries. An editorial that announced the settlement of a dispute between Francis Cardinal Spellman and Eleanor Roosevelt included an exceptional call to avoid ruffling

Protestant feathers: 'In the face of the growing number of conversions to the Catholic Church and its increasing prestige, a certain amount of uneasiness has developed among non-Catholics. To reassure our Protestant friends of our intention of abiding by the letter and spirit of the constitution is a task that requires a great deal of tact and understanding.' The *Digest* even repeated the *Catholic World*'s call to 'handle this Church–State question with a sympathetic understanding of the non-Catholic mind than with a belligerent antipathy'. Furthermore, in a notice of Paul Blanshard's anti-Catholic work, the *Digest* covered its obvious distaste with the pronouncement that 'We luckily have a democratic system under which all subjects can be discussed freely. Even those who deplore Mr Blanshard's words, and attack his opinions vigorously should defend his right to speak' (*Hibernian Digest*, March/April 1954, p.8).

The other voice of change within the Hibernians came in the form of the publication of the first written membership manual in the history of the order. Written by George Reilly, it explained the basis for a recruitment drive that carefully balanced the Hibernians' pride in their tradition with the immediate demands of the postwar fight against communism. In his foreword Reilly explained the ostensible need for such a document:

> Previously, we have depended upon the veteran members of the order to act as mentors and instructors to the new members, but in recent years it has been drawn to my attention by deputy organizers and Division officers that nowhere did we have in compact form a book or manual which a recruit could read in a single evening and from it gain an insight into the background and traditions of the Order he had just joined. (Reilly, *Hibernians on the March*, p.11)

Yet Reilly's manual went beyond a simple summary of pre-existing policy. Images of constancy and respect for tradition were accompanied by an anxiety about the postwar world. The manual's introduction began with the declaration that 'The world of the atom bomb presents a sad and sorry picture of mental bewilderment and spiritual hunger.' Just a few sentences later a bold-typed paragraph announced that 'Christian civilization is reaching the crossroads where a struggle with the rival is inevitable. In the clash, there can be no neutrality for Christianity is at stake' (ibid., p.17).

Such bold proclamations about the fate of the world were new material for the Hibernians, but for Reilly the fight against communism breathed new life into this ancient institution: 'In this struggle, it is imperative that we of the Irish strain know our ideals and our heritage: and here in America Ireland's historic stand is nobly expounded by the Ancient Order of Hibernians.' Reilly began his 'Blueprint for the Future' with a return to the atmosphere of alarm, reminding readers of his introductory statements that 'Christianity stands today at a crossroads', with 'the choice at the moment ... between Christ and anti-Christ' (ibid., p.1). Reilly explained that Irish–Catholic culture stood alone in its survival, compared to the ancient cultures of the Babylonians, Assyrians, Chaldeans and Egyptians. Meanwhile, the inheritors of the Greek culture were 'menaced by the forces of the anti-Christ', while Italian attempts to revive Roman grandeur under Mussolini's paganism left the Vatican as 'an island of faith and sanity in a sea of disillusionment and distrust'.

With so many former lights extinguished, Reilly established that the Hibernians were being called on to play a new role with an expanded mission. The AOH was more important than ever, since, in his words, 'It is one which can save the world and preserve us here. It battled and it conquered the pseudo-cultures of the past; it is full of energy and youth for the battle of the future ... We Hibernians must rally to this glorious command' (ibid., p.54).

Such a charge effectively redefined the institutional responsibility of the AOH. Reilly returned to the Hibernian motto of 'Friendship, Unity, and Christian Charity' in defining 'Our Program', but the raised stakes meant that 'we must be broad ... loving not merely our own members but all God's children, irrespective of their race, unmindful of their color, regardless of their creed' (ibid., p.55). The order to mobilize came as a stark contrast to the previous role of the Hibernians as a mutual assistance society. As Reilly declared: 'our program includes undying opposition to the dictatorships of all varieties and vigorous championship of all the democratic freedoms'. The new crusade pertained to 'every person, not only in own country but all over the world' (ibid., p.56).

The new manual effectively replaced the outdated foe of Protestant nativism with a threat that demanded the attention of the entire nation: the 'Anti-Christ' of communism. Reilly was certain of two things. The first was the need for the AOH to take new steps to expand its membership: 'If we Hibernians are to avoid stagnation and desire to remain a living force to continue to grow and expand, we must make a continuous appeal to those eligible for membership in Order.' This imperative particularly concerned younger members, with the organization needing to 'serve as a rallying point for youth' in order to 'remain an effective force on the American scene' (ibid., pp.60–1).

Their vanguard position in the fight against communism convinced Reilly to widen the Hibernian mission. While prominent local chapters railed against American communists as 'Red termites', the national leadership expanded its mission with a more ecumenical approach to service, citing 'Friendship, Unity, and Christian Charity' as the 'fundamental articles of the Hibernian creed'. These articles carried a new mission that expanded beyond the more modest scope of the former Hibernian role, as Reilly pledged the organization to 'religious and civic tolerance and freedom' (ibid., p.55). Such a mission took Hibernians far beyond parish or diocesan boundaries, as such rights extended 'not only in our country but all over the world' (ibid., p.56).

This started with protests over alleged religious persecution behind the Iron Curtain, touching upon the general sympathy among anti-communists with previously maligned eastern European nationalities. Their attempt to champion the anti-communist cause also gave Hibernians new responsibilities at home, including 'relief, welfare, and memorial services and sick administrations' to non-members as well as members. In fact, Reilly identified this aspect as 'one of the strongest points of the Hibernian program'. The handbook also suggested that Hibernians assert their leadership by 'setting up forums, lectures ... [and] courses for self-advancement and advancement of our neighbors'. This wider approach even hinted at support for civil rights, as Reilly stressed the importance of also honouring 'those of other races who died to preserve the democracy and the freedom that we know today' (ibid., pp.53, 57).

Hibernians on the March also called for a new sense of fellowship among Catholic ethnic groups, identified as the pluralistic centre of American society: 'Hibernians should take the lead in civic celebrations that develop the true American way of life, celebrations such as Columbus Day, Saint Patrick's Day, and all the church holy days.' The mission even meant the sacrifice of traditional antipathies toward Britain. Although the Hibernians were strongly opposed to partition, postwar 'England' (i.e., Britain) was to be more pitied than vilified. American superpower responsibilities took precedence over retribution, and Britain was identified merely as part of an enfeebled Western Europe 'wracked by the economic ills of scarcity, underproduction, and insecurity'. Traditionally WASP institutions such as the Ivy League schools also merited Hibernian assistance, as Reilly called on members to 'aid and constantly publicize the advancement of Irish culture in American colleges and universities such as ... Harvard, Yale, Northwestern, Fordham, Michigan, and in a small way at the University of California'. The matter of Irish neutrality still stood in disfavour in the eyes of the AOH, and Reilly forcefully stated that their ancestral homeland could not afford a similar mistake in the fight against totalitarianism on the left. He announced in his introduction that 'in this clash there can be no neutrality', and later reminded the reader that as 'the choice at the moment is between Christ and Anti-Christ ... neutrality must be fictitious' (ibid., pp.17, 51, 53, 60).

Reilly emphasized the 'fertile intellects' of the 'sons of Gael', declaring that 'a distinctive passion of the Irish is their love of education' (ibid., p.46). The sectarian divisions between parochial and public schools in the United States were obscured by his boast that 'of all the nations represented in American civilization, Ireland has produced a percentage of teachers higher in proportion to their numbers than any other' (ibid., pp.47–8). The universalist ideals that provided the core for the Hibernian world-mission reflected this middle-class orientation:

> We believe every person not only in our country but all over the world has a right to religious freedom, to a good education, to the sanctity of his own home, to marry, to raise a family, to insurance against disease and disaster ... We believe in the right to work and we favor some form of job insurance. (Ibid., p.56)

POSTWAR IRISH–AMERICAN SOCIO-ECONOMIC MOBILITY

The domestic appeal to middle-class Irish America by the Hibernians took place at a fortuitous time, as millions of Irish–American families enjoyed the unprecedented socio-economic mobility that emerged after the Second World War. Memories of the Depression loomed ominously in 1945, as impatient high-school graduates initially spurned higher education to enter the job market before the return of the depressed conditions of the 1930s. Yet the surprisingly flawless transition to a peacetime economy soon boosted American economic confidence and ushered in a socio-economic 'coming of age' for Irish America. The late 1940s began a period of increasing incomes, better houses and burgeoning professional careers. These opportunities instilled middle-class values and aspirations among Irish–American families. Ideological commitments were supplemented by appreciation of a new-found economic security, and a growing share of Irish Americans eagerly embraced the postwar middle class.

American census returns show a steady rise in educational levels and occupational status for second-generation Irish Americans, as American workers enjoyed near full-employment conditions. The reversal of Depression-era joblessness redeemed the hope of American opportunity for a new generation of Irish–American workers and their families, and a prolonged period of postwar prosperity brought them within reach of such achievements as professional careers and houses in the suburbs. The old urban working-class neighbourhoods gradually gave way to a more dispersed residential pattern, sacrificing ethnic colour for privacy and convenience.

The G.I. Bill played an important role in boosting Irish–American fortunes, although this legislative provision was only one of several important factors that created the groundswell of upward mobility for Americans in the late 1940s and 1950s. Andrew Greeley's work at the National Opinion Research Center showed a sharp climb in the Irish–Catholic rates of college attendance, college graduation and white-collar employment that even exceeded the general trend toward upward mobility among Americans (Greeley, *Irish Americans*, pp.131–48). In his explanation Greeley recounted the steady rise in economic confidence and in career opportunities during the late 1940s, soon reflected in upward occupational mobility.

Prompted by postwar prosperity, increasing numbers of Irish–American families started to leave the urban neighbourhoods of their parents and grandparents for the more affluent suburbs, abandoning the ethnically concentrated city neighbourhoods for more homogenized environs (Winsberg, 'Suburbanization of the Irish in Boston, Chicago, and New York', pp.90–104). Irish–American movement into the middle class became a crucial factor in the survival, and even growth, of the middle-class Irish ethnicity promulgated by the Ancient Order of Hibernians, especially when compared to the more strident, but less successful, articulations of working-class militancy from institutions such as the *Gaelic American*, which ended a 48-year run in early 1951 after a self-destructive indulgence in Anglophobic bitterness.

CIVIC RELIGION AND IRISH–AMERICAN CATHOLICISM

The contrasting outcomes of the 1928 and 1960 presidential elections offer two significant milestones in the history of Irish Catholicism in the United States. The selection of Alfred Smith by the body of

Democratic delegates assembled at the national convention in the summer of 1928 provided an historic milestone for Irish Catholics in America. Nativist prejudices had marred the previous meeting of that body only four years before, embodied in the appearance of Ku Klux Klan marchers outside the assembly hall. Although Smith's political career came to an unwelcome end with his opponent's landslide victory that fall, the Democratic victory in the following election brought a host of Irish–Catholic political figures to the national level as part of the Roosevelt administration.

For many older Irish Catholics, Kennedy's historic victory in 1960 represented the realization of a dream deferred over thirty years before. Franklin Roosevelt drew heavily upon Smith's notions of public welfare at the federal level, and it was fitting that the young man who realized Smith's dream came from the family of Joseph Kennedy, one of the Irish–Catholic figures who benefited from the Irish–Catholic breakthrough in national politics in 1928. Smith's ideas of federal involvement in public welfare also played a seminal role in Franklin Roosevelt's New Deal programmes, which helped to redefine the Democratic party through five consecutive successful campaigns.

But the Democratic Party was not the only entity that had been defined between 1928 and 1960. In fact, a second transformation, larger but more subtle, had taken an opposite message from Smith's eventual defeat against Hoover. Irish America itself was subject to revision during the middle decades of the twentieth century, as it dropped the defensive posture that it had needed against successive generations of nativist antagonism to demonstrate a strikingly self-confident leadership role in American politics. Gone were Smith's nasal New York accent, derby and cigar, seen by some as 'provincial'. In their place was J.F.K.'s unmistakable Harvard accent, pinstripe suits and occasional sophisticated cigarette. The Kennedy campaign of 1960 by no means ran away from J.F.K.'s Irish Catholicism, with impressive and outspoken appearances in front of historical adversaries. But by 1960 Irish Catholicism in America was far more palatable for its host society, as Ireland had gone from being a geographic point of origin to an ethnic point of reference.

REFERENCES

Adamic, Louis. *A Nation of Nations*. New York: Harper & Bros, 1944.

Ayer, N.W. & Sons. *Directory of Newspapers and Periodicals 1929–1935*. Philadelphia: N.W. Ayer & Sons, 1936.

Barron, Milton. 'Intermediacy: Conceptualization of Irish Status in America'. *Social Forces*, vol. 27 (1948/9), pp 256–63.

Blanshard, Paul. *American Freedom and Catholic Power*, Boston, MA: Beacon Press, 1949.

Greeley, Andrew. *The Irish Americans: Rise to Money and Power*. 2nd edn, New York: Warner Books, 1988.

'The Success and Assimilation of Irish Protestants and Irish Catholics in the United States'. *Sociology and Social Research*, vol. 72 (1988), pp.229–36.

Irish World. 'Resolutions Passed at the 63rd National AOH Convention'. 3 August 1946, p.4.

McGreevy, John T. 'Thinking on One's Own: Catholicism in the American Intellectual Imagination, 1928–1960'. *Journal of American History*, vol. 84 (1997), pp.97–131.

O'Dea, John. *History of the Ancient Order of Hibernians and Ladies' Auxiliary*. Philadelphia, PA: Keystone Printing Co., 1923.

Patterson, James T. *Grand Expectations: The United States, 1945–1974*. Oxford: Oxford University Press, 1996.

Proceedings of the Ancient Order of Hibernians: 55th National Convention, 1927, Buffalo, New York, July 19–23. Chicago: J.S. Hyland & Co., 1927.

Reilly, A.J. 'Irish Americans', in Francis Brown and Joseph Roucek (eds), *One America: The History, Contributions, and Present Problems of Our Racial and National Minorities*. New York: Prentice-Hall, 1945.

Reilly, George R. *Hibernians on the March: An Examination of the Origin and History of the Ancient Order of Hibernians with a Program for the Future*. San Francisco, CA: Calmar Press, 1948.

Ridge, John T. *Erin's Sons in America: The Ancient Order of Hibernians*. New York: Ancient Order of Hibernians 150th Anniversary Committee, 1986.

Waters, Mary. *Ethnic Options: Choosing Identities in America*. Berkeley and Los Angeles: University of California Press, 1990.

Winsberg, Morton D. 'The Suburbanization of the Irish in Boston, Chicago, and New York'. *Éire-Ireland*, vol. 21 (1986), pp.90–104.

CHAPTER FIVE

Shamrocks and Segregation: The Persistence of Upper-Class Irish Ethnicity in Beverly Hills, Chicago

MARGARET LEE

In 1961 Father Andrew Greeley, a sociology graduate student at the University of Chicago and former pastor of Christ the King in Beverly Hills, Chicago, studied his former parish. He observed the behaviour of Irish Catholics in this community and argued that ethnicity was declining: Catholics intermarried with Catholics of other ethnic backgrounds, but rarely with non-Catholics. Similarly, teenagers formed their social groups around religion rather than ethnicity. But despite this evidence, Greeley concluded that Beverly Hills 'is an Irish community, despite the recent addition of substantial numbers of non-Irish' (Greeley, 'Some Aspects of Interaction', p.42).[1] Evidently, while cross-ethnic ties were growing and ethnicity as a relevant social indicator was declining, distinct Irish ethnicity still persisted in some form – but what were the signs of an 'Irish community' that Greeley witnessed?

Analysing the Irish in Beverly Hills on Chicago's far South Side reveals that Irish ethnicity in the early postwar period permeated the community in terms of both culture and social interaction. Irishness in this period was most obvious in expressions of Catholicism and celebrations of Saint Patrick's Day, displays that were strongly rooted in the parish. Irish ethnicity, however, extended beyond popular cultural display to influence larger neighbourhood processes and individual interaction. Faced with the possibility of African–American neighbours, Beverly Hills residents were unable to unite across ethno-religious divisions in the 1940s and 1950s; even when these barriers were bridged in the 1960s, Irish Catholics continued to rely on their ethnicity and ethnic institutions in coping with racial desegregation.

In this sense, the Beverly Hills Irish challenge long-standing beliefs that ethnic identification faded during the postwar period, leaving behind only a shallow, symbolic ethnicity. Sociologist Herbert Gans first used the term 'symbolic ethnicity' in the 1970s, arguing that for third- and fourth-generation ethnics, ethnicity had greatly diminished, becoming primarily expressive rather than influencing where people lived and worked and with whom they interacted (Gans, *Making Sense of America*, ch. 9).[2]   Thirty years later, Stephen Steinberg similarly advocated the inevitability of assimilation of ethnic groups, with signs of an ethnic revival in the 1970s only '"a dying gasp" of ethnic consciousness on the part of groups already at an advanced stage of assimilation' (Steinberg, *Race Relations*, p.116).[3]   For such theorists, dispersal of inner-city ethnic enclaves into the suburbs aided in the assimilation process, as it was assumed that suburban living would bring ethnics into contact with 'Americans' and obviate the need for traditional ethnic institutions. Yet in Beverly Hills, Irish Catholics continued to self-segregate in terms of housing, education and socializing, suggesting that suburban living had not overhauled ethnic patterns of living in the postwar period.

Moreover, an examination of Irish Catholics in Beverly Hills questions the underlying assumptions of whiteness theories. Whiteness scholars have largely presented whiteness as a homogeneous category with little internal division; that is, once an immigrant group is accepted as white, conflict ceases and they can share equally in the benefits of whiteness.[4] Consequently, the adoption of a white racial identity, for these historians, implies the abandonment of ethnicity. The story of Beverly Hills in the 1950s complicates this trajectory from ethnic to racial identity, however. While Irish Catholics were clearly accepted as white, they did not easily mix with local white Protestants, even when the perceived survival of the community was at stake. In this sense, whiteness neither created unification nor superseded ethnic identity. Beverly Hills's Irish Catholics, then, reveal the persistence of upper-middle-class ethnicity in the postwar period and the continued salience of ethnic identity in a postwar urban environment increasingly infused with questions of race.

Catholicism was a major element of Irish ethnicity in the early postwar period. As Lawrence McCaffrey asserts, 'Irish Catholics diligently practised their religion not only as a sign of faith but also as a symbol of their ethnicity' (McCaffrey, *Irish Catholic Diaspora*, p.194). Devotion to Catholicism and parish life, then, was an obvious way for Irish residents to express their ethnicity. In the 1910s and 1920s Irish

Catholics on Chicago's South Side had begun entering the Beverly Hills neighbourhood, an upper-class Anglo-Protestant stronghold; they immediately formed Catholic parishes to support their ethnic community. By the 1950s the neighbourhood was about equally spilt between Protestants and Catholics – predominantly of Irish descent. For Beverly Hills Irish Catholics, the parish provided the central social and communal life for its members; parishioners attended mass weekly, generously supported their parish through financial contributions and provided the lay leadership for social and charitable organizations.[5] In the late 1950s, moreover, Greeley observed that church life determined residential choices, as the area's Catholics clustered around their parish facilities. Greeley concluded that this purposeful clustering was partly due to the fact that 'the parish plant is looked on by parishioners as much more of a community centre' (Greeley, 'Some Aspects of Interaction', p.91). The extreme devotion of Beverly Hills Catholics to their parish indicated simultaneously an expression of religious belief and ethnicity.

Not only did Catholicism implicitly support Irish ethnicity, Catholic institutions in Beverly Hills reinforced ties to Irish traditions, further blurring the line between religion and ethnicity. St Barnabas and Christ the King, both technically territorial parishes, were largely Irish parishes with Irish–American priests and parishioners migrating from traditionally Irish parishes on the South Side.[6] Moreover, Catholic organizations provided their members with Irish cultural activities. In the mid-1950s the South Side Catholic Woman's Club, a group that encompassed Beverly Hills, repeatedly held events with an Irish theme. In March 1955 the organization hosted a lecture on 'Irish Life and Literature' (*Beverly Review* [Chicago], 17 March 1955). The following year the group held 'a program of Irish songs and melodies', and in 1958 the local newspaper reported that the club would 'View Films of Ireland' (*Beverly Review*, 1 March 1956; *Beverly Review*, 27 February 1958). Similarly, in 1955 the Mothers of Longwood Academy, a Catholic girls' high school in Beverly Hills, hosted a talk on 'Spirituality of Ireland' for one of their monthly meetings (*Beverly Review*, 20 October 1955).

While Catholicism provided Beverly Hills's Irish with a year-round expression of ethnicity, celebrating Saint Patrick's Day in March gave them a more public opportunity to proclaim their Irishness. These celebrations were, for the most part, sponsored through the parishes. St Barnabas held an annual 'Shamrock Festival' to observe the holiday, a gala event that frequently was too large to be held within the neighbourhood. Started in 1948, the *Beverly Review* noted that by 1955,

'The Shamrock Festival with its growing attendance of over 2,000 people has become an outstanding event in the community' (27 January 1955). The evening celebration periodically witnessed the crowning of a 'Shamrock queen', and 'Mr and Mrs Shamrock', and the sale of green carnations (*Beverly Review*, 12 January 1956; *Beverly Review*, 24 April 1958; *Southtown Economist* [Chicago], 3 March 1948). Organizing the event began months in advance, and the local newspaper routinely reported on the planning progress. Other Beverly Hills parishes likewise observed the Irish holiday with community activities, although typically on a smaller scale. In 1950 Christ the King hosted 'Old-fashioned square dancing, with a modern touch added' to commemorate Saint Patrick's Day (*Southtown Economist*, 8 March 1950). St John Fisher, established in 1948, held an annual dance in their school hall, where in 1956 the parish also participated in 'singing of Irish songs' (*Beverly Review*, 11 March 1954).

Indeed, no other holiday was so widely and publicly celebrated. Beverly Hills parishes held Christmas bazaars, but – judging from media coverage – their main public event of each year was Saint Patrick's Day. In fact, the local newspaper suggested that Saint Patrick's Day rivalled Christmas, observing 'The Christmas Holidays are scarcely over when the Parishioners of St Barnabas find themselves busily engaged with plans for their Annual Shamrock Festival' ('The Cover Story, Shamrock Festival', *Beverly Review*, 30 January 1958). Apparently, Irish parishioners quickly moved from Christmas to focusing on preparing for Saint Patrick's Day.

Celebrating the holiday served to unite the area's Irish churches through a parade launched for the far South Side in 1953 (*Southtown Economist*, 18 March 1953). Two years later, the *Beverly Review* reported that 'Business, civic, religious, fraternal and nationalistic groups have banded together to make the parade one of the largest celebrations ever. It will consist of musical units, gayly [*sic*] decorated floats, depicting the history of Ireland entered by the surrounding parishes and other floats of a civic and patriotic nature' (*Beverly Review*, 10 March 1955). Such visual displays conveyed to spectators the celebration of Irish ethnicity; parish floats referred to Irish history and relied heavily upon Irish symbols such as shamrocks and leprechauns. In 1960 the *Beverly Review* printed a photograph of St Barnabas's float for the parade, in which the parish name written inside a large shamrock appeared on the side of the float, indicating the comfortable link between the parish and Irish ethnicity (*Beverly Review*, 3 March 1960).

Although the parade route was outside the bounds of Beverly Hills and ended at St Sabina's parish in neighbouring Auburn-Gresham, the fact that the Beverly Hills newspaper reported on the event indicates that the neighbourhood's parishes and organizations were involved. Moreover, the newspaper explicitly noted that 'the surrounding parishes' participated through recollecting Irish history. In this sense, Saint Patrick's Day brought together parishioners from beyond their neighbourhood boundaries, united through their Irish–Catholic identity. That Chicago's Cardinal Samuel Stritch reviewed the parade and addressed the crowd gathered at St Sabina's only highlighted the convergence of Irish and Catholic on this holiday.

The fact that these observances of Saint Patrick's Day all stemmed from parishes or larger religious associations might suggest that the impetus for celebrating the Irish holiday came from Irish clergy. Yet this does not appear to have been the case. The Shamrock Festival was initiated by parishioners with the consent of the parish priest: Edith Joyce asked Father Norbert O'Connell of St Barnabas about having 'a parish get-to-gether [*sic*] for St Patrick's Day?' When Father O'Connell agreed with this 'excellent idea', according to the *Beverly Review*, 'the "Shamrock Festival" was born' (*Beverly Review*, 28 January 1960). The parish, then, provided the structure for celebrating Saint Patrick's Day, but not the drive behind the observance. Moreover, the popularity of these Irish events indicates that interest in Irish ethnicity was quite high. The *Beverly Review* reported that the Shamrock Festival 'was so successful both financially and socially that the parish has made it an annual event with every man women [*sic*] and child taking part in some activity' (ibid.).

The popularity of Irish ethnicity in Beverly Hills during this period is further illustrated by the extensive coverage provided by the *Beverly Review*, and also in the ways in which non-religious organizations co-opted the message of Saint Patrick's Day. Each year during this period the *Beverly Review* methodically reported on planning for the celebrations, noting even as early as January that events would take place for the holiday in March. Additionally, the cover of the newspaper frequently included photographs of parish planning committees, themes for the annual events, or other images that referred to the Irish holiday. In 1955, for example, the cover showed a photograph of an older policeman, a large bird and a sign for the Saint Patrick's Day parade. An article inside the newspaper explained that the bird was a Kilaloo, a native species of Ireland which Captain William Hennessey had carried to the United States. When customs officials refused to admit the bird, 'reluctantly [Hennessey] had it killed and stuffed and brought the bird here – where he has been the leader of the St Patrick's Day parade ever since' (*Beverly Review*, 17 March 1955).   The *Beverly Review* appeared to revel in the tie to Ireland that the bird represented and the authenticity it provided to Beverly Hills-area Irish events.   While an interesting and unusual story, the inclusion of such articles and information also points toward a strong public interest in Irish ethnicity and in all things related to Ireland.

Beverly Hills businesses and organizations also borrowed from Irish imagery, presumably in order to appeal to potential customers and members.   In 1955 and 1956 business advertisements in the local press celebrated Saint Patrick's Day by including shamrocks, leprechauns and Irish phrases.   Christopher's restaurant announced, 'Erin go bragh and a happy St Patrick's Day to our many wonderful patrons', while a local grocery store proclaimed, 'for St Patrick's Day Shor'n Begorra You'll Save on these' (advertisement, *Beverly Review*, 17 March 1955; advertisement, *Beverly Review*, 15 March 1956). Neither of these businesses had any obvious ties to Irish ethnicity or Catholicism, yet they evidently saw appeals to Irish identity as a way to draw in customers.   At the same time, social organizations in the community gestured toward Saint Patrick's Day, presumably because there was enough support within the organization and the wider public to support Irish-themed events.   The Ridge Country Club, for example, held a fashion show in March 1959 entitled 'Shamrock Silhouette' (*Beverly Review*, 12 March 1959).   The fact that these organizations would hope to win over readers by referencing Irish symbols reveals the popular strength of Irish ethnicity – at least in the days surrounding Saint Patrick's Day.

According to local media, the majority of Saint Patrick's Day events were associated with parishes or religious organizations.   But, as seen through advertisements and the incorporation of the Irish holiday by other local groups, Irish ethnicity pervaded the Beverly Hills community during the month of March.   In 1954 the *Southtown Economist* observed that 'by a shade of coincidence, the Beverly YMCA Youth Service regular party night just happens to be tonight [March 17], demanding an Irish theme' (Patricia O'Mara, *Southtown Economist*, 17 March 1954).   The reporter's language suggests that ignoring Saint Patrick's Day, even in a traditionally Protestant organization, was not acceptable within the Beverly Hills neighbourhood.   While the parish provided much of the structure for public expressions of Irishness, then, the strong interest in Irish ethnicity carried over into the wider community, so that advertising and organizing events around Saint Patrick's Day became an effective means of appealing to Beverly Hills residents.

Interestingly, Beverly Hills parish events articulated a unique Irish identity for parishioners – an Irish veneer on culturally American activities. The Shamrock Festival, in particular, focused on visual displays of Irishness coupled with mainstream upper-middle-class behaviour. The festival relied upon Irish language and symbols to give the celebration a noticeable Irish flavour. The *Beverly Review* reported in 1955 that, 'Just as the Emerald Isle bids you welcome, An Tostal, to the greatest of Irish parties and gayest of all festivals, so do the members of the St Barnabas Woman's Club ... welcome everyone to join in one of the outstanding St Patrick's Day parties of the season' (*Beverly Review*, 3 March 1955).

The newspaper not only compared Ireland and Beverly Hills in celebrating Saint Patrick's Day, but also used Gaelic to highlight the Irish nature of the event. In other years the Shamrock Festival organizers 'extend[ed] to all parishioners of St Barnabas and their friends "Cead Mile Failte" (which means in Gaelic 100,000 welcomes)' (*Beverly Review*, 13 March 1958). Here, use of Gaelic indicated Irishness, but was also translated to encourage those unfamiliar with the Irish language to feel welcome. The use of visual symbols additionally signalled to participants that the Shamrock Festival was an Irish event. Decorations for the celebration included leprechauns, shamrocks, harps and banners declaring 'Erin Go Bragh' (*Beverly Review*, 6 March 1958; *Beverly Review*, 10 March 1960; *Beverly Review*, 12 March 1959). No one could be in any doubt about which ethnic group was represented at this event.

Inclusion of Irish individuals and references to Ireland also marked the Shamrock Festival as an Irish event. In 1952 event organizers especially emphasized their link with Ireland: 'a shipment of living shamrocks was flown in from Ireland and met at the airport by the Irish Consul' for the Shamrock Festival, which 'add[ed] a novel touch to the St Patrick's festivities' (*Beverly Review*, 12 January 1956). In 1959 organizers dubbed the festival the 'Kerry County Fair', suggesting a connection between St Barnabas families and County Kerry in Ireland (*Beverly Review*, 26 February 1959.) The local newspaper made these ties explicit in describing the Irish holiday, stating that 'St Patrick's Day is remarkable not only for its celebration in Ireland, but for its influence in uniting Irish people all over the world; and the parishioners of St Barnabas are no exception' (*Beverly Review*, 6

March 1958). Beverly Hills's Irish Catholics, therefore, used Saint Patrick's Day to reinforce ties to Ireland and to celebrate their own Irishness.

Aside from decorations and titles, though, these events provided little in terms of Irish culture – especially in comparison to lower- and middle-class commemorations of Saint Patrick's Day in Chicago. While occasional references to Irish music appeared in local newspapers, much more common for the Shamrock Festival was modern dance music and card-playing (*Southtown Economist*, 21 February 1954; *Southtown Economist*, 20 March 1955). The 1955 Shamrock Festival, for example, hosted two bands to provide for dancing, 'alternat[ing] the lively conga line and jitterbugging with the soothing rhythm of waltz and foxtrot'; those not interested in dancing 'will be lured to the card tables' (*Southtown Economist*, 16 February 1955). In contrast, celebrations of Saint Patrick's Day across the South Side in the postwar period typically included performances of Irish music and dancing.   While the *Southtown Economist* lamented that 'Southtown's Irish don't observe many of the old customs, such as outdoor games, dances and shamrock picking', many associations in the area did draw upon their Irish heritage to celebrate Saint Patrick's Day, as Chicago's Irish 'are nevertheless still very much aware of the special importance' of the holiday (*Southtown Economist*, 14 March 1945). In 1945, for example, the United Irish Societies of Chicago and another Irish group from Englewood hosted an event in which

> Selections from the national music of Ireland, some of them dating back 1,000 years, will be played. Hugh McCormack will play his Uhlan [*sic*] Irish pipes, Dan Hickey, his accordion and James O'Hara and Paddy Kane, their violins. Theresa Prendergast will present 50 juvenile dancers ... who will entertain the crowd with Gaelic jigs, reels and hornpipes. (Ibid.)

Although this event also included some 'American dance tunes', the entertainments were largely Irish cultural performances – songs, musical instruments and dances.

Additionally, Beverly Hills's Saint Patrick's Day celebrations stressed an upper-middle-class image for what had traditionally been a raucous holiday. The Shamrock Festival put forth a refined and controlled image, aided by the attendance of prominent Chicago figures. In 1952, 'Guests of honor will include Governor Stevenson, Mayor Kennelly and Irish Vice-consul Edward Brennan' (*Southtown Economist*, 27 February 1952). In later years numerous Cook County judges made appearances along with baseball and television stars ('2,400 at St Barnabas Festival'). In 1955 and again in 1958 Mayor Richard Daley and his wife attended St Barnabas's observation of Saint Patrick's Day (ibid.; *Beverly Review*, 13 March 1958). The prominence of these guests suggests that celebrations of Saint Patrick's Day among Beverly Hills parishes were upper-middle-class and respectable events. Photographs appearing in the *Beverly Review* reinforced this impression, showing couples and families dressed in their finest at the Shamrock Festival. In 1958 the newspaper made fancy attire explicit, asserting that 'Many couples and their families will be getting into their best bib and tucker St Patrick's Day evening to attend the Shamrock Festival' (*Beverly Review*, 8 March 1956). Moreover, the festival was repeatedly held in the city's most prestigious country clubs and hotels and awarded expensive prizes to participants – from television sets to mink stoles, to a month-long trip to Europe – highlighting the wealth of the parish and giving the event an air of social superiority (*Beverly Review*, 12 January 1956; *Beverly Review*, 27 January 1955; *Beverly Review*, 11 March 1954).

The annual observance of Saint Patrick's Day illustrated the merging of upper-class behaviour with ethnic traditions, producing a unique celebration that emphasized both the ethnic affiliation and the respectability of the Irish–Catholic community. Participants could pay homage to their Irish heritage and highlight their social success by rubbing elbows with the mayor and governor all in the same night. Although Saint Patrick's Day came around only once a year, and celebrations often only gestured toward Irish cultural traditions, the March holiday publicly marked Beverly Hills as a bastion of Irish Catholicism in the postwar period.

While Saint Patrick's Day provided a means of publicly displaying Irish Catholicism, this ethnic identity permeated the community in other ways as well – particularly in determining the future course and image of the neighbourhood. As racial desegregation moved across Chicago's South Side, Beverly Hills leaders became increasingly concerned with creating a cohesive, organized community to deal with this perceived threat. Such cohesion would have required Catholic and Protestant cooperation, because the area was equally split between religions. Yet, although this community crisis encouraged closer alliances between Irish Catholics and Protestants, long-standing religious and ethnic divisions forestalled such efforts until well into the 1960s. Irish ethnicity, then, was an entrenched identity, not simply an occasional display at community celebrations: it influenced

daily interactions and shaped the responses of Irish Catholics to neighbourhood change throughout the postwar period.

To Beverly Hills residents, threats of a 'black invasion' seemed
increasingly real in the late 1940s and 1950s, especially as they saw
this process taking place in surrounding neighbourhoods. In August
1947, when eight African–American families moved into the
Fernwood Emergency Veterans Housing Project in nearby Roseland,
'Chicago experienced its worst racial violence since the riots of 1919'
(Homer A. Jack, memorandum, 22 August 1947, box 317, Welfare
Council Papers). Families from the area gathered at the housing project, set fires and threw rocks at police who attempted to control the
mob. Municipal officials reported that 'the next two nights saw more
stoning of the project, the smashing of cars and beating of occupants'
(Chicago Commission on Human Relations, *The People of Chicago*,
pp.9–10). The Fernwood project itself was only a mile from the border of Beverly Hills and the violence of the mob extended all the way
to Beverly's border. In 1961 Greeley reported that 'As yet the
[African–American] ghetto is not at the borders of Westwood [Beverly
Hills], but it is no more than a mile away in two directions and perhaps a mile and a half in the third direction' (Greeley, 'Some Aspects
of Interaction', p.27). The presence of African–American communities, particularly the one in neighbouring Morgan Park, gave Beverly
Hills residents the sense that they were being surrounded.
Intermittent interactions with African Americans within the bounds of
Beverly Hills only enhanced residents' fears (ibid.).

In response to the migration of African Americans across the South
Side, many Chicagoans, including Beverly Hills residents, advocated
forming organizations to protect the neighbourhood's interest – but
these organizations could only succeed with the support of the entire
community. After the Fernwood riots, community leaders formed the
Beverly Area Planning Association (BAPA) as an umbrella organization
to coordinate neighbourhood activities. In the fall of 1947 William
Groebe, secretary of BAPA, presented the organization's objective: 'to
get all property in the area now owned by caucasians [*sic*] recorded
under the new restrictive covenant, so that it shall remain owned by
caucasians [*sic*]' (Minutes of Vanderpoel Improvement Association, 4
November 1947, Ridge Historical Society, Chicago).[7] In case there
were doubts about the necessity of this community-wide action,
Groebe 'gave some incidents that have already occurred and explained
some of the dangers that exist now in the frontier areas of Morgan
Park' (ibid.). As he explained, with threats of racial desegregation, it

was necessary for all Beverly Hills residents to participate in neighbourhood organizations, an idea repeated in later years. In a recruitment drive in 1951, a BAPA flier asserted the importance of community-wide participation: 'Since the whole area is only as strong as its weakest part, it is important that every foot of property be organized under the jurisdiction of some individual property owner group' ('An Invitation to Become a Member of the Beverly Area Planning Association, Inc.'). Although never stated in the organization's records, cooperation of both Catholic and Protestant residents was clearly necessary for the community's survival.

A BAPA member organization, the Vanderpoel Improvement Association (representing a portion of the Beverly Hills neighbourhood), further discussed the importance of incorporating all residents to protect the area, 'organizing together to get restricted for caucasian [*sic*] covenants recorded to the titles of every piece of property in the territory'. The neighbourhood association further encouraged 'nearby Associations to invite the unaffiliated residents to join, and in this way the entire area will be ultimately represented' (Vanderpoel Improvement Association minutes, 7 October 1947). Clearly, the leaders of these neighbourhood organizations saw the problem in racial terms: African–American invaders required whites to band together for protection, a process that implicitly mandated cooperation between Catholics and Protestants; neither group could be ignored or secluded in order for restrictive covenants and organization to be effective.

In his study of Beverly Hills, Greeley pointed to one Irish–Catholic resident who explicitly tried to bridge these religious divides for the perceived good of the neighbourhood. While many of the area's leading Catholics were content to socialize within their parish, 'John Larosa' saw a problem in this religious division (Greeley, 'Some Aspects of Interaction', pp.72–3). Greeley writes that Larosa 'deplores the ghetto mentality of his fellow Catholics and has tried to use his position as president of the [Beverly] Improvement Association and the Country Club to promote more communication between the two groups' (ibid., p.72). Larosa used these leadership roles to facilitate contact between Catholics and Protestants even in the social world, where 'he invites non-Catholics from the neighbourhood to his cocktail parties' (ibid.). Although Greeley did not explicitly connect Larosa's activities to the drive for neighbourhood preservation, he repeatedly asserted that Beverly Hills would not survive racial desegregation if it was not able to unite across the religious divide. For

Greeley, then, Larosa served as a necessary forerunner to broader neighbourhood organization and cohesion.

Though neighbourhood leaders advocated bridging Beverly Hills's religious and ethnic divide, achieving such goals among the general population was easier said than done. Tension had existed between Catholics and Protestants in the area since the formation of St Barnabas parish in 1924. Opposition from long-standing Protestant residents to the presence of Catholics in their neighbourhood produced countless lawsuits against the church construction, Ku Klux Klan cross-burnings on church property and physical attacks on parish priests (St Barnabas Parish History, 1978, file; 'Priest Wounded When Attacked By Armed Men', *Bridgeport* [CT] *Telegram*, 9 September 1924; Koenig, *History of the Parishes of the Archdiocese of Chicago*, pp.100–2). Such expressions of hostility were not easily forgotten. As Greeley asserted: 'these events are in the distant past now, but they are remembered at least vaguely by the parishioners … and with resentment' ('Some Aspects of Interaction', p.36). The strength of Irish Catholicism also exacerbated this religious schism: strong parishes meant Irish Catholics had little need to form connections outside of their religious circle. While the local country club membership was about evenly split between Catholics and Protestants, for example, the two groups rarely mixed within the institution during activities such as playing golf (ibid., ch. 8). Greeley concluded that Catholics within Beverly Hills had practically become an 'invisible ghetto'; although Catholics and non-Catholics may have shared many of the same opinions, they existed in separate social worlds (ibid., pp.7–8, ch. 4). Consequently, Greeley argued that while John Larosa advocated socializing across religious lines, he did not actually achieve this goal any more than other Beverly Hills Catholics (ibid., p.72).

Attempts to bridge the Catholic–Protestant divide, then, were largely unsuccessful in the 1950s. In 1959 the Archdiocese of Chicago formed the Organization for a Southwest Community (OSC) in order to preserve the larger South Side region from panic-peddling, block-busting and resegregation through the leadership of Catholic priests and Protestant ministers (McGreevy, *Parish Boundaries*, pp.119–22, 181).[8] Christ the King officially supported the association and Greeley speculated that some parishioners 'might even be secretly proud of the leadership their parish has shown in the new community organization', but the OSC was not popularly supported in Beverly Hills (Greeley, 'Some Aspects of Interaction', p.6). Residents of both faiths were wary of the institution and its cross-religious stance, fearing that it 'might represent a plot by someone in the other group to "take over the neighborhood"' (ibid., p.138). Apparently, community leaders supported the OSC, but, as Greeley observed, 'it was too controversial for the rank and file of either group to become involved with it' (ibid., p.61). Even the OSC, with its preservationist goals, struggled to overcome the long-standing religious barriers among the Beverly Hills public. That these residents were unable to overcome religious divisions in the 1950s points toward the continued importance of Irish ethnicity in the community.

The strength of Irish ethnicity continued into the 1960s, moreover. In 1965 the presence of African Americans in Beverly Hills became a reality and cross-religious relationships finally flourished to calmly manage racial desegregation. Yet even then, Irish–Catholic residents continued to rely on their ethnicity to guide their responses toward racial desegregation. In 1965 Herman Kelly distributed a letter to the parishioners of Christ the King, lamenting that 'Our parish is in a sad state ... a great number of parishioners are indifferent and apathetic on the most important issue of the day, racial justice' (A Fellow Parishioner to Parishioners of Christ the King, n.d., box 16, file 13, Daniel Cantwell papers).[9] While Kelly denigrated the parish for its lax position on racial integration, he still chose to deal with questions of race relations through his parish rather than through other local organizations or media. Kelly's action, although challenging the relationship between Catholicism and racial liberalism, indicated the continued strength of Catholic identity and the influence of this ethnicity on Beverly Hills responses to racial integration. The parish itself remained central to dealing with race relations and providing the structure for community organizing in the 1960s and early 1970s. BAPA records note countless connections between Catholic parishes and approaches to neighbourhood integration. Though Beverly Hills residents had largely moved beyond religious hostility by the 1970s, the Irish–Catholic population still relied upon parish structures and leadership to guide the neighbourhood through continued racial desegregation.

The late 1940s and 1950s for Beverly Hills, then, were a time when attempts were made to bridge the religious divisions within the community, attempts to unite Irish Catholics and Protestants under a unified racial identity in order to stave off perceived threats of African–American residents. The fact that these attempts were not entirely successful points to the continued salience of an Irish–Catholic identity: not just in public and social events such as

Saint Patrick's Day, but in arenas that determined the neighbourhood's future. Moreover, Beverly Hills's Irish represent a challenge to the idea that ethnicity declined in the wake of a developing white identity adopted in response to racial 'others'.[10]   While on the surface Saint Patrick's Day and neighbourhood organizing seem unrelated, in this case they both represent the continued existence of Irish ethnicity in the postwar period, even in addressing questions of race.

REFERENCES

Avila, Eric. *Popular Culture in the Age of White Flight: Fear and Fantasy in Suburban Los Angeles*. Berkeley, CA: University of California Press, 2004.

Beverly Area Planning Association.   'An Invitation to Become a Member of the Beverly Area Planning Association, Inc.'. Beverly Area Planning Association Papers, University of Illinois–Chicago Daley Library, box 3, file 27.

Beverly Review (Chicago). 'St Barnabas Shamrock Festival Celebrated on St Patrick's Day', 11 March 1954.

'St Patrick's Dance', 11 March 1954.

'Planning for the Shamrock', 27 January 1955.

'An Tostal to St Pat's', 3 March 1955.

'Ireland's Saint Reigns at Parade', 10 March 1955.

Advertisement, 17 March 1955.

'This Week's Cover', 17 March 1955.

'Professor Speaks on Irish Life at Woman's Club', 17 March 1955.

'Speak on Ireland', 20 October 1955.

'Pioneers of St Barnabas Shamrock Festival Review History of Annual Affair', 12 January 1956.

'Irish Music', 1 March 1956.

'Stepping Out!' 8 March 1956.

Advertisement, 15 March 1956.

'The Cover Story, Shamrock Festival', 30 January 1958.

'Catholic Women View Films of Ireland', 27 February 1958.

'"Full of Fun"', 6 March 1958.

'Cover Story, "Cead Mile Failte"', 13 March 1958.

'Party Portraits, Eleventh Shamrock Festival', 24 April 1958.

'County Fair Committee', 26 February 1959.

'Ridge Shamrock Silhouette Show', 12 March 1959.

Cover, 12 March 1959.

'The Shamrock Festival is Born', 28 January 1960.

'Afloat for Shamrock Festival', 3 March 1960.

Cover, 10 March 1960.

Chicago Commission on Human Relations. *The People of Chicago: Five Year Report, 1947–1951 of the Chicago Commission on Human Relations.* Chicago, 1952.

Gans, Herbert. *Making Sense of America: Sociological Analyses and Essays.* Lanham, MD: Rowman & Littlefield, 1999.

Greeley, Andrew. 'Some Aspects of Interaction between Members of an Upper-Middle-Class Roman Catholic Parish and their Non-Catholic Neighbors'. MA thesis, University of Chicago, 1961.

Guglielmo, Thomas A. *White on Arrival: Italians, Race, Color, and Power in Chicago, 1890–1945.* Oxford: Oxford University Press, 2003.

Hirsch, Arnold R. *Making the Second Ghetto: Race and Housing in Chicago, 1940–1960.* Chicago, IL: University of Chicago Press, 1998.

Ignatiev, Noel. *How the Irish Became White.* New York and London: Routledge, 1995.

Koenig, Harry C. (ed.). *A History of the Parishes of the Archdiocese of Chicago.* Vol. 1. Chicago, IL: The Archdiocese, 1980.

McCaffrey, Lawrence. *The Irish Catholic Diaspora in America.* Washington, DC: Catholic University of America Press, 1997.

McGreevy, John T. *Parish Boundaries: The Catholic Encounter with Race in the Twentieth-Century Urban North.* Chicago, IL: University of Chicago Press, 1996.

McMahon, Eileen. *What Parish Are You From? A Chicago Irish Community and Race Relations.* Lexington: University Press of Kentucky, 1995.

Roediger, David R. *The Wages of Whiteness: Race and the Making of the American Working Class.* London and New York: Verso, 1991.

Saint Barnabas, Ridge Historical Society, Chicago. Saint Barnabas Parish History, 1978, file.

Southtown Economist (Chicago). 'How Southtown Irish Will Mark St Pat's Day', 14 March 1945.

'St Barnabas Parish Will Hold Shamrock Festival', 3 March 1948.

'Christ the King Altar Guild to Hold Dance', 8 March 1950.

'Club Completes Plans for 5th Shamrock Fete', 27 February 1952.

'Thousands View St Pat's Parade', 18 March 1953.

'St Barnabas Prepared for Irish Festival', 21 February 1954.

Patricia O'Mara, 'Top of the Morning', 17 March 1954.

Patricia O'Mara, 'Welcome to the Shamrock Festival', 16 February 1955.

'2,400 at St Barnabas Festival', 20 March 1955.

Steinberg, Stephen. *Race Relations: A Critique*. Stanford, CA: Stanford University Press, 2007.

Vanderpoel Improvement Association. Minutes, 4 November 1947, Ridge Historical Society, Chicago.

Waters, Mary. *Ethnic Options: Choosing Identities in America*. Berkeley, CA: University of California Press, 1990.

CHAPTER SIX

Irish New Yorkers and the Puerto Rican Migration

EILEEN ANDERSON

Irish and Puerto Rican histories include several moments of contact and overlap, a result of their shared religious beliefs, of the magnitude of their diasporas, and of their history of coloniality. One of the most important spaces in which the two groups have come together is New York City. As early as the late nineteenth century, Manhattan was a gathering place for both exiled Irish and Puerto Rican independence leaders. At the start of the twentieth century the Puerto Rican presence was still relatively small and had a limited number of encounters with the large Irish population. However, beginning in the 1940s the Puerto Rican population of New York increased as 'more than 42,000 Puerto Ricans were estimated to have arrived in the United States every year between 1946 and 1956' (Sánchez Korrol, 'Building', p.1). The mass migration transformed Irish–Puerto Rican relations. As Irish New Yorkers confronted the influx of Spanish-speaking 'newcomers', their feelings fluctuated between understanding and antagonism. The Irish still yielded significant power in the Catholic Church and the parochial schools, in trade-union jobs, and throughout many neighbourhoods of the city. Conflicts often occurred as Puerto Ricans began to integrate, or attempt to integrate, into these places and institutions.

Irish and Puerto Rican authors who write about the 1940s and 1950s tell the complex stories of these intersections. Some, such as activists Joaquín Colón López and Father Joseph P. Fitzpatrick, highlight the importance of mutual support in their speeches and articles. Others, such as Frank McCourt, Piri Thomas and Edward Rivera, demonstrate the frequent misunderstandings that occurred when these two very different cultures converged. The protagonists in these accounts often compare the experiences of the Irish and Puerto Ricans, but never fully identify with the 'Other' community. Colón López recognizes that the Irish have been oppressed in their homeland, yet he finds that they often abuse their power in the United States. Fitzpatrick is an advocate for the Puerto Ricans, who calls for solidarity among the communities. But even a recognition that Irish or Puerto Rican heritage served to set them apart from Anglos was not always enough of a connection to unify the groups. Many times we find little recognition of shared histories and circumstances. The presence of this Puerto Rican/Irish 'Other' often serves only to strengthen their sense of ethnic identity by representing what they were not.

Father Fitzpatrick, a sociology professor at Fordham University, was one of the first community leaders to note the historical parallels between the Irish and Puerto Rican communities. His speeches and homilies often outlined the similarities. He was extremely sympathetic to the hardships that Puerto Ricans faced, which reminded him of his own family history. For instance, in a talk given to the Knights of Columbus in 1952, he called upon the members as 'children of immigrants' to support the Puerto Rican newcomers because

> they are misunderstood, frequently criticized in exactly the same way that all our people were criticized before them. They are called dirty, unkempt, half-civilized; they are considered irresponsible, shiftless; and the crime and delinquency statistics are used to show that they are people prone to crime.
>
> (Fitzpatrick, *The Stranger is Our Own*, p.99)

Fitzpatrick goes on to cite articles from the Irish–American newspapers to demonstrate that identical claims were made about the Irish a hundred years before.

Fitzpatrick wrote and spoke extensively about the New York Irish church leaders and their efforts to incorporate Puerto Ricans into the existing diocesan infrastructures. He notes that difficulties in adjusting to the American church are understandable, as it differed greatly from ways in which the Spanish-influenced church functioned on the Island:

> Many of them, it is true, are poorly instructed in their Faith. But that is not their fault. They come from a tradition where they never had to fight for their Faith as the Irish did for centuries against the English; they come from an area where the priests have been too few to reach them. But they are not to blame for

> this. They come now into our land, where we point with pride
> to the achievements we have made, the Churches we have built,
> the schools we run.   (Ibid., p.101)

Fitzpatrick believed that as the New York Irish had achieved positions
of power in the church and schools, it was their obligation to use those
advantages to help the Puerto Ricans.

The Irish presence in the parochial schools is apparent to protagonist Edward Rivera's *bildungsroman, Family Installments: Memories
of Growing up Hispanic* (1982). Rivera, a teenager in the 1950s,
writes about Irish teachers in the schools and neighbourhoods. At his
school, the nuns and brothers are all Irish; the school colours are
green and gold; and the symbol that they stamp on the books is a
shamrock. Santos, the protagonist, also recognizes the similar dynamics of Irish and Puerto Rican history but receives conflicting messages
(fluctuating between solidarity and superiority) from the religious
communities who teach him. In two vignettes, 'First Communion'
and 'Caesar and Bruteses: A Tradegy', Santos begins to think about his
Puerto Rican heritage in terms of what the Irish nuns and brothers
teach him.

In 'First Communion' one of the nuns offers to buy Santos a suit
for this ritual and he thinks, 'it may have been a nice favor on sister's
part ... putting out all that money for a kid on ADC. For one thing
they were Irish, all of them, so why should they gave a damn for people like me?' (Rivera, *Family Installments*, p.75).[1] Santos appreciates
the gesture, but he later mentions the nuns' history lesson about his
ancestors:

> the Caribs, cannibalistic Indians from the jungles of South
> America ... [who] ate their enemies raw. She [the nun] went on
> to tell us that they hadn't even discovered friction –that's how
> primitive they were. It was the Europeans, the Spaniards, who
> had brought them friction, True Faith and other forms of
> Christian civilization. (Ibid., p.76)

As the boy never hears anything else about Puerto Rican history in
school or at home, this lecture can only add to his existing feelings of
personal and cultural insecurity.

Santos's insight into the situation of the Irish changes its tone and
even approaches an understanding in the humorous vignette 'Caesar
and Bruteses: A Tradegy'. There, one of the Irish brothers tries to
teach Shakespeare to his grade school class. The protagonist is

Brother Cassian O'Leary, whose name is condensed to the more easily pronounced 'Bro' Leary' by the boys. He is a retired sailor who fought in World War Two and is not as well read as the other brothers, who are, in Santos's opinion, younger and smarter. During his classes Bro' Leary calls Dante 'Dandy' and makes mistaken references to Homer and Virgil. Santos feels some form of pity for his teacher; he imagines that he stays up at night worrying, while his better-educated colleagues 'snored in peace and held dreamy dialogues with the smarter angels and the Founding Fathers of the Holy Mother Church' (ibid., p.117). In general, Bro' Leary is liked by his students, who believe he in turn actually feels some affection for them. The narrator notes that 'the Irish always sided with the Irish and the Italians always sided with the Italians and the law was that you always sided with Your Own Kind'. Bro' Leary was the one exception to the rule; however, 'because he had no favorites in class' (ibid., p.11).

His attempt to teach *Julius Caesar* is a complete disaster. Santos tries to read it and is totally lost; he ends up hiding the book under the bed in the hope that the cockroaches will eat it. The school's 'specially ordered edition' is of poor quality and contains errors which make it impossible for any of the students to understand. At school, Bro' Leary's exam makes it clear that the teacher is as alienated by the antiquated English and unfamiliar situations as his students. The exam contains a note at the bottom of the character identification section that says 'Try not to get these mixed up. I know they all sound alike, but that's no excuse' (ibid., p.135). Another questions asks, 'Could this tragedy have taken place in a Catholic country? E.g. Ireland? Italy? Porto Rico? Poland? Why not?' (ibid., p.136). It escapes Bro' Leary's notice that the original play was set in Rome. Bro' Leary's misapplication of Catholic values to an English classic, in a classroom full of Italians and Puerto Ricans, signifies the complexity of the cultural transference between immigrant groups.

For Santos, the story of Bro' Leary is especially significant; his teacher's deficient English skills and ignorance of important literature are a revelation. He notes that O'Leary often struggles for the right words in class and must make a noticeable effort to use correct grammar, which does not come naturally for him. Santos's father has instilled a desire to succeed in the boy, and has made it clear that *el camino al exito* (the path to success) is speaking correct English. The boy's English affects all his interactions. He laments, 'I was timid in school (I was timid everywhere, in fact) and that my English, broken and mispronounced, was a disgraceful version of the real thing' (ibid., p.85). After failing the test on Shakespeare, Santos and his friend Virgilio go on the roof of the school and launch water balloons at their teacher. Bro' Leary, however, blames public school kids, and Santos and Virigilio receive no punishment. But Bro' Leary has disappeared when they come back from spring break. The students are told that he has gone to teach in a school near the Hudson River, but Santos doubts this excuse; he and the other students imagine their teacher has been put away in an institution.

Rivera's story of Bro' Leary and Santos encapsulates the ways in which relationships between Puerto Rican students and their Irish educators continually fluctuated between admiration, fear, respect and complete antagonism. Santos and the other students are certainly afraid of the brothers and their use of corporal punishment, yet they admire their 'perfect' English. Bro' Leary, in turn, is not quite comfortable in his position of authority, and, according to Santos, breaks the rules by not favouring his Irish students. After the water balloon incident, Santos feels slightly guilty about the betraying of Bro' Leary. Ironically, Santos later realizes that he has understood the Shakespearean play: he and Virgilio are the 'Bruteses' who betray the only teacher who had their best interests at heart.

Schools were not the only place where such encounters took place. Puerto Ricans also moved into neighbourhoods that were once pre-dominantly Irish. Throughout the period well-placed Irish politicians such as William O'Dwyer were involved in decisions that were chang-ing the city. Irish-born O'Dwyer was mayor of New York from 1946 to 1950, and one of his most important decisions was to appoint Robert Moses as construction coordinator for the city. Moses had held government posts since the late 1930s, but his new power under O'Dwyer gave him more freedom to expand on his vision for the city. In order to build highways, his agencies divided neighbourhoods and tore down public housing, policies that played a large part in the city's housing shortage of the fifties and sixties and which had immediate effect on the recently arrived immigrants. As Fitzpatrick notes, over-crowding had profound effects on many Puerto Ricans:

> They came into a city which was completely built up not only in terms of homes but also in terms of Churches and parochial schools. In other words, when the Italians, for example, came to New York City, many of them moved into crowded areas of the City which older residents were leaving. But large numbers moved into areas where there was vacant land, where the neighbourhoods

were not yet developed and where the Churches either did not exist or existed in small numbers. This was not the case when the Puerto Ricans arrived. The City was crowded; had little empty land; and the Archdiocese was highly developed with parish churches and parochial schools on every corner of the City.
(Fitzpatrick, *The Stranger is Our Own*, pp.192–3)

The old neighbourhoods, which provided safety and security for immigrants and newcomers, were not as well defined and easily formed as they had been in the past.

The Irish and Puerto Ricans were not only fighting for living spaces; many were also struggling to find even low-wage jobs. Such struggles are evident in both Piri Thomas's memoir, *Down These Mean Streets* (1967) and Frank McCourt's *'Tis* (1999). McCourt was born in Brooklyn in 1930, spent most of his early years in Ireland, and returned to New York in 1949, where he eventually taught in the public school system. Piri Thomas's memoir was the first well-known literary work about Puerto Ricans in New York written by someone from inside the community. *Mean Streets* and its 1974 sequel *Seven Long Times* chronicle a young man's experiences growing up on the streets of Spanish Harlem in the 1930s through the 1950s. They were definitive works for American Puerto Rican writers: as Edgardo Vega Yunqué observes, 'the success of this memoir set the parameters for Puerto Rican Literature in the United States' (Hernandez, *Puerto Rican Voices in English*, p.206). Thomas is consistently praised for the authenticity and gritty realism of his stories about his life on the street, his drug addiction, his involvement in street fighting and basic struggle for survival.

In *Mean Streets* Thomas depicts continual, seemingly inevitable conflict between the Puerto Rican and African–American *ganguitas* over turf. He also remembers fighting with the Irish.

> There was a lot of violence on the streets because of racism. The Italians and Irish hated us with a vengeance. When we had to go to the store, we had to go with convoys of *la ganguita* for protection and if there was a fight, the police came out on the side of the Italians and the Irish and attacked us, who were still boys.
> (Ibid., p.175)

Throughout, the interactions of the protagonist with other ethnic groups result in verbal or physical confrontation and Thomas is forced into defending his right to inhabit the shared spaces.

Thomas, a dark-skinned Puerto Rican, experienced racism on two levels. His ability to be part of the Anglo society in the United States is hindered not only because he is Puerto Rican, but because of his skin colour. His own father (who is dark-skinned as well) denies his African ancestry, as does the rest of his lighter-skinned family. Asked why he never acknowledges this aspect of his ancestry his father responds,

> I ain't got one colored friend ... at least not one American Negro friend. Only dark ones I got are Puerto Ricans or Cubans. I'm not a stupid man. I saw the look of white people on me when I was young man, when I walked into a place where dark skin wasn't supposed to be. I noticed cold rejection turned into indifferent acceptance when they heard my exaggerated accent.
>
> (Thomas, *Mean Streets*, p.153)

His father, then, feels that associating with African Americans will only lead to even more discrimination. As Fitzpatrick points out, race was one of the most important ways in which Puerto Ricans differed from the mainstream:

> Nothing is so complicating to the Puerto Ricans in their effort to adjust to American life as the problem of color. They represent the first group ever to come to the United States in large numbers with a tradition of widespread intermingling and intermarriage of people of different color.
>
> (Fitzpatrick, *Puerto Rican Americans*, p.104)

Racism existed on the Island, but there skin colour was not the only identifying factor.

White society – which for the author clearly included the Irish – discriminated against Thomas, which he believes is because it perceives him to be a black man. The importance of the Irish presence in his subconscious is significant: his references to the Irish community are manifested in racial slurs. Throughout the memoir, he dismisses all white people by using common derogatory terms. He uses the words *blanco* and *blanca*, 'white' and 'paddy' interchangeably (he also incorporates the word 'Charley' after his stay in the South) – but 'paddy' is the term that he uses most often as an insult. For Thomas, the Irish were important, but they were inseparable from the larger Anglo community.

At several points Thomas uses the term 'paddy' to call attention to white racism, and also to define what he is not. The first occurs when his parents decide to move out to the Long Island suburbs. Thomas does not want to leave Harlem; he explains his resistance to his mother by telling her that his friend Crutch had said that 'there were a lot of paddies out there and they didn't dig Negroes or Puerto Ricans' (Thomas, *Mean Streets*, p.81). His mother resists the idea and responds 'Caramba! What ideas! …What for you talk like that? Your Poppa and I saved enough money. We want you kids to have good opportunities. It is a better life in the country. No like Puerto Rico, but it have trees and grass and nice schools' (ibid., p.82). Although the suburbs mean new opportunities for the family, Thomas resists because he knows he will inevitably be rejected by the whites who live there.

An important scene where the word 'paddy' is used to represent all those who discriminate against him occurs during Thomas's job interview with a Mr Christian. Thomas lies when the interviewer asks him about religious affiliation and his church attendance. When asked about his reasons for dropping out of school, the boy invents an excuse; he tells Mr Christian that he needed to help out his family, but to himself he thinks it was '*On account of you funny paddies and your funny ideas in this funny world*' (ibid., pp.100–1). After a few more minutes of questions, Mr Christian quickly informs Thomas that there are no positions currently available and affably tells him he will call him. A short while later, Christian offers the narrator's friend Lucky – who is white – the same job.

Another significant moment occurs when Thomas decides to leave his family to join the merchant marines. He looks up at his brothers and sisters and ponders, 'Maybe if I had come out the same kinda color as them – my eyes swept across my paddy-fair brothers –maybe I wouldn't feel like I do … Maybe I hate them for what I am not' (ibid., p.150). Here the word 'paddy' has been transformed into an adjective, one that clearly refers to skin color and which equates Irishness and whiteness.

This use of the word 'paddy' was also common in African–American communities, and in that sense, may demonstrate how much black Americans influenced Thomas, both linguistically and socially. But it also carries a history of pervasive anti-Irish sentiment in the United States. According to Michael de Nie, 'the construction of the term intended to reflect the peasant nature and Catholicism of the Irish began around 1798 after a failed rebellion of the Irish people against the English' (De Nie, *Eternal Paddy*, p.18). This derogatory significance was frequent in England throughout the 1800s, when 'paddy' became a shorthand phrase used to describe the supposed laziness, drunkenness and uncleanliness of the Irish. The most common usage in the United States reflects these negative connotations and is the term 'paddy wagon', meaning a police van used to pick up large groups of out-of-control intoxicated individuals or other minor delinquents. In this usage, 'paddy' is employed to highlight difference and call attention to the fact that the Irish were not part of English society. Without realizing it, Piri has employed a slur that promotes the kind of historical ethnic discrimination against which he was rebelling.

In Frank McCourt's memoir *'Tis*, as in Thomas's work, the protagonist struggles with his own predetermined status. McCourt needs to come to terms with the fact that he will always be considered a 'Yank' in Ireland and a 'Mick' in the United States, much as Piri Thomas must figure out how to be a dark-skinned Puerto Rican in America. Growing up in the lanes of Limerick, McCourt always felt a certain distinction because he was born in New York, and he dreamed of going back. However, once he arrives he is categorized as an 'off the boat Mick' (McCourt, *'Tis,* p.65) or a 'Paddy-from-the-Bog' (ibid., p.430). As soon as he speaks, he is forced to confront how others perceive his Irishness:

> Why is it the minute I open my mouth the whole world is telling me they're Irish and we should all have a drink? It's not enough to be American. You always have to be something else, Irish–American, German-American, and you'd wonder how they'd get along if someone hadn't invented the hyphen. (Ibid., p.91)

McCourt comes back to New York determined to leave his past behind him, because he associates Irish identity with the poverty and oppression that he has experienced. He refuses to let this dominate his new life, but he is drawn to the Irish bars, with the shamrocks 'the likes of which you'd never see back in Ireland' (ibid., p.27), and later spends his free time in those bars singing patriotic songs his father has taught him.

McCourt is made immediately aware of the opinion that many New York Irish hold of Puerto Ricans. On his second day in the city he asks the doorman of the hotel, where he has just secured a job cleaning the lobby, for directions. The doorman is from Roscommon; he cheerfully gives the information and warns, 'Good luck, stick with your own kind and watch out for the Puerto Ricans, they all carry knives and that's a known fact, they got that hot blood. Walk in the light along the edge of the sidewalk or they'll be lep-pin' at you from dark doorways' (ibid., pp.25–6). The doorman's warning does not influence his thoughts until his landlady also disparages the Puerto Ricans. She tells him not to eat outside on the stoop because 'cock-roaches will come running from all over and people will say we're a bunch of Puerto Ricans who don't care where they eat or drink or sleep'. His Irish colleagues quickly teach McCourt the epitaph used to insult the Puerto Ricans, *spics*. He reflects, 'That's a new word, spics, and I know from the way he says it that he doesn't like Puerto Ricans.'[2]

In many ways, the low status of the Puerto Ricans determines McCourt's position as an Irish person in the city at this time. He quickly incorporates the word 'spic' into his vocabulary, and associates it with his sense of his own place in the power structure. Like Thomas, he understands that his position in the world will be based not only on his personal attributes, but also on how his community compares to others. McCourt's 'place' in the hierarchy is explained to him on his first day at the hotel, when he is told that he is not allowed to talk to the guests unless they speak to him. Then, as soon as he begins to clean up, the Greek waiters start shouting orders at him. After a few days, he begins to lament his situation:

> It's shameful enough going around the Palm Court [hotel lobby] in the black houseman's uniform which means I'm just above the Puerto Rican dishwashers in the eyes of the world. Even porters have a touch of gold on their uniforms and the doormen themselves look like admirals of the fleet. Eddie Gilligan, the union shop steward, says it's a good thing I'm Irish or it's down in the kitchen I'd be with the Spics.
>
> (McCourt, *'Tis*, p.38)

Holding down a difficult and thankless job, McCourt nonetheless takes comfort from seeing those who are in a worse position.

Frankie's co-worker at the hotel, Eddie Gilligan, also tells the young protagonist to stay away from the Puerto Ricans in the kitchen 'cause they wouldn't think twice about pissing in your coffee' (ibid.). However, Gilligan has a brief moment of revelation about the Puerto Rican workers when he thinks about the coffee. He tells McCourt that the previous year 'he saw them [the Puerto Rican dishwashers] pissing in the coffee urn that was being sent to a big lunch for the Daughters of the British Empire'. This, he decides, was a good idea, because it could be seen as retribution for 'what they did to the Irish

for 800 years'. Gilligan brags that at the next banquet he will also uri-
nate in the urn and afterwards announce that 'they have just drank
coffee filled with spick-mick piss' (ibid.). For this brief moment, he
places the Irish and Puerto Ricans on the same level, but it is only a
limited solidarity. The discussion closes with McCourt summing up
Eddie's final conclusion:

> He wouldn't want them marrying his daughter or moving into his
> neighbourhood but you have to admit they're musical and they
> send up some pretty good baseball players, you have to admit
> that. You go down into the kitchen and they're always happy like
> kids. He says, –They're like the Negroes, they don't take nothing
> serious. Not like the Irish. We take everything serious.
>
> (Ibid., p.39)

At no point does McCourt realize the irony that being musical and
good at sports are precisely what the Irish were known for when they
first came to the United States. He also infantilizes the Puerto Ricans
when he compares them to the Irish whose relative 'maturity' leads
them to take themselves too seriously. For both the Puerto Rican dish-
washers and the Irish shop workers, the Daughters of the British
Empire represent an Anglo culture that discriminates against them.
Gilligan may understand himself as excluded by Anglo society, but he
cannot recognize his experiences as similar to those of other ethnic
minorities.

Early in *'Tis* young Frank McCourt is taken to the Democratic
party headquarters by a priest he met during his voyage to New York;
there, the party workers find him his first job, at the hotel. At headquarters, the priest says to a secretary, 'This is a great country and the
Irish owe everything to the Democratic Party, Maureen, and you just
clinched another vote for the party if the kid ever votes, ha ha ha'
(ibid., p.24). In other words, McCourt's Irishness alone is sufficient
reason for the political machine to find him a job. Tammany Hall may
have lost some of its national power, but McCourt's experience in
1949 demonstrates that the Irish still have control of many jobs and
other aspects of civic life.

Joaquín Colón López's *Pioneros Puertorriqueños* is a collection of
articles written about the early years of the Great Migration. Colón
López meticulously documented the difficulties that Puerto Ricans
experienced in trying to preserve the culture of their homeland, while
still participating in the cultural and political life in New York. He,
too, emphasizes the importance of the Democratic party for many dif-

ferent immigrant groups and comments on the far-reaching Irish influence. 'Los irlandeses dominaban la ciudad de Nueva York, especialmente Brooklyn, cuando llegábamos nosotros. Estos hijos de Eire y de Ulster habían desplazado a los holandeses del control público de la ciudad' (The Irish dominated New York City, especially Brooklyn, when we arrived. These sons of Eire and Ulster had displaced the Dutch for public control of the city) (Colón López, *Pioneros Puertorriqueños*, p.46; translation by the author).

Colón López was aware that the Irish in America had endured discrimination and prejudice; he writes that the Irish 'llenaron de gloria y martirologio las páginas de la historia del movimiento obrero en los Estados Unidos' (filled the pages of the stories of the worker's movement in the United States with glory and martyrdom) (Ibid., p.46). But he experiences the Tammany Hall machine first hand, and he recognizes its power. His contempt for the system is obvious and it negates any potential feelings of solidarity that he has for the Irish. *Pioneros Puertorriqueños* consistently illustrates that minority races had to work hard to improve their lives – in part, because they were excluded from the system of ethnic favouritism.

Encounters between Irish New Yorkers and the Puerto Rican immigrant community fluctuated between limited acceptance and outright conflict. Occasionally, internalized social norms, which emphasized group solidarity within their communities, led to moments of recognition and understanding. In these cases, the Puerto Rican 'Other' served as a reminder of their own experiences, because the Irish likewise viewed themselves as outsiders who were not completely integrated into the hegemonic Anglo culture. However, mistrust outweighed these feelings and most encounters became adversarial.

Writing in 1956, Ivan Ilich – at the time a young priest and a colleague of the activist Father Fitzpatrick stationed at a chiefly Irish parish in the Washington Heights neighbourhood that was rapidly becoming a Puerto Rican area – saw clearly the consequences of such 'Othering'. He wrote: 'All this points to the need the Puerto Ricans have to win some more respect for their background. *What they need now is not more help but less categorization according to previous schemes, and more understanding.* Only thus will they make the unique cultural, political, and economic contributions for which they seem destined' (Ilich, 'Puerto Ricans in New York', p.297; emphasis in original). For the newly arrived Puerto Ricans, the Irish were often part of a hierarchy which looked down on them, despite their shared background as colonized peoples.

REFERENCES

Colón López, Joaquin. *Pioneros Puertorriqueños en Nueva York 1917–1947*. Houston, TX: Arte Público Press, 2002.

De Nie, Michael. *The Eternal Paddy:Irish Identity and the British Press, 1798–1882*. Madison, WI: University of Wisconsin Press, 2004.

Fitzpatrick, Joseph P. *The Stranger is Our Own: Reflections on the Journey of Puerto Rican Migrants*. Kansas City: Sheed and Ward, 1996.

Fitzpatrick, Joseph P. *Puerto Rican Americans: The Meaning of Migration to the Mainland*. Englewood Cliffs, NJ: Prentice-Hall, 1971.

Hernandez, Carmen Dolores. *Puerto Rican Voices in English: Interviews with Writers*. Westport, CT: Praeger, 1996.

Ilich, Ivan. 'Puerto Ricans in New York'. *Commonweal*, vol. 64, no. 12 (June 1956), pp.294–7.

McCourt, Frank. *'Tis*. New York: Scribner, 1999.

Rivera, Edward. *Family Installments: Memories of Growing up Hispanic*. New York: Morrow, 1982.

Sánchez Korrol, Virginia. 'Building the New York–Puerto Ricans Community, 1945–1965: A Historical Interpretation', in Gabriel Haslip-Viera, Angelo Falcón and Félix Matos Rodriguez (eds), *Boricuas in Gotham: Puerto Ricans in the Making of Modern New York*. Princeton, NJ: Markus Wiener, 2004.

Thomas, Piri. *Down These Mean Streets*. New York: Knopf, 1967.

CHAPTER SEVEN

From 'Peace and Freedom' to 'Peace and Quiet': The Quiet Man as a Product of the 1950s

EDWARD A. HAGAN

Long reviled as Irish–American sentimentality, John Ford's *The Quiet Man* has recently been discovered by critics to have a previously unnoticed depth that rewards even further excavation.[1] There are notable gaps in earlier criticisms of the 1952 movie. For instance, earlier critics have not acknowledged the screenplay's removal of the story from its Irish nationalist context, which is clear in the 1933 and 1935 Maurice Walsh stories on which it is based. Critics have also not noted that the film makes no reference to World War Two. In addition, those criticisms do not focus on the effacement of the parish priest, Father Lonergan (Ward Bond) as narrator, and do not focus on what he actually does say. As we watch the film, we forget that the story is being told from the priest's memory; its idealizations arise from selective memory, and the dramatic immediacy of film causes us to have a present-tense sense of the story.

Director Ford appears to have intended that we would discover our propensity to forget that the film is at least as much about storytelling and 'making it up' as it is about the story of Sean Thornton (John Wayne) and Mary Kate Danaher (Maureen O'Hara). Ford sets a trap for an audience that – in the aftermath of World War Two – wants to be beguiled into accepting romantic fantasy as realism, but he also leaves the evidence that allows us to see that trap. We need to understand why we want to believe in that false story, as the desire for belief in fantasy particularly marks the film as a post-World War Two artifact.

The Quiet Man records a fading of historical consciousness in both Ireland and America. While the Walsh stories are set specifically in the lead-up to the formation of the Irish Free State and the Great

Depression, the film transforms these into a story seemingly epic and timeless. The apparent mythic story in the film actually reveals the early 1950s as a period in which historical consciousness is dimming because of the perceived desire to be quiet about World War Two, including, perhaps, a studied reticence about Ireland's neutrality in the war. The film removes its story from its historical moment, although it contains scattered historical referents.

The disconnected historical markers in the movie are curious. The Walsh story appeared as a chapter in the 1935 novel *Green Rushes*, and refers to the Black and Tan War; earlier, in the 1933 *Saturday Evening Post* short-story version, it refers to 1916. The 1935 version has the Sean Thornton character involved in IRA activities.[2] The film purges most of the IRA references, though a few bits remain and are somewhat puzzling: Michaeleen Oge Flynn (Barry Fitzgerald) talks of 'sedition' in the film, but his use of the term seems generic, as he makes no direct reference to the IRA. Later, Red Will Danaher (Victor McLaglen) inexplicably asks whether the IRA is involved in his bamboozling. The reference would make sense in the 1933 story, because in that version the central character is presented as having been an active member of the IRA in the aftermath of 1916. Flynn's sedition comment could refer broadly to any Irish revolutionary movement during the preceding centuries. Such broad reference in the film removes historical specificity, whereas the story versions are set in identifiable time frames. 'Physical force' nationalism becomes barroom *craic* in Michaeleen Oge's head. He will drink and talk sedition, but does so with no link either to 1916 or to the Black and Tans.

The economics of filmmaking can partially explain the excisions. A film that requires substantial knowledge of Irish history would limit its American audience. The Irish government, whose cooperation was required, might have wanted to diminish the role of Irish nationalist politics. Ford worked closely with Lord Killanin (later a controversial president of the International Olympic Committee) to advance an Irish film industry and probably would have accepted Irish government desires to downplay nationalist politics. The government would have found a partner in this regard in Republic Pictures. Ford's biographer, Joseph McBride, says that Herbert J. Yates, the owner of Republic, argued that a reference to Irish nationalism 'could make it difficult to play the film in Great Britain and the British Commonwealth' (McBride, *John Ford*, p.513). Moreover Republic would be unlikely to want to address recent American history in its films: if the nation's veterans were determined to keep silent about their war experiences, neither Republic nor Ford would likely seek to break their silence. Finally, Ford may well have seen aesthetic value in leaving only a residue of contemporary Irish and American politics in the film. Most Ford films favour the mythic to the realistic; he often showed the American preference for the legendary, even, or perhaps especially, at the expense of truth. Whatever the reason, the 1952 film provides only fragmentary references to Irish nationalism and no mention at all of World War Two.[3]

However, those surviving remnants of Irish nationalism offer interesting, if possibly unintentional, windows on the question of what the returned American, Sean Thornton, is seeking in Ireland. The wedding toast by the local IRA man suggests one goal; he offers the wish that Sean and Mary Kate may live in 'peace and freedom'. Later Father Lonergan tells us that they want to live in 'peace and quiet'. The change is significant. 'Freedom' is both the goal of Irish nationalism and an iconic American word worth fighting for. We do know that the original script called for the toast to wish the couple the chance to live in 'peace and national freedom' (ibid.). 'Quiet' suggests a less political orientation, especially important because 'quiet' is the defining word in the film's title. Behind Thornton's desire for 'peace and quiet' lies that constellation of postwar psychological hangovers that since the 1970s have come to be grouped under the diagnosis of Post-Traumatic Stress Disorder (PTSD). A desire for peace, of course, would have had a particular resonance in 1952, in the immediate aftermath of World War Two and in the midst of the Korean War. But more important, Thornton killed a man in the ring in a prize fight for, in his words, 'filthy money'; he has gone back to the place of his birth, Ireland, scarred by the memory of the killing and determined to keep his past 'quiet'. Thornton apparently hopes that Ireland will somehow cure the terrible alienation and intense guilt he feels. This element is also new to the film: in Walsh's stories, the Thornton character was a boxer in the United States, but in neither did he kill a man. The killing is a postwar addition to the story; Sean Thornton, like World War Two veterans, has blood on his hands. The shooting script for the movie specifically states that he 'returns to Ireland ... in search of forgetfulness of all the wars of the human spirit he has lived through so far' (Nugent, 'Shooting Script').

When Mr Playfair, the Protestant minister, recognizes 'Trooper' Thornton – the name might be derived from his former military service – as a former boxer, Thornton pleads for silence, and Playfair complies. This reticence is quite contrary to the Thornton character's behaviour in the Walsh stories, in one of which the Mary Kate Danaher character 'thrilled when he showed her ... how to stiffen [the] wrist for the final devastating right hook' (Walsh, *Green Rushes*, p.183). Thornton's conduct in the film resembles that of returning veterans who apparently did not want to tell their stories of wartime horror, and who associated peace with quiet. In fact, quietness is a quality ascribed to veterans of many wars; it has been attested to by Ernest Hemingway in 'Soldier's Home', Paul Fussell in *Wartime* (1989) and, more recently, by George W.S. Trow in *My Pilgrim's Progress: Media Studies, 1950–1998* (1999).

Hemingway's central character, Krebs, developed a need to talk about his World War One experiences, but 'no one wanted to hear about it. His town had heard too many atrocity stories to be thrilled by actualities. Krebs found that to be listened to at all he had to lie, and after he had done this twice he, too, had a reaction against the war and against talking about it' (Hemingway, 'Soldier's Home', p.69).

Fussell discusses the alienation of veterans of World War Two in similar terms. Their silence grew out of their repugnance toward the way the mass media insisted on portraying their experience. He writes:

> What was it about the war that moved the troops to constant verbal subversion and contempt? It was not just the danger and fear, the boredom and uncertainty and loneliness and deprivation. It was rather the conviction that optimistic publicity and euphemism had rendered their experience so falsely that it would never be readily communicable. They knew that in its representation to the laity what was happening to them was systematically sanitized and Norman Rockwellized, not to mention Disneyfied ....The troops' disillusion and their ironic response, in song and satire and sullen contempt, came from knowing that the home front then (and very likely historiography later) could be aware of none of these things.
>
> (Fussell, *Wartime*, pp.267–8)

Fussell argues that, because of the veterans' silence, 'America has not yet understood what the Second World War was like and has thus been unable to use such understanding to re-interpret and re-define the national reality and to arrive at something like public maturity' (ibid., p.268).

Trow also testifies to the quiet of the postwar era:

> I was born *during* World War II, so I saw nothing to do with the

> war itself. My first memory – and it has stayed with me all my
> life – was of this enormous strange quiet following our victory.
> Something enormous had just happened; I happened not to have
> witnessed it, but it had happened; people were living in a kind of
> quiet, suspended, dignified, tense aftermath, very dignified,
> black-and-white.   (Trow, *My Pilgrim's Progress*,
> p.24)

Trow contends that the silence that marked the immediate postwar era
amounted to a denial of context for whatever the soldiers might have to
say.[4]   The post World War Two quiet represented a sea change in
American culture; Americans, particularly under the influence of television, began to cut themselves off from history more pervasively than
ever before. In making this point, Trow closely examines the *New York
Times* for February 1950, especially the serialization of Winston
Churchill's memoir of the Second World War. He notes that there has
been no subsequent serialization of any book, especially not a war memoir, in the daily *New York Times* since 1950, at least not on the front
page of the paper. Thus, Churchill is of the 'old world'; his hero is 'A.W.
Kinglake, who wrote about the Crimean War, and so right on the front
page of the *New York Times*, you get a bit of the early-nineteenth century, early-Victorian writing, making our modern era continuous, in a
way, with the Crimean War – with Agincourt for that matter' (*Pilgrim's
Progress*, p.75). Trow finds the Churchill serialization already *passé* in
1950. Such historical continuity was cut off in the postwar era; returning veterans discovered there was no context in which to present the
text of their stories. In *The Quiet Man*, Ford delivers a film that point-
edly makes us aware of the incompleteness of its context.

Trow's thesis of the sea change in consciousness and Fussell's thesis
– public immaturity – were consequential for both Ireland and
America. Both the Irish and the returned American appear to be juvenile in *The Quiet Man*; but a central reality of childhood and adoles-
cence is that they come to a close, and the film speaks to the end of eras
in both countries. It is time to be quiet when truth cannot be told; Ford
gives us an improbable romantic story of a world that never was. Being
quiet also involves a self-willed isolation, and Sean Thornton is a loner,
an American, acting perhaps in the American tradition of individualism, to cut himself off from society. But he has not come to his decision alone: we must also suspect that the blood-lust of the American
crowd has driven him back to the womb – his birthplace.

If Thornton can be reborn in Ireland, he may be able to sever his ties to his personal history and to the recent history of the United States. *The Quiet Man*, thus, operates as the story of a culture that cannot recall what its most sacred ideals in both politics and religion were, only a generation before. Here, Ireland becomes in the American imagination a place of fairy-tale romance, enacting de Valéra's famously halcyon radio address made in the midst of World War. At least in part, Ford's film gives us de Valera's ideal Ireland – a land where the people are happy children. But while Ford's film accords with de Valera's vision, it simultaneously also shows that ideal is both wildly romantic and painfully ironic.

We perceive Ford's sense of irony in his decision to undermine his story by drawing attention to its teller's inability to control his own telling. Ford uses a limited narration that masquerades as omniscient. He wants us to understand what happens when we claim to be presenting God's view, when we actually know better. We are living in a world that has collapsed, but we are not aware of the collapse because the mechanism of storytelling impairs our consciousness of the narrator's manipulation. In Ford's work we can come to understand the consequences of losing track of narratorial manipulation of a story; in response, we latch on to the story we want to hear. Nostalgia enables the manipulative storyteller to recover a past that no longer exists, or, perhaps, never existed.

Ford's directing is most evident in his framing. We can observe the framing throughout the film, but most especially in the scene in the rain (right after Sean and Mary Kate break away from Michaleen, their escort). They are framed by the arch of a ruined church, and Ford holds the shot long enough for us to catch the idea that the framing is crucial, especially framing that suggests the budding romance is built on the demise of tradition. However, in fact, it is the framing itself we lose sight of. Ford's movie reveals our inability to see how consciousness shapes the picture of what we see. We in fact become absorbed by the immediacy of the scene and lose our awareness of the shaping quality of Hollywood's makers of fantasy. Ford is deconstructing Hollywood's manipulations, even as we can allow our nostalgia to lead us into thinking he is constructing them. Ford gives us the evidence that we should be questioning the framing of his narrator as well as Ford's own framing as director.

We might perceive Ford's questioning of narrative accuracy in the fact that the film changes the place name of Thornton's birthplace to 'Innisfree'. Notably, the speaker in Yeats's 'The Lake Isle of Innisfree' only dreams of such an idyllic place; he remains 'on the pavements grey'. Ford expects us to wake up and see that his story is really about story-telling and its demise, its ossification in times of cultural collapse.

A film that Ford made ten years later, in 1962, *The Man Who Shot Liberty Valance*, helps to illustrate his strategy in alerting us to our preference for the good narrative yarn – at the expense of truth. The narrative strategy of *The Quiet Man* resembles Ford's very direct assault on a crowd's (and his audience's) preference for legend in the later movie. In the opening scene of that movie – a long shot of a landscape – Ford has the camera held steadily in an unmoving position, and it never changes our perspective. The point of observation is static. The train enters the screen from the right and exits from the left. It is bringing US Senator Ransom Stoddard (Jimmy Stewart) back to Shinbone, the Wild West town in which he began his legal career; he is returning for the funeral of Tom Doniphon (John Wayne). Stoddard owes his entire political and professional career to Doniphon, who actually shot Liberty Valance (Lee Marvin), an outlaw who routinely terrorized Shinbone. Stoddard is a man of law, given to a certain wimpy petulance, but also committed to avoiding violence (much as Sean Thornton is in *The Quiet Man*). Doniphon, however, is the one who brought order to Shinbone, which he did at the point of the gun. A key moment in the movie is the apparent shooting of Valance by Stoddard; the truth is that Doniphon actually fired the shot that killed Valance. Because Stoddard is credited with the killing, he becomes the hero of Shinbone and its political leader, and the beneficiary of the legend that grows out of the shooting. The movie then presents the telling to Shinbone's newspaper editor, years later, of the story of what actually happened.

In the closing scenes, the newspaper editor learns that Stoddard did not kill Valance and that the town has been living with a false story – but the editor declares he will not print the story of what actually happened. Here, Ford's comment on history is quite pointed: the West is built on the lie the editor perpetuates. The necessity of the lie in American culture is a *sine qua non* of Ford's work.

As *Liberty Valance* ends, Ford inverts the film's opening by focusing on Stoddard as he leaves town, and we hear the legend that surrounds him repeated by the train's conductor. The final image is a long shot of the train pulling away from Shinbone. But the shot of the train's exit differs in important ways: the camera is obviously handheld, shakes noticeably, and pans slightly to keep the train on the screen, so that it does not pass out of the picture as it did in the opening scene. Ford's camera work suggests that the film should have modified our understanding of storytelling. We should see that the perspective we are getting at the end is human, and therefore shaky – just like the legend of the man who shot Liberty Valance. The train does not leave the picture, so we are aware that the perspective of the camera observer is not godlike. It is as much the result of human activity as the movement of the train, which, in fact, contains the trainman who has asserted the legend of the man who killed Liberty Valance. However, though the movie has undermined the legend, we cannot, like Shinboners, ignore the fact that Stoddard did not kill Liberty Valance. Ford wants us to also see that the storyteller is not the impassive, unbiased observer that the position of the camera at the beginning portends.

This insight into Ford's focus on the role of the storyteller allows us to look at the opening of *The Quiet Man* with greater acuity. It, too, opens with the arrival of a train bearing a transforming outsider like Stoddard – Sean Thornton. However, upon his arrival we immediately hear the voice of the narrator, Father Lonergan. His statement, 'I'll begin at the beginning', suggests a definitiveness to his story as if there is an acknowledged, authoritative beginning that the all-knowing narrator, the parish priest, can enunciate. But, unlike the Stoddard character in the later movie, the process of *The Quiet Man*'s story is that Father Lonergan's voice will disappear over the course of the movie. The story of Sean Thornton and Mary Kate Danaher overwhelms that voice; but as the film moves toward its conclusion, it makes us conscious of its play-acting, in a series of closing stage bows by the actors that break any illusion that we have been watching anything other than a staged fantasy. Ford makes clear that we need to see that the movie offers a legend, but we should see it simply as legend, as made-up, an exercise in storytelling. We should catch on to the device of the storyteller's fake authority. The series of final bows is an especially clear statement that the film's story is a contrived play. In short, the movie drives home how necessary artifice is to creating 'peace and quiet' in Innisfree. Father Lonergan appears to be wrapping up his story when he offers the hope for a life of 'peace and quiet' for Sean and Mark Kate. But his final narrative proclamation is in fact interrupted by the charade of the cheering by all the townsfolk for Mr Playfair and his bishop. We are treated to a most improbable spectacle of 'peace and quiet'. We should also see 'peace and quiet' as a contrived *story* abstracted from the historical realities of 1950s Ireland and America – ironically, a marker of the movie's embedding in that time.

Another 1950s time signature informs this contrived play-acting. Once we see how the crowd manipulates the characters' actions at the end of the film, we should notice that the forces that motivate the characters closely resemble those described in David Riesman's influential theory of the 'other directed' personality, published in his landmark 1950 book, *The Lonely Crowd*. Riesman argued that population changes produced three types of personalities: tradition-directed, inner-directed and other-directed, and theorized that Americans were entering the other-directed stage. Riesman's thesis achieved widespread currency in the early 1950s, so much so that he appeared on the cover of *Time* magazine in 1954. There is no evidence that Ford was keenly interested in Riesman's theory, but it is difficult to imagine he was not aware of his thinking. *The Quiet Man*, in fact, neatly presents both the conflict of the three types of personality that Riesman delineated and the evolution of the characters toward acceptance of other-direction.

Mary Kate Danaher is a tradition-directed character; she is strongly motivated by her allegiance to the tradition of the dowry. Her allegiance must be served for the romance with Thornton to be consummated. Thornton is an inner-directed character, an American individualist who has strongly held personal values derived in part from his mother but also from his own bitter experience in America. Inner-directed character, according to Riesman, results from breakdowns in tradition brought on by population growth and the impossibility of repeating the lives of one's parents. Thornton's return to the Ireland of his birth signifies his disapproval of the mass values of American society; he is instead guided by what Riesman called an 'inner gyroscope' (Riesman, *Lonely Crowd*, p.16).

The Innisfree to which Thornton returns might be regarded as a tradition-directed society; however, Riesman explains, tradition-directed societies do resemble other-directed societies. He writes:

> the other-directed person learns to respond to signals from a far wider circle than is constituted by his parents. The family is no longer a closely knit unit [note the absence of parents for either Thornton or Mary Kate] to which he belongs but merely a part of a wider social environment to which he early becomes attentive. In these respects the other-directed person resembles the tradition-directed person: both live in a group milieu and lack the inner-directed person's capacity to go it alone. The nature of this group milieu, however, differs radically in the two cases.

The other-directed person is cosmopolitan. For him the border between the familiar and the strange – a border clearly marked in the societies depending on tradition-direction – has broken down. As the family continuously absorbs the strange and so reshapes itself, so the strange becomes familiar. While the inner-directed person could be 'at home abroad' by virtue of his relative insensitivity to others, the other-directed person is, in a sense, at home everywhere and nowhere, capable of a superficial intimacy with and response to everyone.

(Ibid., p.26)

Innisfree is hardly insular. The film records the compromise that Thornton must make with his sense of himself and with the place he can cut out for himself in the world. *The Quiet Man* records the increasing cosmopolitanism of Innisfree; it becomes a place in which the border between Catholic and Protestant is bridged; a place in which such recent Irish events as 1916 and the Black-and-Tan War are barely remembered; a place that can enact American movie idylls as effectively as any American place. The boxing flashback in the film presents America as sports-mad; in this regard, Innisfree – in its love of boxing as well as horse racing – seems to be quite like America. Thornton's departure from America has come about through the pressure of American other-direction. He hopes to escape from the crowds that would constantly remind him of his boxing feats, including the killing in the ring for money. Ironically, he finds no difference in the crowds in Innisfree; they require him to forswear his promise never to fight again.

When Thornton is finally faced with the need to deal with both Mary Kate's tradition-direction (the dowry) and with the crowd's insistent desire for a bout with Danaher, he becomes anxious and seeks help from Mr Playfair. Riesman tells us that 'one prime psychological lever of the other-directed person is a diffuse *anxiety*. This control equipment, instead of being like a gyroscope, is like a radar' (ibid.,p.26). In seeking Playfair's advice, we see Thornton developing the radar that allows him to respond to the pressures upon him; it forces him to compromise his pledge never to fight in order to secure the quiet he desires. That Playfair is in contact with Thornton's boxing history is instructive in many ways: the only relevant history in Innisfree appears to be sports history. Playfair fits right in to a community where the priest is apparently more obsessed with catching a fish than with his parishioners, and where a trainman calls the history of All-Ireland hurling championships 'the history of your country'. Sports-gambling thrives in Innisfree, including among the clergy. Michaeleen Oge makes book on the Thornton–Danaher fight; even the gardaí participate. The athletics contest is central to the plot's resolution. Playfair, a former boxer himself, recognizes Thornton as a famous boxer and shows him that he cannot escape the pressure of the crowd. Father Lonergan works on Mary Kate at the same time, and in this way Protestant and Catholic work together to consummate the match of Thornton and Mary Kate.

But what a consummation: a public spectacle of Thornton dragging Mary Kate for a great distance, the demand for the dowry, and the final showdown fistfight of Thornton and Danaher. The public – and the film audience – will have its epic Hollywood battle. The film viewer enjoys the shenanigans and, thus, participates in reducing the Irish to children. And children, of course, have no sense of history.

Crucially, the changes in the film from the two Walsh stories rendered the film more ahistorical. In both story versions the Thornton character returns home disillusioned with 'drudge toil' in the America of the Great Depression. In Ireland, he would think 'of the poor devils [back in America], with dreams of fortune luring them, going out to sweat in Ironville, or to bootleg bad whisky down the hidden way, or to stand in a bread line' (Walsh, 'The Quiet Man' [1933], p.10). In Ford's film there is no mention at all of the Depression. The sole reason cited for Thornton's return is his remorse over killing a man in the ring. The element of having killed a man is an amendment of the Walsh stories, one consistent with postwar trauma. The 1935 story version did in fact refer to silence about war: we are told that the Thornton and Mary Kate characters 'did not speak at all of the Black-and-Tan war. That was too near them. That made men frown and women shiver' (*Green Rushes*, p.183). Ford could find precedence for quiet about war in the original story – but in the film, the silence is wholly displaced from Irish nationalism and revolution, and moved to the political neutrality of the boxing arena.

But Ireland does not allow Thornton to avoid PTSD; indeed, Ireland turns out to be not so different from America. The village of Innisfree is a community in transition from tradition-direction to other-direction. In other-directed societies, Riesman argues, personality, not any staple or machine, is the most important product (Riesman, *Lonely Crowd*, p.46). When Thornton arrives in Innisfree, he is immediately cast as an American who must fit a well-established cliché. Because Thornton does not have a camera or fishing pole, the markers of the tourist American, he appears to be an enigma. He has not completely absorbed identity from his fellow-American country-men, and in this sense we should see him as mostly inner-directed. In fact, he is driven by his mother's voice evoking White o'Morn, the ancestral cottage, as heaven. This fits Riesman's definition of inner-directed quite explicitly; he seems to have developed from his mother the 'inner gyroscope' that brings him back to Ireland. However, we do see that Thornton has developed some other-directed personality traits from his years in America. When he first enters Cohan's Bar, he tries to buy everyone a drink – an act of anonymous congeniality suggestive of other-direction, which we may suspect Thornton learned from American movies. But notably, he must pay obeisance to Irish tradition before his offer is accepted: the people in the bar must establish his genealogy before they will accept his largesse. American other-direction must meet the tradition standard of the crowd – the visitor's member-ship in its ethnicity, and consequently, his unthreatening nature – not the anonymous congeniality of Riesman's 'lonely crowd'.

But the Innisfree of *The Quiet Man* is also in transition. Its strongest force is, in fact, the crowd. Clearly, the whole village has been waiting for the big fight between Thornton and Red Will Danaher to break out, and slyly moving them toward that event. Once it does, we have a pure Hollywood extravaganza, one in which the Irish are hard-drinking brawlers who just love a donnybrook. The Irish are revealed as lovers of spectacle and, thus, are well qualified to take their place in what Riesman calls the new visual world, in which all can be subordinated to a good show – to the eye of the beholder, not the invention of the par-ticipants (Ibid., p.286). Michaleen Flynn puts on his bookie's hat and starts taking bets on the outcome of the fight. The fight itself is punc-tuated with drinks in the bar, and follows upon Thornton's dragging of Mary Kate from a railway car to Danaher's farm to demand and collect her dowry, which they both promptly burn.

The crowd determines both Thornton's and Mary Kate's conduct, and the crowd manipulates the decision of the Protestant bishop to keep the Revd Mr Playfair in the village. This is clearly other-directed behaviour. The decision is based not on any inner convictions about what ought to be done, but on the perceived will of the people, which, of course, has been manipulated by the Catholic priest and his flock. Significantly, Father Lonergan is not motivated by any religious prin-ciple, but by a belief in the need to maintain the parson's place in the community – a value that might be tradition-directed, but which is enacted by using the crowd.

In fact, Father Lonergan and his curate go so far as to cover up their Roman collars. In this gesture, Ford achieves a final storybook amelioration of religious rivalry in Ireland. That the gesture ran counter to actual practice is clear in a 1952 letter to the *Connaught Telegraph*, from a writer from Westport, Mayo, who saw Ford's manipulation as offensive: 'I asked myself why did Cong people allow John Ford [to] direct such misleading and degrading scenes here in Mayo? I ask John Ford since when did any Catholic priest the world over cover and deny the Roman collar? – Never' (*Connaught Telegraph*, 18 October 1952, p.5). The letter writer's complaint had some currency in Ireland and in Irish Catholic America of the day. It reveals an allegiance to tradition, which the film treats as trivial. The letter writer goes on to cite the current Cold War context in which 'bishops and priests died alike for the Roman collar' (ibid.). The letter writer, thus, insists on context; Ford's deeper offense has been to remove that context in order to tell a mythic story of the movement of Irish and American sensibilities to other-direction.

The initially inner-directed Thornton succumbs to other-direction. To do so, he undergoes a reprise of the traumatic event of his life – a boxing match – and in doing so, enacts the often-recorded PTSD cycle of recurring trauma.[5] However, in the fairy-tale world of *The Quiet Man*, there is no nightmare. What happens instead is that Thornton pleases the crowd by fighting Danaher, and he weans Mary Kate of her tradition-direction. In one swoop, Ireland becomes a Hollywood set and, therefore, a place that will become ultimately sensitive to outside pressures. Ireland is welcomed to the world of American childishness. It is hardly surprising that such an outcome would meet some resentment from the Irish. A reviewer in the *Irish Press* in 1952 noted the power of Hollywood to transform Ireland:

> Cinematically this is gloriously presented ...
>
> It's the finest bit of divarshun the Hollywood factory has poured out. And they have as Barry [Fitzgerald] says, 'a fine shteady hand'.
>
> Innisfree is a grand place, a fightin' place and a drinkin' place. You'll find it round the bend of Sunset Boulevard convenient to Gloccamora, Calif.
>
> (*Irish Press*, 9 June 1952, p.4)

It is no small irony that Thornton left America to escape from his role in a spectacle of violence, performed for crowds, only to find that he must play the same role in Ireland in order to purchase the quiet isolation that he desires. Thornton returns to Ireland with Riesman's 'internal gyroscope' that was implanted by his mother. He hears her voice that now draws him back to his childhood cottage, 'White o' Morn'. But he cannot have the cottage on such inner-directed terms: he must bend to the will of the crowd.

In Ford's film, both the Irish and the Americans move into the new, ahistorical future. Ford let us see just where we were in the 1950s, and we are still there. We have entered mythic space, in a quite witting repudiation and denial of history. In such a space we can easily lose consciousness of narratorial manipulation of reality; we can forget that we are in fact listening to a yarn told by Father Lonergan. The result of the romance in *The Quiet Man* is a couple who have a life ahead of them that will meet the idyllic goal of *rapprochement* between Ireland and America, between Protestant and Catholic, between tradition-direction and other-direction – or does their new life not really resolve such former antinomies, but simplify and homogenize all differences? Ford ensures that we can perceive a lingering distaste for the trivialization of values that were once held dear.

REFERENCES

Connaught Telegraph. 'The Quiet Man', letter to the editor, 18.

Fussell, Paul. *Wartime*. New York and Oxford: Oxford University Press, 1989.

Hemingway, Ernest. 'Soldiers Home', in *In Our Time*. New York: Collier, 1986, pp.69–77.

Irish Press. 'John Ford Shows Us Us', review of *The Quiet Man* signed 'L. MacG', 9 June 1952.

McBride, Joseph. *John Ford: A Life*. London: Faber & Faber, 2003.

Nugent, Frank. 'Shooting Script: Production #1912: "THE QUIET MAN" DELUXE by Frank Walsh' (1951). Republic Pictures. Margaret Herrick Library, Academy of Motion Pictures, Los Angeles.

The Quiet Man, directed by John Ford. 1952; Republic Pictures.

Riesman, David. *The Lonely Crowd: A Study of the Changing American Character*. New Haven and London: Yale University Press, 1950.

Trow, George W.S. *My Pilgrim's Progress: Media Studies, 1950–1998*, New York: Pantheon, 1999.

Walsh, Maurice. 'The Quiet Man'. *Saturday Evening Post*, 11 February 1933.

—— *Green Rushes*. New York: Frederick A. Stokes, 1935.

CHAPTER EIGHT

Ahead of Their Time: Irish–American Women Writers 1945–1960

SALLY BARR EBEST

The postwar years were pivotal for American women. As Susan Hartman argues in *The Home Front and Beyond*, 'the 1940s contained developments which sharply set off that decade from the preceding one and which established patterns that would shape women's lives for some years to come' (Hartman, *Home Front*, p.ix). Feminist scholars provide sometimes scathing findings regarding the treatment of American women during this period; however, little has been written about how the postwar era influenced Irish–American women. Well-known historical works by Kerby Miller, Lawrence McCaffrey, Hasia Diner and Janet Nolan provide the prewar context; unfortunately, the studies written by men devote little time to women, while those by women tend to stop around 1920. Luckily, Irish–American women writers of the time fill in the gaps. An examination of their writings unsettles the popular notion of Irish–American 'girls' and housewives during the early postwar era characterized by naïveté or conformity. Such writers as Maeve Brennan, Maureen Howard and especially Mary McCarthy challenge any notion of the submissive Irish–American woman, married or not. When juxtaposed with Irish–American and feminist histories, their memoirs and novels not only paint a vivid picture of women's lives in transition, but also offer a valid and heretofore unexamined picture of Irish–American women writers at mid-century.

The decade preceding World War Two set in motion many subsequent social changes, for the Depression not only cost many men their livelihood, but also impacted on women's lives. Despite financial stresses, 85 per cent of married women stayed at home (ibid., p.16). The 15 per cent who worked outside the home were 'viewed as self-ish, greedy women who took jobs away from male breadwinners' (ibid., p.17). American society and government policy of the time openly discriminated against working women: most jobs and relief projects were reserved for men.

In the early 1900s married Irish–American women, like women all over the country, were discouraged from seeking work outside the home (Mageean, 'Making Sense and Providing Structure', p.234). Although many worked before marrying, they were forced to 'retire' when they married (Nolan, *Servants of the Poor*, p.xi). Notably, before marriage Irish–American women were among the most employed of their gender. As early as 1892, this demographic represented 'a sizable presence' within the workforce (ibid., p.1). Not all were in low-status occupations; although Irish-born women constituted the largest number of nannies and housekeepers during the early twentieth century (Katzman, *Seven Days a Week*, p.66), they also made up the majority of teachers. By 1910 Irish–American women represented 'one of the largest single ethnic groups among public elementary school teachers in Providence and Boston ... fully a third of the teachers in New York and Chicago ... [and] 49 percent of San Francisco's primary and grammar school teachers' (Nolan, *Servants of the Poor*, p.2). By 1939, 70 per cent of Chicago's schoolteachers were Irish–American women (ibid., p.92).

Janet Nolan writes that 'Teaching ultimately allowed daughters ... of immigrants to leave the working class and enter the educated lower middle class' (ibid., p.137). Their ascent was central in the assimilative process: 'Rather than being footnotes to the history of the Irish in America, teachers are at the center of that experience' (ibid., p.138). Lawrence McCaffrey agrees, noting that education 'placed the Irish in the vanguard of American women marching toward economic independence and professional stature' (*Textures of Irish America*, p.32). Among teachers and nurses, writes McCaffrey, 'Irish women became prominent . . . essential to public as well as Catholic education and health' (ibid., p.32). Many owed their success to nuns, who provided a rigorous education as well as strong, positive role models for young Irish–American women. McCaffrey maintains that due in large part to the nuns' influence, by mid-century Irish–American women had become 'the most successful members of their sex in the United States. As educators, school administrators, union leaders, nurses, physicians, and lawyers, they added a women's leadership dimension to American society' (ibid., p.77).

Significant numbers of Irish–American women also worked in publishing, writing novels and short stories for women's magazines and
occasionally for mainstream outlets (R. Ebest, *Private Histories*,
pp.58ff.). These authors were among the 15 per cent of *married*
American women working outside the home. This figure is more significant than it may seem at first glance. In the 1940s approximately
66 per cent of Irish Catholics were lower class and only 9 per cent
were upper class. Their education consigned them to these strata, for
57 per cent of the Catholic population had no more than a partial high
school education. Only 7.1 per cent of Catholics were among the
professional class, as opposed to 11 per cent of Protestants (Schneider,
Religion in 20th Century America, pp.228–32). Irish–American
women writers resided among upper-class professionals because they
held college degrees. Indeed, after the war, when an influx of returning soldiers displaced the majority of women working in publishing,
Irish–American women retained positions on the major intellectual
journals and magazines.

The most prominent among this group was Mary McCarthy. A
descendant of John McCarthy, an Irish immigrant who settled in
Newfoundland in 1837 (Brightman, *Writing Dangerously*, p.49), Mary
was born to Roy and Tess McCarthy in 1912. When her parents died
in the influenza epidemic of 1920, Mary and her brothers were taken
in by their abusive Irish–Catholic relatives in Minneapolis – an experience that forever tainted her view of Catholicism. McCarthy married immediately after graduating from Vassar; nevertheless, she
worked from 1937 through 1962 as a writer and editor for the
Partisan Review, the most intellectually élite 'old boys' club' in New
York City. 'Over a fifty-year period, only 12 per cent of the essays in
the *Partisan Review* were by women' (Showalter, *Inventing Herself*,
p.179). McCarthy's prominence in this imbalanced work environment is all the more striking given the low stature of women contributors there: in the *Partisan Review Reader*, a collection of the 'best and
most representative' essays published from 1939 to 1944, only 14 of
the 92 selections are by women. However, 36 per cent of these were
written by three Irish–American women: McCarthy and poets Louise
Bogan and Marianne Moore.

In the war years prohibitions against women working changed rapidly: '[b]etween 1940 and 1945, the female labor force grew by more
than 50 per cent', three-quarters of whom were married (Hartmann,
Home Front, p.21). By war's end, 'wives for the first time comprised
almost the majority of women workers' (Chafe, *Unfinished Journey*,

p.13). But as the war wound down, the same forces that had encouraged women to work ensured that they returned to their presumed
true calling as wives and mothers. The responses to this retrenchment
varied: ironically, some Irish–American women who were themselves
professional writers supported the move. Betty Smith's novels – *A
Tree Grows in Brooklyn* (1943), *Tomorrow Will be Better* (1948) and
Maggie-Now (1958) – reiterate the belief that when women married,
they quit working outside the home (Scott, 'Women's Perspectives',
p.90). The preoccupations of Smith's heroines novels are 'romance,
marriage, childbirth, and death' (Ibid., p.92). Smith told *Good
Housekeeping* that 'Mating "means the desire for children – and that
is important. Nature gives us the love instinct solely for the purpose
of propagating the earth"' (qtd in ibid., p.93). Other Irish–American
novels of the time, such as Mary Doyle Curran's *The Parish and the
Hill*, Mary Deasy's *Hour of Spring* and Ellin Berlin's *Lace Curtains*, all
published in 1948, sound a comparable note, featuring various versions of the fresh-faced, aspiring girl hero. In a 1948 interview with
The Boston Post, Curran describes her novel by saying:

> mine isn't a love story. There isn't a drop of sex in it ... it is my
> family of whom I am writing ... My mother was born in Ireland.
> She taught her children the true Irish value of life. We learned
> Irish folk lore and poetry, and we were not ashamed of our Irish
> background ... My mother believed in education for her chil-
> dren, moral and intellectual ... [W]e must return to those values.
> (qtd in Halley, 'An American Story', n.p.)

While it might be argued that a majority of women's fiction of the
time included similarly conventional ideas, Mary McCarthy's *The
Company She Keeps* (1942) instead offered sordid details of a
divorcee's dalliances, most notably in her short story, 'The Man in the
Brooks Brothers Suit', which recounts Meg Sergant's seduction by/of
an unattractive travelled salesman, Mr Breen, during their cross-coun-
try train trip to the west coast. Meg, divorced and engaged to a new
man, coolly analyses the seduction and her alternating feelings of
pleasure and disgust for both herself and Breen. Intermittently self-
aware, at one point she realizes, 'Dear Jesus . . . I'm really as hard as
nails.' Vowing to redeem herself, she goes to bed with Breen again,
thinking, 'This . . . is going to be the only real act of charity I have ever
performed in my life; it will be the only time I have ever given anything when it honestly hurt me to do so' (McCarthy, *Company She
Keeps*, p.114). McCarthy's frank departures from conventional fare

were by no means commonplace; nevertheless, her work suggests that at least one Irish–American woman writer was countering romanticism and pathos with realism and satire.

Chafe notes that, 'as late as the 1950s, more than 70 per cent of all American families consisted of a father who worked and a mother who stayed at home to take care of the children' (Chafe, *Unfinished Journey*, p.436). Among the exceptions were a number of prominent Irish–American women who maintained professional lives. Louise Bogan, granddaughter of an immigrant from Derry, began judging applications for Guggenheim Fellowships in 1944, a job she held into the 1960s; she also served as Fellow in American Letters of the Library of Congress, Consultant in Poetry to the Library of Congress, and consultant on *belles-lettres* to Doubleday publishing. She taught at the Universities of Washington and Chicago, New York University and Brandeis while continuing to publish prodigiously and win awards (Bogan and Limmer, *Journey Around My Room*, pp.xxxi–xxxiii). Mary Doyle Curran, whose mother was from Kerry, may have written novels that sang the praises of housewifery, but she herself taught at the University of Massachusetts at Boston, Queens College and Wellesley. In the same years, Irish-born Maeve Brennan wrote for *Harper's Bazaar* and later became a staff writer for the *New Yorker* (Bourke, *Maeve Brennan: Homesick at* The New Yorker).

Later authors have written memoirs in which they attribute their careers to the role models provided by their Irish–American mothers who worked outside the home after marriage. Novelist and memoirist Caryl Rivers's parents met in law school in the 1930s. Her mother 'left work when [Rivers] was born [in 1937], but returned to practice at a large law firm in Washington shortly afterward' (Rivers, *Aphrodite at Mid-Century*, p.10). Memoirist Maureen Waters' mother worked at Macy's. Novelist Mary Gordon recalls watching enviously as her mother carefully dressed and applied makeup for her job as a legal secretary. 'Early on,' she writes, 'the word "work" took on for me a gravity, a luster, like the stone in a monarch's signet ring. "Work" was a word I savored on my tongue like a cool stone' (Gordon, *Circling My Mother*, p.18). Work, then, was not only a key to Irish–American assimilation; in many cases, it also differentiated Irish–American women from their counterparts.

Another key was education, which for Irish–American women (and men) was likely to mean a Catholic school. John Cogley observes that in the early twentieth century

> Nowhere else in the world were so many Catholic children drilled in the catechism as thoroughly as in American parochial schools; nowhere did the notion of Catholicism as embodying a tidy system of rules and regulations covering practically every aspect of life gain stronger hold on the faithful . . . and the 'siege mentality' the schools inculcated was often carried over to life outside the classroom. (Qtd in Ebest, *Private Histories*, p.140)

The influence of these lessons in the larger culture was particularly potent following World War Two, when the American–Catholic population of 25 million equalled the combined membership of the six largest Protestant religions (Wuthnow, *Restructuring of American Religion*, p.18). Most American Catholics, Irish or otherwise, saw a gradual assimilation into the middle class in these years, as evidenced by an increased number of Catholics with college educations (ibid., p.86). For men, and for some women, these trends were dramatically accelerated by the benefits awarded by the GI Bill of Rights.

Literature by Irish–American women of this era reflects the combination of religion and education. Among American writers of both genders, this cohort is unique for their inclusion and discussion of what Alice McDermott has termed 'Catholic themes, Catholic language' ('Confessions of a Reluctant Catholic', p.12). Mary McCarthy rejected her faith at the age of 11; nevertheless, her early Catholic training is evident throughout her *oeuvre*. Although McCarthy grew further and further from the mores of her Catholic girlhood, she could not escape herself. An 'infamously autobiographical writer', her heroines inevitably reflect her childhood beliefs, for 'All are effectively Catholic.' According to Stacey Donohue, 'all of McCarthy's characters are unable to mediate between the traditional definitions of femininity embraced by the church, and the modern revisioning, an Irish Catholic fatalism and a belief in free will' (Donohue, 'Reluctant Radical', p.91). Her heroines 'declare their sexual freedom, intellectual independence, and are willing to compete in the world with men, but ultimately they are undermined by self doubt, shame and an internalization of Catholicism, which lead to a desperate search for someone to tell them what to do, and some structure to tell them how to do it' (ibid., p.93).

A similar ambivalence runs through Maureen Howard's memoir of a 1950s childhood, *Facts of Life*. Her parents were devout Catholics, but they tended to mock 'the world we came from . . . the *Catholic Messenger* with its simpering parables of sacrifice, its weekly photos of saintly missionaries and their flock of mocha children with souls like ours, rescued for eternity' (Howard, *Facts of Life*, p.12). Still, for her parents' generation, 'Religion was a serious business' (ibid., p.13). Perhaps as a result, Howard finds that her 'religious periods have been genuine only as dramatic exercises' (ibid., p.35). Her first novel, *Not a Word About Nightingales* (1960), displays this pattern. As Durso writes: 'Irish Catholic culture ... is an integral part of the set upon which Howard's stories play out, but it is there more for mood and dramatic effect than anything else' ('Landscapes of Memory', p.57).

Immigrants and second-generation Irish often preferred to ignore their cultural heritage. Mary McCarthy and Maureen Howard distanced themselves from the Irish. McCarthy associated the Irish with the abusive relatives who took in her and her brothers after their parents' death, whereas Howard picked up on her mother's disdain. 'Oh, the Irish,' her mother would say. 'We were taught to take the Irish lightly,' Howard explains (*Facts of Life*, p.11). Elizabeth Cullinan's family was even more vehement: 'Mother hated the Irish,' she explains in an interview. 'We were supposed to be above all of that' (qtd in McInerney, 'Forget About Being Irish', p.99).

Maeve Brennan's ambivalence is suggested by her choice of settings, for some of her best stories take place in the Dublin suburbs. However, Brennan's underrated American stories reveal 'a satiric preoccupation with the ways of the privileged' (Palko, 'Out of Home', p.74; Bourke, *Maeve Brennan: Homesick at* The New Yorker, p.182). After her marriage to the *New Yorker* editor St Clair McKelway, Maeve and 'Mac' moved to his home in Sneden's Landing, an artists' colony in upstate New York. In *New Yorker* stories published between 1953 and 1956, Sneden's Landing becomes Herbert's Retreat. Some of the stories feature *nouveau riche* women such as Leona Harkey and bitchy, parasitic theatre critic Charles Runyon, but they are viewed through the 'derisive eyes' of their Irish maids. Although Brennan herself may have been counted as one of the upper class, her accent opened her to many of the stereotypical assumptions attributed to the maids. 'Grotesque and often repellent, Maeve's portraits clearly show the women's suffering humanity, not least in the way they persist in referring to themselves as "girls". Their only power lies in their ability to tell stories, and it is this that Maeve celebrates and participates in, when she writes about Herbert's Retreat' (Bourke, *Maeve Brennan: Homesick at* The New Yorker, pp.183–4).

The Irish–American embrace of Catholic education contributed to the palpable division between 'us' and 'them'. Recalling her formative years in the 1950s, Caryl Rivers notes that 'The nuns made it clear that prolonged exposure to non-Catholics was not healthy. They gave off a subversive perfume; unseen, like radiation, but deadly' (*Aphrodite*, p.129). The Church spelled this out clearly: '*It is a sin to attend a non-Catholic service*' (Ibid., p.130); 'We were urged to have Catholic friends, to attend none other than Catholic schools, to date Catholic boys, and if we married one, to live in Catholic neighbourhoods (ibid., p.137); 'Our minds were kept innocent of anything but praise for the Church' (ibid., p.154). Maureen Waters writes of growing up at mid-century knowing 'our souls were in mint condition, bright and glittering although vague in detail ... We kept them that way by a continual round of devotions: Mass on Sundays and holy days, rosaries, novenas, stations of the cross, little acts of self-denial' (Waters, *Crossing Highbridge*, p.69). She adds that 'in a curious, paradoxical way [the nuns] encouraged independence' (ibid., p.9). They demanded hard work and concentration, which in turn fostered autonomy. Moreover, Waters's lay teachers introduced her students to such progressive figures as Dorothy Day and Ammon Hennessey, to the Catholic Worker movement, and encouraged debates about Christian writers such as Augustine and Thomas Aquinas (ibid., p.81).

By the 1950s 'the Irish immigrants had begun to enter the economic mainstream, even though this move threatened their ethnicity and sense of group unity' (Takaki, *Different Mirror*, p.163). Like other baby-boomer Irish Americans, Alice McDermott, born in suburban Long Island in 1953, was raised in a family that chose not to self-identify as hyphenated Americans. Nonetheless, growing up, McDermott attended parochial schools and religious icons dotted the house; she even slept with a rosary beneath her pillow until she was a teen (McDermott, 'Confessions', p.13). Conversely, third-generation Irish–American Madeleine Blais, born in 1947, identifies strongly with her ethnic and religious background. Her memoir *Uphill Walkers* tells of growing up in the 1950s; when her widowed mother needed a job, the Blais girls wondered 'if we should say a novena ... We believed that good things happened not so much because you lifted yourself up by your bootstraps, the Protestant explanation, but when luck and prayer collided in heaven' (Blais, *Uphill Walkers*, p.75).

Blais's contemporary, Mary Gordon, born in 1949, was raised by an exceedingly devout Catholic mother: from 1935 until her death more than sixty years later, Anna Gordon was a member of the Working Women's Retreat Movement. For these women, mostly widowed or unmarried, this group 'provided a situation, in which their spiritual life could be taken seriously', brought similarly minded women together, and provided, in essence, a room of their own where they could get away from their families. Several times a year, the women travelled around the country to meet, usually in a convent, attend Mass, listen to sermons and talks by the priests, and visit their friends (Gordon, *Circling My Mother*, p.105). These retreats led not only to enduring friendships among some of the women, but also with some of the priests. Unlike the current climate in which priests are almost by default considered suspect, Gordon notes that clergy in the mid-1950s, 'were treated like princes – no, like kings ... Nothing was too much to do for them.' She continues: 'You will say that I am naïve, that many of these women served priests sexually,' but the ethnic composition of the mid-century church provided a crucial distinction. 'I am talking of the American Church in the triumphalist years of 1920–60, a church entirely under control of the Irish, who had no toleration for the wink-wink, nudge-nudge, "we're all human after all", "a man's a man" comprehension found in other parts of the world' (ibid., pp.131–2).

Irish–American women of the postwar years – particularly those whose memoirs suggest they had professional and creative aspirations – provide a record of the period that more than confirms Betty Friedan's findings in *The Feminine Mystique*: 'After World War II, this mystique of feminine fulfilment became the cherished and self-perpetuating core of contemporary American culture ... If a woman had a problem in the 1950s and 1960s, she knew that something must be wrong with her marriage, or with herself' (Friedan, *Feminine Mystique*, pp.18–19). Forced to give up their jobs, their new-found independence and the accompanying satisfaction, many women developed feelings of anger, frustration and guilt. In their accounts of domestic pressures, thwarted ambitions, divorce and depression, a striking prescience stands out among these writers. Although they suffered from the exertion of patriarchal authority in a specifically Irish–Catholic context, their writings speak to a wider experience.

Novels by Maeve Brennan and Mary McCarthy reflect these issues. Brennan focused on marriage and motherhood, neither of which was fulfilling. In the posthumous short-story collection, *Springs of Affection*, Rose Derdon is an unhappy middle-aged woman who has been married to her husband Hubert for twenty-seven years. Bourke suggests that this couple might be confused with Brennan's parents (*Maeve Brennan: Homesick at* The New Yorker, p.172); however, she goes on to note that while the setting reflects Maeve's childhood home in Dublin, Rose and Hubert are 'fully realised fictional characters, entirely under the control of their creator' (ibid., p.172). Bourke argues that their portrayal reveals, rather, 'the emotional landscape of Ireland' (ibid., p.173). But this landscape is not so different from the America that Brennan knew: housewives are unhappy; husbands are resentful. Rose and Hubert alternately long for and loathe the other, even going so far as to dream of the other's death. Hubert so dislikes his wife that he avoids her whenever possible. 'Her pretensions, the pitiful air she wore of being a certain sort of person, irritated him so much that he could hardly bear to look at her on the rare occasions – rare these days, anyway – when they went out together' (Brennan, *Springs of Affection*, p.72). Yet he never confronts her, preferring instead the silence and avoidance McCaffrey attributes to Irish men, for when he finds himself about to address the issue, Hubert

> would have to stop himself, because he could begin to feel his anger against her getting out of hand. The anger was so dreadful because there seemed to be no way of working it off. It was an anger that called for pushing over high walls, or kicking over great towering, valuable things that would go down with a shocking crash. (Ibid., p.78)

Mary McCarthy's novels and memoirs display a marked disregard for the sanctity of marriage. In scenes more graphic than 1950s readers of women's novels were accustomed to, McCarthy's works explicitly address sex, usually adulterous sex. *A Charmed Life* (1955) – a *roman à clef* (in parts) satirizing McCarthy's relationship with Edmund Wilson (Brightman, *Writing Dangerously*, p.243) – is perhaps most notable for the sex scene between Miles/Wilson and Martha/Mary after both have remarried. Maureen Howard's memoir, *Facts of Life*, is less graphic but more cynical. In her determination to be the ideal wife, Howard became 'the compliant young matron' (*Facts of Life*, p.75). As a young faculty wife, she played the role even as she clung to the hope that someday she would move beyond 'the hot competition in the *hors d'oeuvres* department' (ibid., p.76). In fact, she *was* moving along, for in 1960 she would publish her first novel, *Not a Word About Nightingales*, which describes a man's attempts to flee his wife and conventional job, only to return in the end to resume the 'dull garment of his past' (ibid., p.61). Despite favourable reviews, Howard apparently saw the work as a reflection of her life at the time.

> I wrote a mannered academic novel, actually a parody of that
> genre and so at a further remove from life. If there is any
> strength there . . . it can only be in what I wanted that book to
> reflect: a sense of order as I knew it in the late fifties and early
> sixties with all the forms that I accepted and even enjoyed: that
> was the enormous joke about life – that our passion must be con-
> tained if we were not to be fools. (Ibid., p.80)

But Howard does not seem to be laughing.

In the 1950s thousands of women began seeking psychiatric help:
'the married ones were reported dissatisfied with their marriages, the
unmarried ones suffering from anxiety [about their status] and, finally, depression' (Friedan, *Feminine Mystique*, p.25). This decade saw
the introduction, acceptance, application and misapplication of
Freudian theory, which 'led women, and those who studied them, to
misinterpret their mothers' frustration, and their fathers' and brothers' and husbands' resentments and inadequacies, and their own emo-
tions and possible choices in life' (ibid., p.103). Questions regarding
women's unhappiness were answered within a 'Freudian framework',
which led to only one conclusion: 'education, freedom, rights are
wrong for women' (ibid., p.123).

Irish–American women writers were not immune to these pressures. Despite their Catholic upbringings, the Irish–American women
writers discussed here appear to greatly exceed the national probabil-
ities for divorces in their time. They also embraced the fad of seeking
psychoanalysis to understand themselves. Caryl Rivers would later
write, 'I would love to see the data on how many female alcoholics
and frigid wives evolved out of that crazy indoctrination' (*Aphrodite*,
p.185). Mary Doyle Curran divorced her first husband; over the
course of her life, she suffered from depression and alcoholism for
which she sought help through psychoanalysis. Louise Bogan married
and divorced twice; she also suffered from 'nervous breakdowns' and
depression and was hospitalized three times over a thirty-year period.
Maeve Brennan married and divorced; she too suffered from mental
illness during her last years and had to be institutionalized. Mary
McCarthy married four times, divorced three. She began undergoing
psychoanalysis while married to Edmund Wilson, ultimately seeing
three different psychoanalysts before declaring them unnecessary
(Brightman, *Writing Dangerously*, p.229). Maureen Howard married
twice, divorced once, and also sought analysis at one point.
Describing her early married life, she writes sardonically, 'Look, I'm

perfectly happy ... I've finally learned not to want things I cannot have' (*Facts of Life*, p.174).

The memoirs of Caryl Rivers and Maureen Waters, born before the war (1937 and 1939 respectively), adumbrate the feminist concerns of their baby-boomer successors. Rivers's childhood games alternated between arguing and fighting. 'I was convinced that being a girl was an O.K. thing. Could I not do anything the boys could do, and do it better? Except, of course, pee on target' (Rivers, *Aphrodite*, p.20). Rivers grew increasingly disenchanted during high school. To her, the nuns' insistence upon the rhythm method implied that it was 'a woman's duty to be a brood mare, even if it destroyed her health, her marriage, her family life, and kept them all in bleakest poverty'. The idea that it was 'Better to die in the state of grace than to commit [the] mortal sin of using contraceptives' was unacceptable (ibid., p.185).

Maureen Waters had similar experiences. 'Nobody played with dolls,'she writes. 'What a strange group of girls we were, children of immigrants, fighting for a toehold in the promised land' (*Crossing Highbridge*, pp.14–15). As Waters grew older, these attitudes grew stronger. A teenager in the 1950s, the 'last thing in the world I wanted to be,' she writes, 'was a housewife. In high school my electives were math and science; I wouldn't be caught dead in home economics' (ibid., pp.16–17). The last straw occurred at her all-girls college. Because there were no males, the female students became responsible for responding to the chaplain during Mass, a role Waters assumed with pleasure. However, when she learned that she would not be allowed on the altar, that she would have to kneel 'on a pretty little *prie-dieu* just outside the sanctuary', she rebelled. 'Despite the thrust of my religious upbringing or, paradoxically, because of it', she writes, 'I expected to be treated like everyone else, men included' (ibid., p.95).

America experienced a spike in divorces after World War Two, jumping from approximately 16.7 per cent in 1936 to 26.4 per cent in 1946 (Day, 'Patterns of Divorce', p.511). Despite the Catholic pro-hibition against divorce, these figures varied little between Catholics and Protestants, averaging 21 and 25 per cent respectively (Robinson, 'Religious Tolerance'). But divorce rates dropped in the 1950s, when 'almost 80 per cent of American households contained husband–wife couples' (Gerson, *Hard Choices*, pp.206–7). It would be a mistake to infer that these statistics reflect overall marital satisfaction, for couples of the day separated much more often than they divorced (ibid., p.205), and there is enormous anecdotal evidence to suggest countless

unhappy marriages. Nor do these statistics suggest a general acceptance of divorce among Catholics. Mary Gordon notes that her mother,
a legal secretary, explained that her boss did not '"handle divorce".
She said this as if divorce were a particularly nasty, possibly toxic
species of effluvia, which they very well knew better than to touch'
(*Circling My Mother*, p.23).

In an earlier generation, 'Irish immigrant servants of the rich ...
sent their daughters ... to serve the poor in American schools' (Nolan,
Servants of the Poor, p.138); in the postwar years, Irish–American
women writers continued that legacy of self-improvement. Despite
marital and psychological problems, Irish–American women writers at
mid-century outperformed their unhyphenated peers: while Catholic
families were encouraging their daughters to postpone marrying, the
average marriage age of American women in 1959 dropped to 20, and
was still dropping into the teens. Fourteen million girls were engaged
by 17 (Friedan, *Feminine Mystique*, p.150). While many
Irish–American women went to college and worked throughout their
lives, overall the proportion of women attending college in comparison with men dropped from 47 per cent in 1920, to 35 per cent in
1958. 'A century earlier, women had fought for higher education; now
girls went to college to get a husband' (ibid., p.150). The works discussed here not only confirm these statistics, but also relate aspects of
Irish America that challenge its conventional portrayal as a conformist patriarchy in which women were at most housekeepers or nannies,
their parents pious simpletons or atavistic ethnics. This variegated
picture of mid-century Irish America offers a convincing response to
the traditional monolithic view.

In other words, the memoirs and autobiographical fiction by
Irish–American women writers who came of age in the postwar years
afford us a glimpse of what life was like among the 15 per cent of
American women who married and kept on working. They established careers that granted them membership into the top tier of
Catholic professionals, the 9 per cent of Catholics in the upper class.
That they did so during the conservative, sexist postwar era probably
accounts for their above-average rates of marriage, divorce and psychoanalysis – the wages of the 'sin' of working-while-married.

REFERENCES

Blais, Madeleine. *Uphill Walkers: Portrait of a Family*. New York:
Atlantic Monthly Press, 2001.

Bogan, Louise and Ruth Limmer. *Journey Around My Room*. New York: Viking, 1980.

Bourke, Angela. *Maeve Brennan: Homesick at* The New Yorker. New York: Counterpoint, 2004.

Brennan, Maeve. *The Springs of Affection*. Boston, MA: Houghton Mifflin, 1997.

Brightman Carol. *Writing Dangerously: Mary McCarthy and Her World*. New York: Harcourt Brace, 1994.

Chafe, William. *The Unfinished Journey: America Since World War II*. Oxford: Oxford University Press, 1991.

Day, Lincoln H. 'Patterns of Divorce in Australia and the United States'. *American Sociological Review*, vol. 29 (August 1964), pp.509–22.

Donohue, Stacey. 'The Reluctant Radical: The Irish–Catholic Element', in Eve Swertka and Margo Viscusi (eds), *Twenty-Four Ways of Looking at Mary McCarthy*. Westport, CN: Greenwood Press, 1996, pp.87–99.

Durso, Patricia Keefe. 'Maureen Howard's "Landscapes of Memory"', in Sally Barr Ebest and Kathleen McInerney (eds), *Too Smart to be Sentimental: Contemporary Irish American Women*. South Bend, IN: University of Notre Dame Press, 2008.

Ebest, Ron. *Private Histories: Irish Americans, 1900–1935*. South Bend, IN: University of Notre Dame Press, 2004.

Frank, Elizabeth. *Louise Bogan: A Portrait*. New York: Columbia University Press, 1986.

Friedan, Betty. *The Feminine Mystique*. New York: W.W. Norton, 1963.

Gerson, Kathleen. *Hard Choices: How Women Decide about Work, Career, and Motherhood*. Berkeley, CA: University of California Press, 1986.

Gordon, Mary. *Circling My Mother: A Memoir*. New York: Pantheon, 2007.

Halley, Anne. 'An American Story: Mary Doyle Curran (1917–1981)'. 2003. Unpublished MS in the possession of the author.

Hartmann, Susan. *The Home Front and Beyond: American Women in the 1940s*. Boston, MA: Twayne, 1982.

Howard, Maureen. *Facts of Life*. Boston: Little, Brown, 1975.

Katzman, David M. *Seven Days a Week: Women and Domestic Service in Industrializing America*. Chicago, IL: University of Illinois Press, 1981.

Mageean, Deirdre. 'Making Sense and Providing Structure: Irish–American Women in the Parish Neighborhood' in C. Harzig (ed.) *Peasant Maids–City Women*.Ithaca: Cornell University Press, 1997, pp.223–60.

McCaffrey, Lawrence J. *Textures of Irish America*. Syracuse: Syracuse University Press, 1992.

McCarthy, Mary. *The Company She Keeps*.New York: Dell, 1942.

McDermott, Alice. 'Confessions of a Reluctant Catholic'. *Commonweal*, Vol. 127, number 2 , 11 February 2000, pp.12–6.

McInerney, Kathleen 'Forget About Being Irish': Family, Transgression, and Identity in the Fiction of Elizabeth Cullinan', in Sally Barr Ebest and Kathleen McInerney (eds), *Too Smart to be Sentimental: Contemporary Irish American Women Writers*. South Bend, IN: University of Notre Dame Press, 2008.

Nolan, Janet. *Servants of the Poor*. South Bend, IN: University of Notre Dame Press, 2004.

Palko, Abigail L. 'Out of Home in the Kitchen: Maeve Brennan's Herbert's Retreat Stories'. *New Hibernia Review*, Vol. 11, number 4 (Winter 2007), pp.73–91.

Robinson, B.A. 'Religious Tolerance'. www.religioustolerance.org/chr_dira.htm.

Rivers, Caryl. *Aphrodite at Mid-Century: Growing Up Catholic and Female in Post-War America*. New York: Doubleday, 1973.

Schneider, Herbert Wallace. *Religion in 20th Century America*, Cambridge, MA: Harvard University Press, 1952.

Scott, Bonnie Kime. 'Women's Perspectives in Irish–American Fiction from Betty Smith to Mary McCarthy' in Daniel Casey and Robert Rhodes (eds) *Irish–American Fiction: Essays in Criticism*. New York: AMS, 1979, pp.87–104

Showalter, Elaine. *Inventing Herself: Claiming a Feminist Intellectual Heritage*, New York: Scribner, 2001.

Takaki, Ronald. *A Different Mirror: A History of Multicultural America*. New York: Little Brown, 1993.

Waters, Maureen. *Crossing Highbridge: A Memoir of Irish America*. Syracuse: Syracuse University Press, 2001.

Wuthnow, Robert. *The Restructuring of American Religion: Society and Faith Since World War II*. Princeton, NJ: Princeton University Press, 1988.

PART THREE
REARTICULATING THE MEANINGS
OF IRISHNESS

CHAPTER NINE

Ireland as a Past Life:
Bridey Murphy and Irish–American
Tourism to Ireland, 1945–1960

STEPHANIE RAINS

In the 1950s very few Americans had travelled to Ireland by any means, whether by sea or air. In 1956, however, a remarkable phenomenon burst upon America popular culture – Morey Bernstein's book *The Search for Bridey Murphy*, in which the possibility of an entirely different means of travel to Ireland became a national sensation. The phenomenon was that of past life recall, induced by hypnosis. Bernstein's book provides a transcript of conversations with his subject:

> Now I want you to drift on back ... I want you to go back to the time before you were born, even back before you were born into this lifetime ... All right. Now rest and relax. Be very comfortable. You're going to enjoy this very much. It's going to be a lot of fun. Now I want you to go back to that life experience in Ireland when you were Bridey Murphy. Now, can you remember that lifetime in Ireland, when you were Bridey Murphy?
> (Bernstein, *The Search for Bridey Murphy*, p.16)

Scholars have only recently begun to examine the role of the tourism industry in helping to construct Irish–American identity during the 1950s. A conspicuous theme in the promotion of tourism to Ireland was the many ways in which travel to Ireland was represented to the diaspora as a journey 'back in time' or 'back home'. In the light of this representation, it is particularly important to examine the Bridey Murphy sensation of 1956, in which a Colorado housewife apparently recalled, under hypnosis, a previous life in nineteenth-century Ireland – a story that prompted what *Life* magazine described as a national 'hypnotizzy' of fascination with past-life regression in the United States (*Life*, 19 March 1956). The significance of such tourist representations of Ireland, however, must first be situated in the political economy of its tourism industry during the postwar period.

Throughout the 1950s tourist travel from America to anywhere in Europe was still a luxury consumer expenditure. This era saw the beginnings of mass international tourism by Americans not only because of the development of commercial passenger jets, but also because of the strong dollar and the lower costs of living abroad compared to those in America. Travel information published in the American press in the early 1950s indicated that a ten-day bus-tour around Ireland, including first-class accommodation, would cost $94.08, or approximately $734 at 2007 prices.[1] However, international travel costs were still very high. In 1953, for example, a summer season tourist-class return flight to Ireland cost $434, roughly equivalent to $3,364 at 2007 prices. Even travel to Ireland by steamship, which continued as a frequent method of travel throughout the 1950s, cost $330 for summer travel, roughly equivalent to $2,557 at 2007 prices (Zullo, 'Ireland Looking Forward to Huge Tourist Invasion', *Chicago Tribune*, 15 February 1953).

Because of these high costs, as well as the greater time commitment required for American tourists to visit Ireland, US visitors were always outnumbered by visitors from Europe. Irish tourism officials sought tourists from the United States, but they did so because the value of American visitors to the Irish tourism market was based upon their proportionately higher purchasing power per capita when compared to other visitors. Indeed, throughout the 1950s American visitors to Ireland never comprised more than 1.8 per cent of all tourists, but they provided up to 16 per cent of tourist revenue, making them a valuable target market (Rains, 'Home from Home', p.199).

In particular, later-generation Irish Americans – those born in the United States – were especially valuable to the Irish market. Irish-born Americans who visited Ireland were much more likely stay with family or friends, thus removing them from the economically important hotel, restaurant and consumer-attractions market. This division among the already small Irish–American tourist numbers was reflected in the Bord Fáilte official designation of such tourists as 'visiting friends and relatives', or VFRs. While such visitors often stayed in Ireland for longer than the average tourist – which meant that they were likely to spend more money in total – the promotions of the time make clear that the marketing of Ireland to American tourists in the

1950s already placed particular emphasis upon later-generation Irish Americans, who would stay in hotels and spend money on organized leisure activities. Indeed, there is evidence of a concerted policy by Bord Fáilte (established in 1952) to expand greatly the numbers of later-generation Irish Americans visiting Ireland. Throughout the 1950s, for example, such mainstream American newspapers as the *New York Times* and the *Chicago Tribune* published regular feature articles each year on tourism to Ireland. Many of these appear to be derived from Bord Fáilte press releases, giving detailed package-tour information and costs, as well as publicity for officially organized tourist attractions. By the mid-1950s these newspapers were printing promotional photographs credited to the Irish tourist authorities, typically depicting Irish pastoral scenes.[2] By 1954 tourism was listed as Ireland's principal source of foreign-exchange income, earning $84m a year, of which $6m was attributable to visitors from America (Doyle, 'Ireland Bids for Increase in Travel Trade', *Chicago Tribune*, 6 June 1954; Deegan and Dineen, *Tourism Policy and Performance*, pp.17–21).

The following year Bord Fáilte spent $250,000 on tourist advertising (nearly $2m at present value), much of it designed to attract wealthy tourists who would spend above-average amounts during their stay, described by the *Chicago Tribune* as the 'class tourist ... who spends money for the top grade article' (Doyle, 'Ireland Sets its Sights for Class Tourists', *Chicago Tribune*, 12 June 1955). Throughout the 1950s this 'class tourist', as envisioned by the Irish tourist authorities, was a later-generation Irish American.

One of the most prevalent methods of marketing Ireland to later-generation Irish Americans was to present their first visit as itself a 'return' to their cultural home. The An Tóstal festival, established in 1953, was perhaps the most literal example of this marketing technique. An Tóstal was translated, in press releases and advertising literature to the United States, as meaning 'at home'. The literature was quite clear that the Irish nation was 'at home' to visitors.[3] By extension, however, the An Tóstal festival, which was explicitly linked to promoting the tourist industry, also implied that Irish Americans themselves would be 'at home' in their ancestors' homeland. As Mary E. Daly explains, 'The 1953 souvenir handbook emphasized the festival's aim of "keeping 'open door' to men and women of Irish birth and origin from all parts of the world, who have come back to renew their contact with our country"' (Daly, 'Nationalism, Sentiment and Economics', pp.268–9).

Other aspects of the Irish tourist apparatus also incorporated narratives of the Irish–American 'return' to Ireland. Promotional films
were widely used during the 1950s by the international tourist industry, and several were made that promoted Ireland. These include *The
Hills of Ireland* (1951), *The Spell of Ireland* (1954), *The Irish In Me*
(1959) and *O'Hara's Holiday* (1960). These films generally took the
form of a travelogue through Ireland, highlighting notable tourist destinations and activities. Little archival information is now available
regarding the production and distribution policies behind the travelogues of this era. The distribution of the films appears to have been
controlled by Bord Fáilte and other 'traffic operators', such as airlines
and major tour operators. Not only were they shown at conventions
and trade fairs in the United States, they were also loaned out to interested groups through Bord Fáilte's lending libraries of travel information. These groups could include diverse professional or social organizations in the United States who were considering taking a tour group
to Ireland. One group known to have been a regular user of these
films, and a frequent organizer of visits to Ireland, was the
Irish–American 'parish associations'. The centrality of the Catholic
Church to the Irish–American diaspora, and the large number of Irish
clergy working in their parishes, appears to have created a definable
audience for both the travelogue films and group tours to Ireland. On
19 August 1953, for example, a cruise liner sailed from New York to
Cobh carrying 431 passengers on a pilgrimage to Ireland led by the
Catholic archbishop of Boston, and on 9 August 1955 another 'pilgrimage', this time organized by the Irish Institute of New York, flew
to Ireland ('Pilgrimage to Ireland Sails', *New York Times*, 19 August
1953; 'Pilgrimage to Ireland; New Yorkers Fly to Ould Sod in
Chartered Dutch Plane', *New York Times*, 9 August 1955).

Some of the films had limited releases in United States cinemas,
especially those based in Irish–American areas. In May 1951, for
example, *The Hills of Ireland* began its screening at the 55th Street
Playhouse in New York, as part of a programme of Irish-themed films,
and in May 1954 its sequel, *The Spell of Ireland*, was premiered at the
Baronet cinema in New York (Crowther, 'Screen in Review', *New York
Times*, 22 May, 1951; A.W., 'A Visit to Ireland Shown at Baronet',
New York Times, 11 May 1954).[4]

One of the principal distinguishing characteristics of these tourist
travelogues was the implication that a visit to Ireland, for an Irish
American, would prove to be an experience which would extend far
beyond the strictly market transaction of the standard tourist econo-

my. In *O'Hara's Holiday*, for example, the eponymous O'Hara (a New York policeman) is not only depicted enjoying some of the popular tourist destinations of Ireland, but is also shown succeeding in tracing his Irish ancestors and becoming engaged to Kitty, an Irish girl who he meets during his holiday and takes home to New York with him at the end of the twenty-minute film. *The Irish In Us* tells the story of Sheila, an Irish–American adolescent who visits Ireland to spend a summer in her family's village and meet her Irish grandfather for the first time. The film places great emphasis on the spiritual and cultural impact of this visit; Sheila is described as having discovered her 'true' home in Ireland. *The Spell of Ireland* adopts a documentary tone that was unusual for such films, and was also substantially longer. However, the 1954 film does insert a fictional sequence into the scenes in which the narrator visits Donegal – which he identifies as his home county – during which the entire tone of the film shifts abruptly to a remembrance of his Irish childhood, including unheralded voice-over reminiscences by his mother in a style strikingly similar to early scenes in *The Quiet Man*, released two years earlier.[5]

There were many other texts of the 1950s which were not, in the strictest sense, tourist advertising, but which must be considered as influencing Irish America's understanding of Ireland as a destination. These include travel articles in such prominent American newspapers as the *New York Times* and the *Chicago Tribune*, as well as magazine feature articles on the country in *National Geographic* and *Life*. In May 1951 *National Geographic Magazine* published Dorothea Sheats's lengthy article 'I Walked Some Irish Miles', illustrated with nineteen photographs, nine of which were colour Kodachrome images highly reminiscent of the John Hinde postcards that so defined tourist representation of Ireland during the 1950s and 1960s.[6] (Most of the photographs in the article are credited to Sheats herself. However, it is striking that the Kodachrome photograph most reminiscent of Hinde's postcards is credited to Harry Dugan, the director of the films *The Hills of Ireland* and *The Spell of Ireland*, discussed above.)

Sheats's *National Geographic* article well illustrates the extent to which, by the 1950s, the dominant representation of Ireland to an American audience was of a place to which Irish Americans might 'return' as tourists. At the very beginning of her article, she explains that 'I had just eight weeks for "going back" to an Ireland I knew only in song and story; my grandparents sailed from there to America before I was born' (Sheats, 'I Walked', p.678). Notably, Sheats's article returns to the issue of ethnic heritage in its closing paragraph, when she explains: 'my last chat was with [an employee] of the Irish Folklore Commission. He gave me a kind of benediction. When he asked me where my people came from in Ireland, I told him that I didn't know. "No matter," he said. "'Twill be written in God's Book." And so it will' (ibid.). After downplaying her own ties of ancestry over the course of the article, Sheats nonetheless concludes by suggesting that Ireland makes a special, indeed spiritual, claim on the descendants of immigrants.

Life's most well-known feature on Ireland during the 1950s was certainly Dorothea Lange's celebrated photo essay, titled 'Country People of Ireland', published in March 1955. Consisting of twenty black-and-white photographs with detailed captions, Lange's piece also focused on the connections between contemporary Ireland and the ethnic heritage of the diaspora. In the very brief introductory paragraph to the photographs, Lange refers to the first image in the essay, that of a 15-year-old Ennis boy with a donkey-cart. She says:

> The forefathers of the Irish around the world who are celebrating St Patrick's Day looked very much like the smiling lad above from County Clare in western Ireland. He is of the seed stock, the rural people of the towns and countryside who for 100 years and more have been exporting Irishmen ... His people live to the ancient Irish ways and a visitor finds them, as the following pages show, humorous, direct and generous – good ancestors to have.
>
> (Lange, 'Country People', p.135)

Tellingly, the syntax of this statement implies that the Irish people whom Lange encountered and documented in her essay were *themselves* the 'ancestors' of the contemporary diaspora. By extension, therefore, a visit to Ireland by Irish Americans becomes an opportunity for the latter to, in effect, meet their ancestors – rather than people of their own era.

Exactly a year after publishing Dorothea Lange's photographs of Ireland, *Life* was again sending reporters to Ireland – although on a quite different journalistic mission. In January 1956 Morey Bernstein, a Colorado businessman and amateur hypnotist, published *The Search for Bridey Murphy*, in which he claimed to have used hypnosis to successfully regress a housewife from Pueblo, Colorado to her past life as a nineteenth-century Irish peasant girl. During several recorded sessions of hypnosis, Virginia Tighe – a 27-year-old woman who was married to a local car dealer – had apparently recalled vivid memories of her previous incarnation as Bridey Murphy.[7] She claimed to have been born in Cork in 1798 and to have died in 1864, after spending most of her life in Belfast.

The Search for Bridey Murphy became an instant national sensation. It outsold its first print run within a matter of weeks, and would go on to sell more than 200,000 copies, spending twenty-six weeks in the *New York Times* bestseller lists. In addition to the book, Bernstein also issued an LP of the hypnosis sessions, which sold 30,000 copies, and a movie of the same title was rapidly released that same year. The phenomenal success of the Bridey Murphy story – termed a national 'hypnotizzy' by *Life* – soon generated other spin-off artefacts and practices. The press reported a fashion for 'come-as-you-were' costume parties, in which guests were to dress as their own previous incarnations. A 'reincarnation cocktail', as well as an 'ectoplasm punch' were invented; newspaper cartoons showed parents greeting newborn babies with 'welcome back' signs; and several popular songs referenced the story, including *The Love of Bridey Murphy* and the parodic *The Quest for Bridey Hammerschlagen*, by comedian Stan Freberg.[8]

The mainstream press greeted the Bridey Murphy story with considerable scepticism. The *Denver Post* and the *Chicago Daily News*, along with *Life*, sent reporters to Ireland to investigate the factual information in Virginia Tighe's hypnotized recollections. And yet while the coverage in the mainstream press was generally incredulous at best, its extent, and the press's tenacity in attempting to disprove Bernstein's claims, both indicate the scale of the nation's 'hypnotizzy' over the subject of reincarnation.

In a 2006 article on the varieties of 'hypnotizzy' that preoccupied Americans during the 1950s, Robert Genter has analysed the ways in which the use of hypnosis to 'discover' Virginia Tighe's previous life as Bridey Murphy fitted into Cold War concerns within American society about 'communist brainwashing'. He offers detailed evidence that in the aftermath of the Korean War there was considerable anxiety about the use of hypnosis against American soldiers (Genter, '"Hypnotizzy" in the Cold War', p.155).[9] Genter also argues that anxieties in the 1950s about the use of hypnosis or brainwashing by agents of the Cold War were also connected to increasing concerns regarding a perceived similarity between such activities and those of the advertising industry in modern American life. This would result, by the end of the decade, in such publications as Joost Meerloo's book, *Rape of the Mind* (1956), in which a direct connection was made between communist brainwashing and the advertising industry's techniques, Vance Packard's *The Hidden Persuaders* (1957), an exposé of psychological manipulation by Madison Avenue, and Erving Goffman's *The Presentation of Self in Everyday Life* (1959), in which he critiqued the conformist and bureaucratic nature of modern American life, arguing that it was leading to a society of alienated and fractured individuals.

These issues, therefore, place the Bridey Murphy sensation within a framework of American cultural anxieties about the threat of hidden controls over both the individual and general populace, whether from the external menace of communist brainwashing, or the internal peril of industrial society and the power of advertising. Certainly, some contemporary reviewers of Bernstein's book appeared to connect it explicitly to the Cold War, such as the *Chicago Tribune* review, which described the book as taking the reader 'on a weird adventure thru [*sic*] the most ponderous iron curtain of all – the human mind – and into the mysterious, unknown realms of hypnosis' (Blakesley, 'Adventure in Hypnotism; Woman Recalls Prior Life', *Chicago Tribune*, 8 January 1956). Genter argues that the story of hypnosis allowing Virginia Tighe to recover her previous identity as Bridey Murphy served as an 'antidote' to prevailing stories of its use as a manipulative and possibly hostile force in modern society, suggesting that '*The Search for Bridey Murphy* portrayed the unconscious as an unexplored, open terrain and argued for the reconnection of the individual to a deeper spiritual heritage' (Genter, 'Hypnotizzy', p.165).

And yet an aspect of the ways in which the Bridey Murphy phenomenon operated within the cultural context of 1950s America that Genter overlooks is the significance of Virginia Tighe's past life having been specifically Irish. If part of the explanation for the national sensation caused by *The Search for Bridey Murphy* was its capacity to 'domesticate' the previously threatening spectre of hypnosis – as well as to provide a reassuring heritage for a populace feeling increasingly disconnected and anxious – then the specific nature of that reassurance is noteworthy. Virginia Tighe's 'memories' of her previous life as a nineteenth-century Irish peasant girl can therefore be read not only in terms of Cold War geopolitical anxieties, but also in terms of the predominant representation of Ireland during the 1950s as a pre-modern idyll.

Through feature films and ever-increasing tourist advertising, Ireland in this period was being presented as a place where Americans could escape from such pressures of modern life as work and social fragmentation – but also, and, most striking, seemingly escape from time itself. Tourist advertising and American press coverage of Ireland strongly and consistently emphasized that it had not been subject to the 'progress' of modern American consumerism or working life. Ireland was represented as having retained not only a *Gemeinschaft* of close-knit communities that were hospitable to visiting strangers, but also a distinctly pre-industrial relationship to time. The 'unhurried' and 'leisurely' pace of Irish life was a frequently invoked theme, and was one of the most evocative ways in which Ireland was depicted to Americans as existing 'outside of time'. *Vogue* magazine, for instance, described the country in 1953 as having agreed to 'a sort of voluntary turning back of the clock' (O'Higgins, 'Ireland: The Grand Meander', p.113). In particular, this 'timelessness' in Irish life of the 1950s was presented as a contrast to the industrialized clock-time of contemporary American working life. Concomitant with its 'timelessness', Irish life was also depicted as non-consumerist and uncommodified – a state idealized in tourist advertising as an opportunity for visiting Americans to escape from the relentless pressures of time, work and consumption at home in order to experience an almost spiritual renewal – especially if they could claim an ancestral link to the country. In Sheats's article for *National Geographic*, for example, she not only comments in the opening lines that in Ireland 'nobody seems to care' about time, but also approvingly quotes a Patrician Brother she meets as saying: 'But Ireland is a spiritual country, not materialistic, as is so much of the world. Isn't that what you've found?' (Sheats, 'I Walked', p.662).

If such feature films as *The Quiet Man* and explicitly touristic films such as *The Irish In Me* and *The Spell of Ireland* portrayed the Irish–American relationship to Ireland as centring on the inherited memories of the diaspora, then the Bridey Murphy sensation was, in many ways, a logical extension of these representations. In *The Irish In Me* the 12-year-old Irish–American girl visiting Ireland for the first time is inducted into her cultural heritage through the stories of her emigrant father and the narrative voice-over of her grandfather in Ireland. In both *The Quiet Man* and *The Spell of Ireland*, Irish Americans returning to Ireland rely on the stories of their Irish mothers to construct their own responses to Ireland itself; their experience is, in effect, filtered by the memories and narratives of their Irish–American heritage. In the case of Bridey Murphy, the Irish–American woman Virginia Tighe was apparently able to by-pass the inherited memories and narratives of her parents' or grandparents' generation, and instead lay claim to memories of her own Irish past and heritage, in the form of a previous life.

In other words, the 'hypnotizzy' in American popular culture surrounding Bridey Murphy can be read not only as a reassuring domestication of the Cold War theme of 'brainwashing', but also as a utilization of ethnic heritage in order to effect this domestication. Ireland's representation to Irish America during the 1950s as a place that continued to reflect their ancestral past in its lack of modernization (and in particular in its lack of consumer modernity) may have made it especially appealing as a location for consolatory 'past lives' – both the past lives of diaspora family history and, more dramatically, those of reincarnation.

The eventual public emergence of more rational explanations for Virginia Tighe's hypnotized 'memories' underscores the importance of these *imaginative* uses of Irishness in American popular culture of the time in fuelling the national craze that surrounded the Bridey Murphy story. Initially, Tighe had been described in the press as not having Irish origins. However, investigative journalists not only discovered that her parents were of Irish descent, but more important, that one of her immediate neighbours during her Chicago childhood had been an Irish immigrant called Bridie Murphy Corkell, who died in 1957 at the age of 65 (*Chicago Tribune*, 10 August 1957). The past life 'memories' Tighe recounted to Bernstein while under hypnosis were most likely to have been childhood memories of Corkell's stories of Ireland – albeit memories that were later than those of the reincarnated Bridey Murphy. Virginia Tighe's second-hand memories of Irishness were in fact very similar to those represented in *The Quiet Man* or *The Spell of Ireland*: they were narrativized accounts of an Irish childhood that had become deeply embedded in her memory. Indeed, even the transposition of time in Virginia Tighe's memories – from that of the 'real' Bridie Murphy's early life in Ireland (which would have been in the early twentieth century) to that of the 'recalled' Bridey Murphy of the early nineteenth century – suggests just how mutable the concept of historical time was in relation to Irish–American 'memories' of Ireland.

There is, of course, a tremendous irony in the appeal of an 'outside of time' construction of Irishness to Irish America as an escape not only from the anxieties of the Cold War but also from the effects of modern, commodified culture. Throughout the 1950s the Irish government and other tourist authorities were vigorously promoting an idyllic and unmaterialistic representation of Ireland precisely in order to commodify Irishness in the pursuit of foreign-exchange earnings and economic growth. A range of official agencies pursued a variety of active policies to encourage the growth of American tourism in Ireland, as well as the sale of specifically Irish-branded goods to the American market. Daly notes that by the early 1950s the international export of 'altar vestments and religious objects' made in Ireland was being promoted by the Irish trade board (Daly, 'Nationalism, Sentiment and Economics', p.278).

The official tourist advertising of Ireland trod a careful line, however, between presenting the country as 'outside of time' – and therefore an escape from the pressures of modern life – and simultaneously providing reassurance to potential visitors that they would find all of modernity's major comforts available to them during their visit. The promotional films and the newspaper articles that were clearly derived from Bord Fáilte press releases, balanced images of a pre-modern society with direct reassurances that hotel accommodation was modern (especially in the vital area of bathroom and plumbing arrangements), that restaurant menus were varied and plentiful, and that Ireland's transport infrastructure was highly developed.

The careful balancing of modern and pre-modern images of Ireland for potential visitors – including the positioning of the country as an ancestral 'home' for later-generation Irish Americans – reveals a deliberate strategy by the Irish tourist authorities that must be considered in the context of wider government objectives of the time. During the 1950s successive Irish governments made concerted efforts to boost their dollar earnings. The promotion of Ireland as a tourist destination, with Irish Americans as the most lucrative target market for this strategy, was integral to this process. Simultaneously, trade groups, both governmental and private, made consistent attempts to promote Irish commodities in the American market, often in ways linked to the tourist industry. In the postwar years Irish manufacturers and retailers took part in a variety of international trade fairs and merchandizing promotions in the United States, designed to increase Irish exports to the American market. In November 1949, for example, Gimbels Department Store in New York held a two-week 'Salute to Ireland' promotion organized in collaboration with American Airlines, featuring Limerick lace, tweeds, Aran knitwear and even 'ecclesiastical objects' ('Wares of Ireland to be Put on View', *New York Times*, 13 October 1949). Irish companies and government departments exhibited at the United States International Trade Fair in Chicago in August 1950, and in 1952 another New York department store, Franklin Simon, organized a promotion of Irish fabrics, also with the participation of the Irish government ('Ireland Joins in Fair', *New York Times*,

2 May 1950; 'Tweeds and Linens Linked in Display', *New York Times*, 28 February 1952).

The An Tóstal festival, notwithstanding its stress on home-coming and the deep-seated bonds between Ireland and its diaspora, was another deliberate attempt to generate income from the Irish–American market. The festival's origins, in fact, were located in a proposal made to the Irish government by Pan American Airlines, designed to increase tourist traffic on their routes into Shannon Airport (Daly, 'Nationalism, Sentiment and Economics', pp.266–9). Indeed, Shannon Airport was the focus of several innovative and aggressive attempts to increase Ireland's foreign-exchange earnings. The Shannon Free Zone, with no import tariffs for manufacturers and distributors, was established at Shannon Airport in 1947, at a time when American airlines were rapidly increasing their routes and passenger numbers through the airport ('First Customs-Free Airport Opened', *Irish Times*, 22 April 1947). This approach was later extended to retail shopping within the airport, resulting in the opening of the first 'duty free' airport shop in 1951.[10] In 1953, for example, a bottle of Irish whiskey cost the equivalent of $5 in a bar or shop in Ireland, but only $1.47 at the Shannon Duty Free shop (*Chicago Tribune* 15 February 1953). The appeal of such discounted shopping to American visitors was demonstrated when sixty-eight women, leaving Shannon after a three-week European tour organized by the American Telephone and Telegraph Company in 1953, bought 250 bottles of whiskey in just one hour at the 'duty free' shop. By 1954 a 'duty free' mail-order retail business had begun operating out of the Shannon Free Zone, specifically aimed at selling Irish products to the American market by distributing 35,000 catalogues to the United States in its first year (*New York Times*, 7 November, 1954).[11] The end result of these economic innovations at Shannon was an international trading structure strikingly encapsulated within the promotional film *O'Hara's Holiday*, when O'Hara, having explained the principles of 'duty free', exclaims, 'Shannon – it's more than an airport, it's an idea.'

Shannon Airport was indeed an idea, as O'Hara proclaimed – and it was an idea born of unmistakably 'modern' economic motivations. The interlocking policies of transatlantic stop-overs; the establishment of the An Tóstal festival at the initial urging of one of the airport's principal American airlines; the instituting of 'duty free' shopping and business operations; and the careful marketing of such 'Irish' commodities as Irish coffee (and therefore whiskey), tweeds and other fabrics, all worked to increase the numbers of Irish–American visitors to Ireland, and to persuade them to spend more money while they were in the country. As such, Shannon Airport was an idea rooted in the unequivocally materialist concerns of consumer capitalism, and more specifically, the boosting of foreign-exchange earnings for the Irish economy.

The 'Bridey Murphy' sensation of the mid-1950s suggests that Irish ethnicity had, within the American popular imagination, become associated with concepts of authenticity, picturesque heritage – and even with an escape from the pressures of Cold War politics and the manipulations of consumer culture. However, the development of such Irish tourist institutions as Shannon Airport, the An Tóstal festival and Bord Fáilte itself suggests that not only was contemporary Ireland eager to participate in precisely those manipulations of consumer culture from which it was presumed to be free, but also that it was precisely its 'uncommodified' national image which was being utilized in order to achieve these economic ends.

REFERENCES

Bernstein, Morey. *The Search for Bridey Murphy*. New York: Doubleday, 1956.

Brean, Herbert. 'Bridey Murphy Puts Nation in a Hypnotizzy'. *Life*, 19 March 1956, pp.28–35.

Chicago Tribune. Zullo, Joseph, 'Ireland Looking Forward to Huge Tourist Invasion', 15 February 1953, p.D1.

Doyle, James, 'Ireland Bids for Increase in Travel Trade', 6 June 1954, p.E20.

Doyle, James, 'Ireland Sets its Sights for Class Tourists', 12 June 1955, p.J27.

Blakesley, Richard, 'Adventure in Hypnotism; Woman Recalls Prior Life', 8 January 1956, p.D7.

'Obituary 2', 10 August 1957, p.19.

Daly, Mary E. 'Nationalism, Sentiment and Economics: Relations between Ireland and Irish America in the Postwar Years', in Kevin Kenny (ed.), *New Directions in Irish–American History*. Madison, WI: University of Wisconsin Press, 2003.

Deegan, James and Donal A. Dineen. *Tourism Policy and Performance: The Irish Experience*. London: International Thomson Business Press, 1997.

Genter, Robert. '"Hypnotizzy" in the Cold War: The American Fascination with Hypnotism in the 1950s'. *Journal of American Culture*, vol. 29, no. 2 (June 2006), pp.154–69.

Gibbons, Luke. 'Back Projections: John Hinde and the New Nostalgia', in Luke Gibbons (ed.), *Transformations in Irish Culture*. Cork: Cork University Press, 1996, pp.37–43.

Goffman, Erving. *The Presentation of Self in Everyday Life*. New York: Doubleday, 1959.

http://historical-debates.oireachtas.ie/D/0139/D.0139.195306160034.html

http://www.measuringworth.com/uscompare

http://www.shannonireland.com

http://www.shopshannon.com

Irish Times. 'First Custom-Free Airport Opened', 22 April 1947, p.1.

Lange, Dorothea. 'Country People of Ireland'. *Life*, 21 March 1955, pp.135–43.

Meerloo, Joost. *The Rape of the Mind: The Psychology of Thought Control, Menticide, and Brainwashing*. Cleveland, OH: World Publishing, 1956.

New York Times. 'Wares of Ireland to be Put on View; Thousands of Articles Made There to Be Included in a Show at Gimbels, Oct. 31', 13 October 1949, p.31.

'Ireland Joins in Fair; Will Have Exhibits in Chicago at International Trade Show', 2 May 1950, p.53.

Crowther, Bosley. 'The Screen in Review', 22 May 1951, p.37.

'Tweeds and Linens Linked in Display; Products of Ireland Shown by Franklin Simon in Four Matching Colors', 28 February 1952, p.24.

'Pilgrimage to Ireland Sails', 19 August 1953, p.20.

A.W., 'A Visit to Ireland Shown at Baronet,' 11 May 1954, p.25.

'Pilgrimage to Ireland; New Yorkers Fly to Ould Sod in Chartered Dutch Plane', 9 August 1955, p.23.

O'Higgins, Patrick. 'Ireland: The Grand Meander'. *Vogue*, vol. 121 (April 1953), pp.113 ff.

Packard, Vance. *The Hidden Persuaders*. New York: D. McKay, 1957.

Rains, Stephanie. 'Home from Home: Diasporic Images of Ireland in Film and Tourism', in Michael Cronin and Barbara O'Connor (eds), *Irish Tourism: Image, Culture and Identity*. Clevedon, OH: Channel View Publications, 2003, pp.196–241.

—— *The Irish–American in Popular Culture, 1945–2000*. Dublin: Irish Academic Press, 2007.

Sheats, Dorothea. 'I Walked Some Irish Miles'. *National Geographic Magazine*, May 1951, pp.653–78.

FILMS

The Hills of Ireland, directed by Harry Dugan, 1951. Celtic Films [United States].

The Quiet Man, directed by John Ford, 1952. Republic Studios [United States].

The Spell of Ireland, directed by Harry Dugan, 1954. Celtic Films [United States].

The Search for Bridey Murphy, directed by Noel Langley, 1956. Paramount Pictures [United States].

The Irish In Me, directed by Herman Boxer, 1959. Universal International Colour/Dudley Pictures Corporation [United States and Ireland].

O'Hara's Holiday, directed by Peter Bryan, 1960. Tribune Films Incorporated [Ireland].

CHAPTER TEN

Ignorable Irishry:
Leprechauns and Postwar Satire

JAMES SILAS ROGERS

Ruth Barton, in a 2004 article titled 'It Came from Glocca Morra', surveys a series of horror films that began in 1993 and continued through five lurid motion pictures – among them *Leprechaun Back 2 the Hood* (2003) – all of which feature malevolent leprechauns. As Barton notes, this series is all the more surprising in light of the innocuous earlier cinematic representations of the folkloric figure. 'Prior to then,' she observes, 'the cinematic leprechaun was most famously associated with Disney's *Darby O'Gill and the Little People*, released in 1959. In this, he is played by Jimmy O'Dea as a fully-fledged trickster whose main dramatic function is to ensure that Ireland is seen to be a space in which the magical can happen and a benevolent irrationality rules' (Barton, 'It Came from Glocca Morra', p.28).

Barton is quite right that the Disney film stands somewhere near the peak of an American popular culture tradition of representing lep-rechauns, and Irishness more generally, as inane. Any glance at a rack of Saint Patrick's Day greetings cards will reveal that leprechauns have come to serve as a default icon of Irish culture in the United States, and for the most part, such familiar images as 'Lucky' (first introduced by General Mills in 1963 for the new cereal Lucky Charms) or the Notre Dame mascot (drawn by commercial artist Ted Drake in 1964) function in much the same way as the infamous cast-iron lawn fig-urines functioned for American blacks – as infantilized and derogato-ry stereotypes. Yet, these reductive figures are emblematic of more than racist stereotyping; looked at more closely, they stand as a complex encoding of ethnic and racial representation, and of the represented group's own negotiation with and reworking of received imagery. *Darby O'Gill*, in fact, might be better considered as a decisive end to a literary tradition in which the leprechaun figure was employed in a nuanced, dialogic and transgressive manner.

The postwar era witnessed a clear body of writing in which leprechauns were used to put one culture into conversation with another: America speaking with Ireland, perhaps, but more important, America in conversation with unadmitted parts of its own experience. While not disruptive in the way that the later schlock-and-shock films present the leprechaun, those found in the works discussed here were faintly – and at times not so faintly – subversive of mainstream culture. At some levels, leprechauns in mid-century America played a role similar to blackface minstrelsy in the nineteenth century, a site in which complicated negotiations of identity, mockery, critique and even a deflected respect for the supposedly inferior group were played out in a non-threatening manner. David Roediger has said, in discussing what he calls the 'oppositional culture' of blackface, that

> the hugely popular culture of blackface likewise developed by counterpoint. Whatever his attraction, the performers and the audience knew that they were *not* the Black dandy personified by Zip Con. Nor were they the sentimentalized and appealing preindustrial slave Jim Crow. Blackface could be everything – rowdy, rebellious, and respectable – because it could be denied that it was anything. (Roediger, *Wages of Whiteness*, p.116)

Likewise, the leprechaun and the Irish could offer barbed observations on mainstream culture, with the safety net that they could be dismissed as nothing more than quaint.

Leprechauns in American popular culture are frequently confused or conflated with the *sidhe* or fairies, of which the folklore tradition is vastly more extensive. The fairies dwell in both the spirit realm and in the real world; Irish folklore and literature abounds with stories of stolen children, or of individuals who have seen 'the other side' and have ever after been disappointed in the world as it exists. Leprechauns, too, turn up in mid-century tales of 'crossing over' between cultures if not between worlds, for Ireland, in these years, was indeed another land. After fifty years of mass tourism to Ireland it is now difficult to conceive of how unfamiliar Ireland appeared to most Americans right through the end of the 1950s. Before the establishment of Aer Lingus's regularly scheduled transatlantic service in 1958, before the efflorescence of the tourist industry under Bord

Fáilte, and before the election of John F. Kennedy and his famous
'roots' trip to New Ross in June 1962, Ireland was remarkably exotic.
In the near absence of any objective correlative for Ireland, it was easy
for an imagined Ireland to trump reality. As a noncombatant in the
recent war, Ireland provided a sort of secular analogy to that 'other
side', a still-pastoral, still-eccentric, still-spiritual counterpoint to an
America growing used to being a world power, and uneasily register-
ing its own uneasiness with the corporatization and efficiency that
were the legacy of the war effort.

Despite the recent reassessments of that decade by Brian Fallon and
others, or the romance that has come to attach to the bohemian
Dublin of Behan and J.P. Donleavy, Ireland in the 1950s was scarcely
idyllic.[1] Yet for Americans obsessively fearful of communist infiltra-
tion and the threat of nuclear attack, and – in the eyes of many – stam-
peding towards conformity and blandness, the Ireland of the
American imaginary presented an attractive alternative. In this context the unlikely figure of the leprechaun – and by metonymy, Ireland
and the Irish – helped to establish a substitute reality. Sometimes leprechaun figures showed a world that was exquisitely simple. More
often, though, in the popular culture of the day leprechauns and Irish
figures functioned as innocents in America, whose naïveté allowed
them to comment on contemporary life. Often, the leprechaun figure
served as, in effect, a guide or mediator whose task it was – sometimes
naïvely, as a *picaro* who stumbles into unfamiliar situations, and sometimes knowingly – to explain one country to another.[2]

There is, in fact, a sort of Ur-source for the American understanding of the leprechaun. Those mid-century writers who employed folklore in a bombastic, self-parodying manner had not learned their subject matter by immersing themselves in the archives of the Irish
Folklore Commission. Rather, their versions of the folk figure
descend from one source, James Stephens's *The Crock of Gold* (1912).
In this tale – which is at bottom a philosophical, albeit comic, novel
featuring mythology and folklore – almost all of the male characters
relentlessly banter about high-blown ideas. Stephens's book was written with a serious purpose, as a fictionalized exploration of how the
mind-forg'd manacles of society, law and custom conspire against
Truth. However sober Stephens's purposes may have been, the book
sold for its comic qualities, and sold well indeed. *The Crock of Gold*
was a stunning success in the United States. A survey of the Library
of Congress Catalog finds that from its publication in 1912 until 1947
it appeared in no fewer than forty-six American editions, including

three special editions for the Armed Forces during the war years.

But in what seems to be the fate of much Irish writing, any thought-provoking ideas behind Stephens's fable are trumped by its self-mocking tone. In a sense, it is has suffered the same fate as another classic satire of Irish origins, *Gulliver's Travels*, as it is routinely classified today as a children's book.[3] Stephens's leprechauns, philosophers and demigods draw near to serious conversation, but the ideas go nowhere. Throughout, the blend of mock profundity and heavy-handed dialect short circuit or deflate any genuine engagement with the concepts being presented. There is an unrelentingly antic quality to the proceedings. The Irish philosophers may be men of great learning, but at another level they are clueless; they do not know where their children came from, and it is only the pragmatic attentions of their devoted wives that allow them the leisure to ponder and pontificate.

The Crock of Gold's leprechauns are both mischievous and fatuous. These are precisely the qualities of the character Og, the leprechaun in *Finian's Rainbow*, a musical comedy that opened on Broadway in January 1947, where it would run for another 725 performances and be revived again in 1955.[4] Written by the Syrian–American Fred Saidy and the Jewish–American lyricist Yip Harburg, *Finian's Rainbow* is almost a parody. A dreamy Irishman, Finian McLonergan, who has stolen the lepechauns' pot of gold, comes to America, where he hopes to bury it near Fort Knox and watch it grow. His plans are complicated by a pursuing leprechaun, by the inconvenience of his daughter Sharon falling in love with a union organizer, and by the designs of a land-grabbing bank corporation. He incurs the wrath of a blustering, racist United States senator – who is later turned into a black man when Finian's daughter unknowingly wishes this while standing above the buried pot of gold. An unusual plot, to say the least: as Harburg's biographers noted, *Finian's Rainbow* is 'surely the only American musical written in the shadow of Marx on the fetishism of commodities' (Myerson and Harburg, *Who Put the Rainbow?*, p.223). Yet under all of the shamroguery and other foolishness, *Finian's Rainbow* creates a carnivalesque moment in which the usual conventions and assumptions of society are suspended. As such, it uses Ireland to introduce a space in which it is possible to express concerns about what America is becoming.

The playwright freely admitted that Stephens's book had provided at least some of the inspiration for the musical comedy; in a lecture given in the 1970s, Harburg recalled that during the process of conceiving the play, he 'was reading James Stephens's *The Crock of Gold*,

a beautiful book with all the lovely Irish names and the leprechaun ...
I love Irish literature – James Stephens, Sean O'Casey. I felt easy working with Irish ideas' (ibid., p.222).[5]

Finian's Rainbow offers an idea of Ireland – apotheosized in the
song 'How Are Things in Glocca Morra' – that contrasts with the
rapaciousness and ruthlessness of America and the capitalist economy.
The authors stated that their first goal, when they set out to write the
play, was to satirize the system of credit. 'Gold made us think of the
pot of gold,' says Yip. 'The pot of gold reminded us of leprechauns,
those mythical shoemakers who repaired only left shoes and their legendary crock of gold, which was good for three wishes. ... The wishes
gave us our conflict and a chance to kid the credit system' (Wolf, *New
York Times*, 9 March 1947). Throughout, the Irish characters show a
flair for 'kidding' in a way that reduces societal conventions to absurd-
ity: in one comic passage, Finian and Sharon get the better of their
creditors by explaining that their gold is already buried near Fort
Knox, which differs only slightly from what the Federal Reserve system plans to do.

Other elements of American life proved susceptible to being
refracted through naïve Irish eyes. Early on, Sharon asks her Finian:
'But, Father, are there no poor in America, no ill-housed, no ill-clad?'
He replies: 'Of course, Sharon. But they're the best ill-clad and ill-
housed in the world' (Harburg and Saidy, *Finian's Rainbow*, p.16).
And an indictment of racism is central to the tale. Harburg remarked,
'Take the racial question, for instance ... In *Finian's* it is all presented
through the eyes of a leprechaun – through a completely unbiased and
child mind which can't understand all this human foolishness about
the color of a man's skin' (Wolf, *New York Times*, 9 March 1947,
p.X1).

In the end, the purloined crock of gold and its attending leprechauns' wishes – having brought prosperity and harmony to Finian's
settlement of Rainbow Valley, Missitucky – turn to 'worthless dross'
when the last of the wishes is used up; there is no lasting pot of gold,
and, as Finian says, 'This little boom is founded on an illusion'
(*Finian's Rainbow*, p.140). The play ends with Finian giving a raptur-
ous description of the wonders of atomic energy and then heading off
to Oak Ridge, Tennessee, to follow a new rainbow. Whatever social
analysis Harburg and Saidy may have hoped to have slipped into
Finian's Rainbow, the 1947 musical has entered the American repertoire for its comedy and broad farce.

Within a year of *Finian*, the husband-and-wife writing team of Guy and Constance Jones, who made a specialty of introducing folkloric or otherworldly figures in such novels and screenplays as *Mr Peabody's Mermaid* and *The Ghost and Mrs Muir,* introduced another leprechaun to American in the 1948 novel *There Was a Little Man.* In this book a glib and ambitious American advertising man named Fitzgerald on his way to London is aboard a plane that makes a forced landing in the west of Ireland. There, his ad-man associates repair to the bar to scheme on how to turn advertising into an irresistible soulless machine-like process –'it is a matter of finding the right formula', one of them says, 'Now we operate scientifically' (Jones, *Little Man,* p.30). Fitzgerald, who is half-Irish, recognizes the opportunity that a new age of advertising provides. But he holds private misgivings about the get-ahead ethos of his associates, whom he describes as

> a brash crew, loaded with degrees but not with manners; opinionated but without much knowledge. To him, they had no warmth, no curiosity, no enthusiasm. For this crowd, it [the trip to London] was just another assignment. No matter where they went, they traveled within the four walls of their own convictions.
> (Ibid., p.10)

Uneasy with his crass companions, Fitzgerald wanders off to the nearby woods and encounters Horace, the Leprechaun of Ballybun. In a complicated exchange, Fitzgerald succeeds in capturing the leprechaun's pot of gold, which, in a moment of largesse, he then gives back, thereby incurring the leprechaun's unwavering devotion.

While Fitzgerald is about this negotiating with Horace, the plane is repaired; his colleagues, unwilling to wait while there is business to be conducted elsewhere, take off without him. When he realizes that he has wound up somewhere so backward he must wait several days even to send a cable, Fitzgerald regrets his earlier misgivings; he bawls, 'I've just chucked away my chances for the best job I'll ever have in my life' (ibid., p.43). Stranded, he finds himself drawn to the pastoral charms of Ireland, and particularly to a rustic beauty named Norah. But he continues to read Ireland through the lens of go-getter America.

In due course, Fitzgerald gets back to America, and reverts to climbing the corporate ladder as a speech-writer with one startling success after another; he seems to have developed a Midas touch, owing – whether he knows it or not – to Horace's blessings. Any early suggestion that Fitzgerald was inclined towards an examined life appears to be fading fast before his worldly success. One promotion follows another; he becomes engaged to a beautiful career woman; he purchases a charming Connecticut retreat at a bargain price. Then Horace shows up. Norah, too, soon re-enters his life, having suddenly been called to America to collect an inheritance. As the tale continues, Horace works in the background to save Fitzgerald from selling his soul to the corporation and the American dream.

The climactic chapter is titled 'The Dead Leaves'. As the chapter opens a mini-epiphany occurs to Fitzgerald, when, in spite of his hurry, he stops for a red light.

> Fitzgerald crossed with the crowd. He decided to feel that was symbolic: He was always crossing with the crowd when the light changed. If you bucked the crowd, you got run over. Particularly in New York. (Ibid., p.202)

Back at his hotel, he meets Horace, who has been out sightseeing in New York. But Horace, too, has been struck by the crowds: 'I've the fancy that if I fell down in the street they'd walk right over me and never know it' (Ibid., p.209). The Irish Horace, however, keeps his own clock and will not take orders from a Pavlovian green light. He has in fact found the Irish cops of New York particularly sweet-tempered:

> Faith, only this afternoon I asked one of them the way to St Patrick's and he stopped his work to take me across the street, because the light had changed color and a big lorry was chasing me. 'And how's the weather in the old country,' he asked me, and with as sweet a smile as I've ever seen. (Ibid., p.209)

In New York, Fitzgerald spends increasing time with Norah. The Irish girl possesses a deeper wisdom than the rat race can offer; at one point she says to him: 'You're not happy, poor man ... I've seen that for myself. You don't like your job. You should leave it' (ibid., p.214). But Fitzgerald feels trapped:

> It's too late. I don't want any part of my job, but it's too late. You've done this to me Norah. Being with you is like looking into a well of clear water, where I see myself too plainly. I don't like what I see. I reached for my pot of gold, and I got it. It's nothing but pebbles: pebbles and dead leaves. (Ibid., pp.214–15)

As the book winds down, Fitzgerald realizes that his beautiful fiancée is a mercenary fake, that his politically ambitious employer is a sham, and that his astounding material success is not bringing him happiness.

He quits his job and moves to Ireland, where he opens a country inn with a new wife, none other than Norah.

Such disillusionment with the American gospel of success – 'pebbles and dead leaves', an echo of Finian's 'worthless dross' – is a powerful condemnation, if taken at face value. But the critique comes packaged in farce and preposterousness. In certain particulars, *There Was a Little Man* resembles the most celebrated anti-corporation novel of the 1950s, Sloan Wilson's *The Man in the Gray Flannel Suit* (1955). In each book introspection leads an upwardly mobile speech-writer to jettison his career in favour of what today might be called 'family values'. Wilson's book is, by any critical standard, superior to the Jones's at every level – not least because its critique of contemporary America is explicit, rather than deflected through a nonsense figure.

By choosing to point out uncomfortable realities by means of a character who lacks the social standing to be listened to, Guy and Constance Jones replicated a standard strategy of blackface. As William Stowe and David Grimsted wrote in their important review essay 'White–Black Humor':

> Certainly, minstrelsy played on and influenced the social stereotypes of Black. Just as certainly, however, black-face, corked or real, seemed to audiences a mask which allowed deep expressions of emotions of loss and longing, as well as ridicule of social and intellectual platitudes and the discrepancy between American dreams and American realities. The black mask, like the sentimental or farcical format, distanced things enough so that truths could be expressed which would have been profoundly troubling or socially dangerous if presented or taken in serious form.
> (Stowe and Grimsted, 'White–Black Humor', pp.82–3)

Similarly, an appraisal of America through a leprechaun and an innocent Irish lass is almost by definition unreliable and juvenile. But commentary from such a source is not necessarily commentary that can be easily dismissed: the most trenchant observer of King Lear, after all, is his fool.

In America, a juvenile characterization became a key element in representing the Irish. In the Irish tradition leprechauns are small, but they are creatures with agency of their own and do not act in childlike or silly ways. James Stephens's leprechauns were not to be dismissed: they had the power to make real trouble. But the leprechauns encountered in mid-century American popular culture were in many cases infantilized.

An explicit instance of such infantilization comes in a 1950 children's book by Frances Frost, *Then Came Timothy*. Frost, a sometime poet and fairly successful children's book author throughout the 1940s and 1950s, lived most of her life in Northern New England; this particular children's book takes place on 'Singing Cow Island' off the coast of Maine. Frost creates an idyllic world in which two children, Kathy and Philip O'Kelly, are raised in a self-sufficient island community by their Irish-born grandparents; Grandfather Rory O'Kelly in particular is a lovable old storyteller. Even by the standards of children's literature, the narrative of *Then Came Timothy* has an ersatz, improvized quality; the first of many surprises in this little book is the arrival of the leprechaun Timothy Sweetfern, described thus: 'He was about two inches tall and he wore tight green trousers and a green jacket with flibberty-gibbet tails. His pointed green hat was cocked jauntily on the side of his head' (Frost, *Then Came Timothy*, pp.35–6). Timothy has sailed to America in an eggshell, thereby making good on one of Grandfather's quaint stories.

Yet, even this minor and forgettable children's book sets up an allegory for a society under stress. In fact, Timothy arrives in this island community just as a sort of petty juvenile delinquency is disrupting the lobster fishing; incomprehensively, someone has been stealing lobsters and cutting lobster pots lose from their buoys. As the story lurches along, Timothy sets up a stake-out that eventually captures the miscreant, who turns out to be 16-year-old Joey O'Shea.[6] Timothy presides over a benevolent informal island court that takes pity on Joey, realizing that he has not been properly served by his family. Quite consciously avoiding the formality of the law, Timothy extracts promises from the offender and the community alike to do better by the youngster. An early expression of the national outcry over juvenile delinquency that would eventuate in films such as *The Wild One* (1953) and *Rebel Without a Cause* (1955), as well as Senate hearings in 1954, *Then Came Timothy* resolves with 'Singing Cow Island' having been remade in the image of an idyllic leprechaun's Ireland – a self-contained place where social pathologies can never again take root. Ireland, then, despite its substantial history of treachery, violence and suffering, was still capable of being imagined as a place of childlike innocence. A radically innocent Ireland is, in fact, exactly what Sean Thornton initially thinks he can find in *The Quiet Man*, the 1952 film in which John Wayne/Sean Thornton retreats from America – where, in the course of fighting his way out of the hell of the steel mills, he has killed a man in the ring – to find sanctuary in Ireland.

Another satirical work of the 1950s may be relevant here: the 1955 novel by Leonard Wibberley, *The Mouse That Roared*, which became widely known when turned into an hilarious 1959 movie in which Peter Sellers plays three different parts. The plot involves a miniscule, beleaguered European nation called the Duchy of Grand Fenwick that declares war on the United States in order to lose and be awarded massive foreign aid – but which inadvertently wins the war by capturing the latest super-bomb during a full-scale practice alert. There is an Irish note in this David *vs.* Goliath story. Lost in the movie, for instance, is the fact that Wibberley – born in Ireland in 1915 and a monoglot Irish-speaker until he was eight – dedicates the book with the note, 'To all the little nations who over the centuries have done what they could to attain and preserve their freedom. It is from one of them that I am sprung' (Wibberley, *The Mouse That Roared*). And when, at the end of the book, the dreadful 'Q-Bomb' is turned over to a multinational body called the Tiny Twenty, it is the Irish representative who seems to do all the talking.

While mocking the supposed largesse of American foreign policy, *The Mouse That Roared* also attacks both the ersatz nature of American culture and American economic imperialism: the reason Grand Fenwick is in dire financial straits, in fact, is that American mass-production has subverted its principle export, the ancient wine Pinot Grand Fenwick, by introducing a cheap California knock-off called Pinot Grand Enwick – at the sight of which one outraged member of the Court exclaims, 'The dogs ... rich as they are, with abundance on every hand, they still seek to deprive us of our only source of livelihood. For a few dollars more for themselves they would beggar every man woman and child in Grand Fenwick' (ibid., pp.45–6).

The Mouse That Roared is farce, of course – but not so farcical as to prevent Wibberley from reintroducing the same themes in a more explicitly Irish vein in his next book, the 1956 young person's novel *McGillicuddy McGotham*. Here, the butt of Wibberley's satire is American economic brashness. The story concerns a leprechaun, one inch tall, sent to the United States as 'Envoy Plenipotentiary from the Kingdom of the Little People' in order to stop New World Airlines from expanding the runway at Foynes Airport by cutting across land that 'belongs to the Leprechauns and must not be touched' (Wibberley, *McGillicuddy McGotham*, p.58).

There are plenty of other targets for satire in this story – among them television game shows and a golfing president who seems a lot like Ike – but the derision is ham-fisted at best, and *McGillicuddy*

McGotham has deservedly been forgotten. Despite the supposed power of satire in the Irish literary tradition, nothing in this foolish story has any sort of an edge to it. What we have, then, is a pattern that becomes a distinctly Irish–American trope: satire and social commentary that overtly asks not to be taken seriously. When Irishness was employed to critique America in the 1950s, it was usually done in a wilfully ineffectual manner, so imbedded in humour and farce that the edge of its satire was blunted.

A conspicuous instance of how Irish-inflected commentary on America was lost on its audience – or put another way, of how the Irish note of opposition was 'defanged' by its own presumed ridiculousness – can be found in Edwin O'Connor's 1956 novel *The Last Hurrah*, which along with *The Quiet Man* was the Irish ethnic phenomenon of the 1950s. *The Last Hurrah*'s Irish politicians, who proved so appealing to the public, speak to us out of a prison of their own blarney, their own cultivation of a paltry and often risible self-invention. One of the most commercially successful political novels ever written, O'Connor's novel tells the story of a larger-than-life silver-tongued political boss and latter-day Irish tribal chieftain named Frank Skeffington. *The Last Hurrah* was widely understood to be based on Boston's James Michael Curley; the real mayor first threatened litigation, then came to relish the novel, and eventually described his fictional counterpart as 'a pale carbon copy' of himself. Curley's willingness to forgive the satire because it ultimately proved so engaging is, in many ways, exactly what the larger public did as well.

Charles Duffy's recent biography, and the testimony of O'Connor's close friend John V. Kelleher, make clear that the author had more than comedy in mind. O'Connor wrote the novel as a thoroughgoing condemnation of the blandness and inauthenticity that he believed had come to dominate American life. In the fictional election his opponent assiduously avoids meeting the public in order to appear on television as often as possible, in carefully staged shows called 'At Home with Kevin McCluskey'. The packaging of the candidate extends to hanging a portrait of Pope Pius XII in his living-room and renting an Irish setter to replace the real family dog. The platitudinous script of one of these televised conversations confirms Skeffington's earlier assessment of his opponent: that he is a 'six-foot hunk of talking putty' (O'Connor, *The Last Hurrah*, p.156).

Yet when the people speak, the talking putty wins in a landslide. In a post-election conversation, the nephew of the defeated Skeffington receives a lecture in the new realities of politics from one of those bloodless new campaign consultants. The nephew says: 'From the way you're describing it, almost anybody could have beaten my uncle.' The devastating answer comes: 'Almost anybody did' (ibid., p.376). In the popular response to the novel, such bleak comments on America's present and future were almost never heard. Rather, readers responded almost exclusively at the charm, wit and flamboyance of its Irish main character.

Charm seems to be the only commendable attribute of the Irish to survive when, as the 1950s closed, the Walt Disney studios introduced an immensely influential work involving a leprechaun, *Darby O'Gill and the Little People* (1959). Nearly twenty years in development, *Darby O'Gill* drew its initial inspiration from a turn-of-the century series of whimsical short stories by the Irish–American writer Herminie Templeton Kavanagh. As has happened to many works brought to the big screen by Disney, the story was much altered. Though Disney himself, as well as his writers and artists, visited Ireland looking for 'background', the reality is that the film's plot draws heavily on Stage Irish conventions and just as heavily on the formula to which the Disney studio adhered. For instance, the significant element of Roman Catholic practice that runs through the stories was largely excised in the movie. And in a small but significant change, the adjective in the title was modified: the 'Good People' of the Kavanagh's 1903 book became 'Little People' in the film, underscoring the inconsequentiality of the Irish figure.

In fairness, *Darby O'Gill* is not utterly juvenile: there is a certain dark energy in the film (small children often find it frightening), in part because it conflates leprechauns with the *bean sí*, the traditional omen of death, and also in an extended scene of music and dancing that evokes dionysian madness. The film is often visually striking as well, owing to Disney's expertise with special effects, and the leprechauns are not all ridiculous: they are portrayed as having an attractive other-worldly panache and, tricky though they may be, as having basically good hearts. Nonetheless, the leprechaun leader, King Brian Connors, is immature in important ways. He is powerless to resist music and dance, and especially powerless to resist alcohol. An extended scene of ludicrous song-swapping, in which Darby captures King Brian by getting him drunk until after sunrise, could hardly be a more naked portrait of Irish irresponsibility.

Despite considerable promotion, including advance showings of portions on the Disney television show, *Darby O'Gill* appears to have been a financial disappointment in its original release (Disney financial figures are closely guarded secrets) (ibid., p.55). Its most lasting effect on Hollywood probably is that it launched the career of actor Sean Connery. *Darby O'Gill* was adapted for screen by an American entertainment corporation, and was in fact filmed entirely in southern California. But in the 1959 film the emergent trope of using Ireland to unsettle American assumptions is nowhere to be seen. In terms of its effect on the American understanding of Ireland, and of the leprechaun in particular, the unrivalled cultural penetration of the Disney empire has essentially displaced all previous iterations of the figure.

Admittedly, *Finian's Rainbow* and the other, much less prominent works discussed above were rarely understood as social commentary. But understood or not, these works *did* propose an Ireland that could, and did, comment on America. They introduced Irish figures who registered the losses, the dubious trajectories and sometimes the deceits of American life. The horror films of fifty years later may have reinvented the leprechaun as a bloodthirsty slasher; but in mid-century America, leprechauns were already slipping a needle under the skin, and sometimes, twisting a dagger.

REFERENCES

Barton, Ruth. 'It Came From Glocca Morra!' *Film Ireland*, vol. 27 (March/April 2004), pp.28–31.

Bradley, William L. 'Walt Disney's Ireland', in Donald McNamara (ed.), *Which Direction Ireland? Proceedings of the 2006 ACIS Mid-Atlantic Regional Conference*. Newcastle: Cambridge Scholars Press, 2007, pp.49–68.

Duffy, Charles. *A Family of His Own: A Life of Edwin O'Connor*. Washington, DC: Catholic University of America Press, 2003.

Frost, Frances. *Then Came Timothy*. Eau Claire, WI: E.M. Hale & Co., 1950.

Harburg, E.Y. and Fred Saidy. *Finian's Rainbow: A Musical Satire*. New York: Random House, 1947.

http://www.en.wikipedia.org/wiki/Finian's_Rainbow

Jones, Guy Pearce and B. Constance. *There Was a Little Man*. New York: Random House, 1948.

MacHale, Des. *The Complete Guide to The Quiet Man*. Belfast: Appletree Press, 2000.

Mercier, Vivian. *The Irish Comic Tradition*. Oxford: Clarendon Press, 1962.

Myerson, Harold and Ernie Harburg. *Who Put the Rainbow in the*

Wizard of Oz?: Yip Harburg, Lyricist. Ann Arbor, MI: University of Michigan Press, 1993.

O'Connor, Edwin. *The Last Hurrah*. Boston: Little, Brown, 1956.

Ó Giolláin, Diarmuid. 'The *Leipreachan* and Fairies, Dwarfs and the Household Familiar: A Comparative Study'. *Bealoideas*, vol. 52 (1984), pp.75–150.

Pyle, Hilary. *James Stephens: His Work and an Account of His Life*. New York: Barnes & Noble, 1965.

Roediger, David R. *The Wages of Whiteness: Race and the Making of the American Working Class*. London and New York: Verso, 1999.

Stephens, James. *The Crock of Gold*. New York: Macmillan, 1940; first published 1912.

Stowe, William F. and David Grimsted. 'White–Black Humor' [review of Toll, *Blacking Up*]. *Journal of Ethnic Studies*, vol. 3 (1975), pp.78–96.

Wibberley, Leonard. *The Mouse That Roared*. Boston: Little, Brown, 1955.

—— *McGillicuddy McGotham*. Boston: Little, Brown, 1956.

Wolf, Arlene. 'How they made that "Rainbow"'. *New York Times*, 9 March 1947, p.X1.

CHAPTER ELEVEN

Unnatural Law:
William McGivern's Rogue Cops

TONY TRACY

The Irish cop has been a recurring character in American film for most of its history, though one usually restricted by the narrow requirements of stereotype. As American society became more homogenized and conservative during the immediate postwar period, cinema became less ethnically diverse. Jews were among the first groups to be elided; in 1944 screenwriter Ben Hecht had complained that the previous twenty years had witnessed 'the almost complete disappearance of the Jew from American fiction, stage, radio and movies' (Hecht, *Guide for the Bedeviled*, p.16). Assimilation, anti-Semitism and acculturation conspired in creating cultural invisibility and weakening. Irish types and representations remained surprisingly resistant to such challenges, although not immune to their pressures.

This chapter sets out to explore a neglected entry in the long representational history of Irish–American law enforcement at this pivotal moment of supposed 'ethnic fade'. In the 1950s several films appeared adapted from the crime novels of William P. McGivern, a Chicago-born Irish–American, veteran and the husband of the Irish novelist Maureen Daly.[1] *Shield for Murder* (1954), *The Big Heat* (1953), *Rogue Cop* (1954) and *The Darkest Hour* (1954) may be situated within a brief subgenre of American film from the early 1950s which presented neurotic and then openly corrupt police figures.[2] What sets the McGivern adaptations apart is the recurring presence of troubled and often objectionable Irish–American protagonists.

These protagonists are most notable in *Rogue Cop* and *The Big Heat*, which were released by rival studios on 1 September 1954. Both productions played down any ethnic dimension to the stories by casting classic 'American' actors – Robert Taylor and Glenn Ford respectively. The screenplays removed specifics of ethnic background wherever possible. Nonetheless, between the films and their source narratives there remains sufficient detail to encourage the recuperation of such elements in the analysis of McGivern's mid-century Irish–American cops.

It is not until the 1950s that big-city police officers attracted significant interest from American writers and film-makers, who had until recently preferred the hard-boiled detectives of Chandler and Hammet (Panek, *American Police Novel*, p.41). McGivern's police characters share with men like Sam Spade and Philip Marlowe both a loner instinct and a sense of pessimism to which McGivern often adds a strong dose of bitterness. He writes of men who have worked all their professional lives in the service of the law, but have become disillusioned with its corruption and bureaucratic inertia. This pervasive sense of frustration gives rise to explosive individual action anticipating the vigilante cops of such 1970s films as *Dirty Harry* and *Brannigan*, the latter co-scripted by McGivern.

In portraying lawmen unbound by traditional margins, these characters represent a new variant of the stereotypical 'wild' Irishman and reflect the influence of Mickey Spillane's mould-breaking *I, the Jury* (1947) – a novel of unregulated male violence that clearly anticipates *The Big Heat*, in particular. To established *film noir* elements of pessimism and dread, McGivern's novels add issues of class confusion and failed ambition in a recognizable, if generally muted, ethnic context. The result is an often complex meditation on the Irish–American psyche.

Deborah Thomas proposes that *film noir*'s treatment of the urban landscape grew out of a sense of strangeness with its roots in the massive immigrant waves in the early part of the twentieth century, 'which seemed to make the city no longer the locus of American "civilization" but rather of antithetical "otherness"' (Thomas, 'How Hollywood Deals With the Deviant Male', p.21). 'Film Noir,' she continues, 'is defining as "reality" the world as perceived by the white American male, the genre's usual protagonist.' While Thomas states that by the time *film noir* was being made, the 'foreign' connotations of the city were simply a given and no longer tied to actual foreigners, her insights point up the ambiguous relations between the Irish and the city, which is illuminating in the context of McGivern's *noir* fictions. His Irish belong to a group that was not only central to impressions of foreignness and challenges to 'civilization' in the American city, but also, since at least the 1890s, a group with deep ties to the forces of regulation, namely the police. McGivern's protagonists move back and forth across the line of order and regulation with ease, presenting us with fluid and unfinished constructs of masculine identity that vacillate between polarities of 'civilization'/'whiteness' and 'otherness'; between assimilated American values and immigrant destabilization.

However, in his positive recuperation of a distinctly Irish–Catholic upbringing and formation, McGivern reverses these earlier conjunctions. Many of his characters find truth and degrees of redemption not in denial of their 'otherness', but in recognition and re-acquaintance with their own traditions in a cityscape that has corrupted older moral certainties.

Rogue Cop

Rogue Cop is McGivern's most foregrounded treatment of the socio-religious background of the 1950s Irish–American police officer.[3] The rogue cop of the title is Mike Carmody (renamed Chris Kelvaney in the film and played by MGM star Robert Taylor), who offers his influence and muscle to the illegal gambling interests of Dan Beaumont (George Raft) and crime boss Ackerman (Robert F. Simon). When Mike's honest cop brother Eddie (Steve Forrest) catches a low-life criminal named Delaney at the scene of a murder, Beaumont and Ackerman exert pressure that he not be identified in court. Delaney has some kind of hold over the gangsters that they wish to avoid bringing to light. Although Mike tries to convince Eddy not to testify, his younger brother refuses – primarily because he sees Mike's corruption as having betrayed their father's pride and honour. But when Eddie is subsequently shot dead by the gangsters, Mike sets out to avenge the murder regardless of the danger to himself or to his now destroyed reputation.

McGivern's story might appear simply a well-crafted entry in the *I, the Jury* tradition of personal revenge. But McGivern reveals himself to be attempting a wider inquiry by his interest in the spiritual subconscious of his central character. In this, *Rogue Cop* reflects what Andrew Greeley, in framing his discussion of Catholic writers, has called a 'Sacramental Imagination'. Though writing in the culturally lowbrow and thematically profane confines of the American crime genre, McGivern is nonetheless best understood as working within this tradition. 'The Catholic imagination is different from the Protestant imagination,' writes Greeley. 'The Catholic "classics" assume a God who is present in the world, disclosing Himself in and through creation ... The Protestant classics, on the other hand, assume a God who is radically absent from the world, and who discloses [Himself] only on rare occasions' (Greeley, *Catholic Myth*, p.45). McGivern's characters and plot are clearly informed by Catholic structures of thought, particularly in his recurrent return to the themes of moral choice, transgression and forgiveness, and in his ambivalent representation of male-dominated institutional hierarchies. His *noir* thrillers grow from a 'sacramental imagination' especially in those moments where corrupt characters find themselves to be living a graced existence, albeit in often secular and disguised forms. This is the same tension Stephen Schloesser finds in his discussion of 'polluted protagonists' as recurring figures of grace in twentieth-century Catholic writing, whose 'indeterminacy – and thus the possibility and mystery of their pollution – made them capable of being "modern sacraments"' (Schloesser, 'Inventing the Catholic Novel').

Rogue Cop is a variation on the fraternal 'Cain and Abel' conflict that has occupied cinematic portraits of Irish–American brotherhood from the Cagney–O'Brien partnerships of the 1930s to the treacherous animosity in *The Departed* (2006). At the heart of these narratives is the potency of individual choice, a central value in American definitions of self. With such choice comes an inevitable conflict with authority, which is of course central to much Hollywood cinema, particularly Westerns. In American culture this theme finds added dimension in the often unspoken conflict between the ties of the old country and the opportunities of the new, the pull of tradition against opportunities of modernity. Werner Sollors has noted that 'America is a country which has placed great emphasis on consent at the expense of descent definitions. The widely shared public bias against hereditary privilege has strongly favored achieved rather than ascribed identity' (Sollors, *Beyond Ethnicity*, p.45). McGivern's stories take place in the middle of this cultural imperative. At crucial moments, his cops feel the competing pulls of ascent and descent. These competing forces form around American cultural and cinematic conceptions of the individual, the hero – the Protestant man alone, if you will – in conflict with the soured hero as part of a group, a community often pulling the protagonist back to the values of his youth and even childhood.

But those communities of origin are not a paradise lost. As key the institutional church may have been, in *Rogue Cop* and *The Big Heat* it fails to make an impression on the hardened and vengeful adult central characters. The tired words of parish curates (Fr Ahern and Fr Masterson respectively) are less potent than the underlying values and faith that have become obscured by American capitalism's corrosive endorsement of individual success over the collective values of society. Thus we have a society caught between the linked social and spiritual aspects of the old world and the rampant materialism of the postwar period. McGivern's polluted protagonists stand between these two worlds.

Rogue Cop introduces the subtext of descent early in the novel, but it is significantly diminished in the film, which, while it cannot omit the shared childhood of the central relationship of the two brothers, avoids McGivern's more theological themes. Following Dan Beaumont's request that Mike Carmody stop his brother from identifying Delaney, McGivern introduces a flash of interior dialogue: 'A phrase came into his mind from his forgotten religion and forgotten values: "Let this chalice pass from me!" ... Why had those words occurred to him' (McGivern, *Rogue Cop*, p.25). The phrase is from the gospel passage referred to as 'The Agony in the Garden', where Jesus attempts to escape his destiny: 'My Father, if it be possible, let this chalice pass from me. Nevertheless not as I will, but as you will' (Matthew 26:39). Within this passage lies the primary struggle of Christian faith; the renouncement of the physical world in pursuit of a higher spiritual kingdom. Significantly, Carmody does not remember the second part of the quotation. It is the return of a repressed memory. 'He didn't want this job and in some intuitive manner he was afraid of it. But there was no one he could ask for help ... Why had those words occurred to him' (McGivern, *Rogue Cop*, p.25). *Rogue Cop* blends into its generic framework of crime and violence motifs of messianic destiny in the figure of Carmody, binding together the lapsed lawman and lapsed Catholic who begins a corrupt cop but who, through the persistence of 'moral memory', contains the potential for redemption.

In the novel and film, Mike Carmody defends his actions as a crooked cop by contrasting his success (visually established by Taylor's expensive suits and movie hero demeanour) with his father's foolish commitment to honesty: 'The stubborn old fool ... He'd been sure he had a stranglehold on happiness and eternal bliss' (ibid, pp.58–9). His father and he fell out when the old man discovered that Mike was on the take and there was 'an emotional clash between a man of faith and a man of reason' (ibid., p.72). Mike, however, sees himself as better than his father, his brother and the other honest cops in the precinct;

he contends that he has had the courage and cunning to increase his income and influence. The threat to Eddie's life and his conflict with the gangsters bring Mike's isolation into focus in a new way. In common with the more existential tendencies of the *film noir* anti-hero he realizes:

> He was alone now, cut off from everyone. There would be no half measures; Karen, Ackerman, Fr Ahern, even Eddie himself, they were all raged against him, watching his futile efforts with contempt. But I've always been alone he thought ... he had thrown away the hollow props of faith and family because he had to stand alone. (Ibid., p.106)

Following Eddie's murder, it is precisely these 'hollow props' that trouble his heretofore complete independence. Standing in the living-room of the family home, Mike fulfils Andrew Greeley's view of Catholics as people who 'find our houses and our world haunted by a sense that objects, events and persons of daily life are revelations of grace' (Greeley, *Catholic Imagination*, p.1):

> The gentle eyes of the Madonna stared at him reproachfully; the silent piano and empty chairs made him guiltily aware of the old rupture between him and his father. He picked up a stack of sheet music and looked at the titles. It was the old Irish stuff ... Why did he cherish these bitter memories? Each one told the same poignant story of betrayal and death ... of people dying grandly in fruitless battles for betrayed causes. They belonged a thousand years in the past; why were they important to him in America? (*Rogue Cop*, p.161)

This is a revealing passage. It explores both the maintenance of the old culture in the midst of the new and also the split allegiance of the immigrant. What Mike, in asking 'why were they important to him in America', fails to grasp is that his father's maintenance of the Irish folkloric and pietistic tradition gave him structure and substance in the new land; the move to America did not represent a 'rupture' with the past so much as a kind of fulfilment, partial though that might have been. Later, the parish priest Father Ahern develops this theme, uniting the 'betrayed causes' of Irish history with the promise and opportunity that America offered for these first-generation immigrants: 'Can't you understand their bitterness when their sons went wrong over here? Instead of being grateful for a country to love and live in, some of the sons seemed bent only on spoiling the place' (ibid., p.183).   The binding force between the old country and the new, between the dead father and the wayward son, is Catholicism. The elderly priest suggests that Mike try to come back to the congregation from which he has drifted – a suggestion Mike finds anathema to his secularized identity: 'I'd be nothing if I turned into a confused sinner, begging for forgiveness ' (ibid., p.184).

Yet, both the film and the novel end on a note of forgiveness. Having shot the gangster leaders and suffered a gunshot himself, Chris Kelvaney (Mike Carmody's name in the film) is taken away by ambulance. By his side is one of the cops from the precinct. 'Do you forgive me?' he asks, 'Could you do that?' 'Sure,' says his colleague, not understanding the full meaning of the injured man's request. 'Now get some sleep.'

This physical suffering offers a kind of redemption that nonetheless remains vague in its origins and object. Why ask the cop for forgiveness? In the tradition of the *noir* anti-hero, the rogue cop dies alone; punished, certainly, but also deprived of any meaningful moral resolution beyond his suffering. The novel's ending is similar but without the hollow ambiguity. Carmody emerges unscathed from the gunfight and in the final scene is preparing to go into Lt Wilson's office to face the consequences of his corruption. The least he can expect is that he will be thrown off the force; his help in breaking up the criminal gang and in apprehending his brother's killer has offset some of his crimes. As he waits in the station corridor a misty recollection takes hold of him: 'This is what it felt like as a child when he waited at the confessional. Fear, yes, but something else. And the other thing was a sweeping relief that came from the anticipation of forgiveness' (ibid., p.224). Rather than becoming 'nothing' in his turn towards forgiveness, Carmody now welcomes the possibility of return. The rogue cop finds redemption not through mere physical suffering, but by acknowledging his moral corruption by the secular city. It is only when he acknowledges his 'polluted' nature in light of the structures of his Irish–Catholic background that he can find peace in his contemporary existence. Father Ahern – who seemed so anachronistic in the midst of crime and vengeance – is vindicated. To be a full American one must also be fully aware of one's origins; to deny the latter is to impede the former.

The Big Heat

Published the year after *Rogue Cop*, *The Big Heat* represented McGivern's attempt to explore another dimension of police corruption;

this time from the perspective of a virtuous officer.[4] The plot revolves around another Irish–American cop, Detective Dave Bannion, and like the earlier novel it is structured as a revenge narrative initiated by the murder of a close family member. A police clerk named Deery (Tom Duncan in the film version) has committed suicide. Bannion is sent to the dead man's house to investigate; there, he meets the apparently distraught wife). Although the circumstantial evidence seems incontrovertible, Bannion remains suspicious. When a former mistress of Deery's is found murdered, Bannion's superior stonewalls his growing doubts. Following an obscene phone call to his home warning him off further investigation, Bannion confronts crime boss Mike Lagana at his palatial home and beats up his bodyguard. Soon afterwards Bannion's wife Katie is killed by a car bomb intended for him. He is asked to turn in his police badge pending an investigation, at which point he realizes that the department is corrupt and decides to avenge his wife's murder on his own. In the course of his 'freelance' investigations he comes in contact with Debbie, moll to the violent criminal Vince Stone, an accomplice of Lagana. When Stone throws boiling coffee in her face, she flees to Bannion's hotel seeking shelter and protection. After Bannion tells her that Deery's wife is blackmailing Lagana with a list of corrupt police officers left by her dead husband, Debbie repays Bannion's sympathetic treatment of her by killing Mrs Deery, thereby exposing the depth of the police collusion with criminal elements. She dies soon afterwards in a gunfight at Stone's penthouse apartment, where the gangster is shot dead by the police. At the close, Bannion walks away into the dawn.

The Big Heat vividly enacts the analysis of policing later presented by Herbert Packer in his influential article 'Two Models of the Criminal Process'. Packer contrasted what he called the 'crime control model', designed to protect the rights of the average citizen by stressing the efficient apprehension and punishment of criminals, and the 'due process model', designed to protect the rights of the accused by presenting obstacles to carrying them past each step in the legal process. Of the former he stated: 'The value system that underlies the Crime Control Model is based on the proposition that the repression of criminal conduct is by far the most important function to be performed by the criminal process' (Packer, 'Two Models', p.9). *The Big Heat* takes the 'Crime Control Model' to an extreme, but with one important distinction: it is applied by an uncorrupted police officer who feels it necessary to circumvent the fatally compromised structures of the police department. In stepping outside police procedure and the limitations of presumed innocence Bannion rejects outright the precepts of 'due process'. McGivern's story presents this break from acceptable norms of justice as being an heroic consequence of the barbarous murder of Bannion's wife and the apparent collusion of the police force in its qualified response to her death. McGivern's women depart from the norms of the genre. Unlike the conventional *noir* presentation of women, where they are either 'presented as prizes, desirable objects' or caught in dead-end marriages of 'routinized boredom and a sense of stifling entrapment' (Harvey, 'Woman's Place', p.27), the women in McGivern's stories, and *The Big Heat* in particular, are presented in less misogynistic terms. Although never agents of change, they are often independent, even if vulnerable and frequently victimized. In almost all instances, his women want to create or be part of a family rather than women who destroy one. And in nearly every case, central male characters fail them, often with fatal consequences.

The Big Heat, like *Rogue Cop*, opens in the fraternal enclosure of the police station, but the ambience differs greatly. Whereas Carmody's colleagues barely conceal their contempt for his criminal associations, Bannion is introduced as likeable, physically imposing and respected. Untainted by the temptations that surround him, he remains a career detective out of a deep sense of vocation that is as conventional and uncomplicated as is his love for his family. In both the novel and its film adaptation, McGivern and director Fritz Lang take pains to establish his credentials as an ideal American: a doting father, loyal husband and dedicated detective. The film shifts his family home from a modest city apartment in Philadelphia to a more salubrious Californian bungalow, but the admirable portrait remains the same: we should be so lucky, to have cops as honest and hardworking as Dave Bannion.

As in other McGivern stories, Bannion's Irish ancestry is suggested rather than overt; it remains in the traces. The film and novel both refer to his wife as 'a genuine Irish blow-top', but the film dilutes the family's heritage by changing the daughter's name from Bridget to Joyce. Unlike Carmody, Bannion is a college-educated Irish American. An earlier draft of the novel placed several philosophy books on the shelves of the dead police clerk Deery, where Bannion notices them on his first visit: 'The books struck Bannion as curious ... There was a tract by St John of the Cross which Bannion remembered reading in his third year at Notre Dame and several other philosophers: Kant, Spinoza, Santayana' (McGivern, 'Big Heat typescript draft', p.10A). In the published novel, McGivern gives the books to his central character instead.

This establishes Bannion as educated and reflective, characteristics in sharp contrast to the menace and violence which he exhibits in the second half of the story. In the early, domestic scenes his philosophical formation offers a foil to an often grim professional existence. 'I read philosophy because I'm too weak to stand up against the misery and meaninglessness heartbreak I run into every day on the job,' he muses. 'I'm no scholar ... I don't want to listen to idols being smashed, I want something that puts sense into life' (McGivern, *Big Heat*, p.22).

Bannion's choice of philosophers is strongly Catholic. It is notably mystical in tone, and thus less dogmatic than the Natural Law tradition of Thomism that dominated American Catholic thinking of the 1950s, suggesting that Bannion has an educated but worldly mind that has less use for Catholic dogma than for its spiritual heritage. But like Mike Carmody, he remains a Catholic at heart, if not in action. The realities of police work may have detached his faith from organized religion, but he has not yet given way to the outright cynicism of the typical *noir* figure. He is drawn to 'St John of the Cross, Spinoza, Santayana – the gentle philosophers, the one's who thought it was natural for a man to be good' (ibid., p.22), and particularly moved by St John's 'Ascent of Mount Carmel', the mystical description of the 'dark night of the soul' between death and full communion with the Almighty. The writings of St John emphasize the incompleteness of man and the incomprehensibility of God. In a bold gesture, McGivern counterpoints the darkness of the *noir* cityscape to the 'darkness' of the soul's wanderings without God.

Twice in the novel – first, before the death of his wife and then following the death of Vince Stone – Bannion intones a specific passage from St John's text: 'Oh happy chance! In darkness and concealment, my house being now at rest ... Oh night that guided me.' The passage thus brackets the 'dark night' of Bannion's revenge, and links the idea of home with that of spiritual fulfilment. The pivotal moment of the story, the death of Katie, results in Bannion abandoning the family home. As he is about to leave, he is visited (in the film) by a fellow cop who advises him to 'stop hating'. In a similar tactic to Father Ahern's home visit in *Rogue Cop* , the novel introduces a young Father Masterson. The priest suggests that the detective bring at least one book with him – and chooses the St John text. But Bannion's outlook has changed: he is no longer interested in St John's eventual progress to communion with God, and instead quotes a passage on spiritual abandonment. McGivern thus manages to parallel the mystical journey of St John with Bannion's secular one.

What is perhaps most disturbing in both novel and film is that Bannion only seems to recover some element of faith – and notably, outside of the family structure – through the violent revenge of his wife's murder. Bannion's personalized 'due process' approach may appear vindicated by his exposure of corruption in the police department. But if we pay close attention, we note that Bannion does not in fact shoot Vince Stone in cold blood – although he goes to Stone's apartment with this intention. This is left to the legitimate forces of law and order, and is justified by Stone's shooting at the police to avoid arrest. The novel ends with Debbie's death:

> Bannion came out of the hospital into the cold, still, purple gray light of dawn. He stood on the sidewalk for a few moments, breathing deeply, and then he turned and walked slowly toward the centre of the city … Something had ended this morning, he knew. Now he was starting over, not with hatred but only sadness. (Ibid., p.189)

Fritz Lang's film avoids this ambiguous ending. It concludes with Bannion back at his desk in the police department, answering another call and going out to begin another homicide investigation (with the ironic instruction to a subordinate to 'keep the coffee warm'). To be sure, this ending captures the dogged and heroic nature of the character – but it alters McGivern's cathartic conclusion and the source of Bannion's redemption. Debbie Thomas sees the *noir* city as 'no longer an objective rendition of American cities of the time [but] more profitably understood as the projection outward of an internal terrain ' (Thomas, 'How Hollywood Deals', p.21). This is exactly how Bannion's spiritual passage through a city of night has been. Key to that journey from disillusion to hope is Bannion's reconnection with community following his bitter rejection of humanity in the wake of his wife's death. When, towards the close of the book, a police colleague asks him, 'You did it alone, didn't you?' he replies, 'I thought so at first … Lonely figure against the mob. That wasn't it, Inspector. I had help, all I could use … All the decent people in the city, I guess.' To which the Inspector replies, 'I'm glad you see that' (*Big Heat*, p.179). Looked at in this way, *The Big Heat* can be read not so much as a justification of masculine violence as force of renewal than as a rejection of the frontier understanding of American heroism.[5]

In *Beyond Ethnicity*, Werner Sollors writes that 'American ethnicity … is a matter not of content but of the importance that individuals ascribe to it' (*Beyond Ethnicity*, p.35). This may be generally true –

but the crime novels of William P. McGivern suggest another approach to questions of descent. For his characters, the past may be 'another country', but the legacy of Irish Catholicism continued to ensure that the way they did things in that other country continued to have significance and resonance in 1950s America.

Although outwardly works of generic significance – particularly in their film adaptations – McGivern's novels can also be read as investigations of mid-century Irish–American masculinity. Distanced from the experience of earlier generations, his protagonists are 'ambiguous' Americans whose ties to the country and the values of their forbearers are tenuous at best. The characters' continued presence in the traditional Irish enclave of the police force brings them in contact with a changing America, one that is less interested in ethnic heritage than in individual ambition. His cops find themselves encumbered by the claims of their heritage – most often articulated through the characters of a priest from their parish.

The fact that these stories and films appeared in the postwar years is an essential key to their reading. At a time of great change in American society, the Catholic church exerted enormous cultural power and influence, and especially on the film industry. The novels' clear conflation of Catholic with American values signals this shift in status and mainstreaming. Charles Morris has noted the tension between these two claims:

> The grand compromise that emerged from the years of ideological struggle was a [Catholic] Church that was *in* America, decidedly *for* America and its founding principles, including religious liberty, but most emphatically not *of* America, or at least the America of slippery attachments and unrooted values...The apogee, the golden moment, of the grand American Catholic compromise can be pinpointed to a narrow couple of decades in mid-century.
>
> (Morris, 'Letter to Jackie')

Yet, even as this 'grand compromise' was effected, there began to emerge in the wider culture questions about American social values and the primacy of material success and individualism. At the beginning of the decade, David Riesman's *The Lonely Crowd* (1950) expressed concern about the growing conformity of American society, a critique directly related to the theme of police corruption in the McGivern works under discussion here.

In contrasting 'tradition-directed', 'inner-directed' and 'outer-directed' Americans, Riesman anticipated the choices facing

McGivern's protagonists. Mike Carmody's father was surely a 'tradition-directed' individual, but Carmody himself is caught between the 'inner-directed' self-reliant individual who lives according to his own values and ambitions (even if he perverts these qualities as a corrupt policeman), and the 'other-directed' conformist formed by contemporary society who 'wants to be loved rather than esteemed' – seen both in the middle-class conformism of Bannion's life and in the tacit acceptance of corruption in the police departments found in both novels. Inner peace is found not in the recovery of the 'inner-directed' individual, as Riesman had hoped, but in a healthy tension between tradition and individuality. McGivern's central Irish–American characters can be seen as moving between these poles of identity, uncertain of their place in American society.

REFERENCES

Greeley, Andrew. *The Catholic Myth: The Behavior and Beliefs of American Catholics*. New York: Touchstone, 1997.

The Catholic Imagination. Berkeley, CA: University of California Press, 2001.

Harvey, Silvia. 'Woman's Place: The Absent Family', in E. Ann Kaplan (ed.), *Women in Film Noir*. London: British Film Institute, 1978.

Hecht, Ben. *A Guide for the Bedeviled*. New York: Charles Scribner's Sons, 1944.

McGivern, William. *Rogue Cop*. New York: Pocket Book, 1951.

—— *Shield for Murder*. New York: Dodd Mead, 1951.

—— *The Big Heat*. New York: Dodd Mead, 1953.

—— *The Darkest Hour*. New York: Dodd Mead, 1954.

—— 'The Big Heat', typescript draft dated 'Rome Jan–Feb 1952', p.10A. William McGivern Collection, Howard Gotlieb Archival Research Center, Boston University.

Morris, Charles R. 'On Top of the World', in *American Catholic: The Saints and Sinners who Built America's Most Powerful Church*. New York: Time Books, 1997, pp.196–227. 'Letter to Jackie: How US Catholics Became the Exemplary Americans'. *Boston College Magazine* (2002), http://bcm.bc.edu/issues/winter_ 2002/ll_jackie.html

Packer, Herbert L. 'Two Models of the Criminal Process'. *University of Pennsylvania Law Review*, vol. 113, no. 1 (1964), pp.1–68.

Panek, Leroy Lad. *The American Police Novel: A History*. Jefferson, NC: McFarland & Co., 2003.

Riesman, David. *The Lonely Crowd: A Study of the Changing American Character*. New Haven, CT and London: Yale University Press, 1950.

Schloesser, Stephen. 'Inventing the Catholic Novel'. *Explore*, vol. 5, no. 2 (2002), pp.9–19.

Sollors, Werner. *Beyond Ethnicity: Consent and Descent in American Culture*. Oxford: Oxford University Press, 1986.

Thomas, Deborah. 'How Hollywood Deals with the Deviant Male'. *CineAction*, no. 13 (August 1988), pp.18–28.

FILMS

The Big Heat, directed by Fritz Lang, 1953. Columbia Pictures.

Rogue Cop, directed by Roy Rowland, 1954. Metro-Goldwyn-Mayer.

Shield for Murder, directed by Howard W. Koch, Edmond O'Brien, 1954. Aubrey Schenk Productions.

CHAPTER TWELVE

Beyond St Malachi's, There is Nothing: Edward McSorley and the Persistence of Tradition

CHRISTOPHER SHANNON

In *Beyond the Melting Pot* (1963), Daniel Patrick Moynihan wrote what still stands as the definitive epitaph for postwar Irish–American literary culture. At times waxing lyrical on the humble yet hard-earned achievements of Irish–America's working-class past, Moynihan nonetheless offers a pitiless account of the cultural impoverishment of Irish–America's middle-class present.

> *Reilly and the 400* was fun, but it was not *Riders to the Sea.* When it emerged that the American Irish did not see this, their opportunity to attain a degree of cultural ascendancy quite vanished. After that began a steady emigration from the Irish 'community' of many of the strongest and best of the young. This migration was as devitalizing in America as it was to the Irish nation overseas (Moynihan and Glazer, *Beyond the Melting Pot*, p.248).

Essentially, Moynihan's critique was that Irish America's communal rejection of the achievements of Irish literary modernism had left it with little more than the musical comedies of Harrigan and Hart to claim as its contribution to American culture. Moynihan lays the blame for this cultural failure squarely at the feet of the Roman Catholic Church, whose dogmatic theology and repressive Victorian sexual code allowed no place for the intellectual and artistic creativity of Irish modernism. In Moynihan's view, the postwar American economic boom left the Irish the most pitiful of Americans: cut off from working-class vitality, yet unable to embrace the best of middle-class intellectual life, the American Irish found themselves trapped in the mediocrity of generic mass culture, perhaps the most conformist people in an age noted for mass conformity.

Moynihan's sociology contains a good deal of truth, yet it suffers from a stunted sense of cultural possibilities. The alternatives he presents are as stark as they are predictable: the repression of received communal and religious traditions or the liberation of aesthetic modernism. The effortless domestication of modernism in the generations since Moynihan's writing suggests the need to rethink these alternatives. In the decade and a half following the end of World War Two, Irish America may not have produced a full-blown alternative literary tradition, but it did produce one writer who suggests an alternative aesthetic, Edward McSorley. Largely forgotten, McSorley nonetheless left behind a small but substantial body of work that points the way out of Moynihan's cultural conundrum.[1] His three novels – *Our Own Kind* (1946), *The Young McDermott* (1949) and *Kitty, I Hardly Knew You* (1959) – forge a distinct aesthetic clearly indebted to the realist modernism of James T. Farrell, yet rooted in an authentic urban Catholic understanding of truth as inseparable from membership in a community rooted in place and religious tradition. McSorley's writing may not have been 'representative' of Irish–American literature in the postwar years, but it nonetheless stands as a sign of a persisting communal sensibility.

The urban, ethnic milieu of McSorley's novels makes it difficult to situate him in a postwar context generally characterized by suburbanization and assimilation. His novels are set in the early twentieth century, but they have a contemporary, rather than historical, feel about them. *Our Own Kind* and *The Young McDermott* explore the theme of lost innocence, but never make the mistake of equating an individual coming-of-age with any facile cultural rupture. Willie McDermott, the main character, experiences many changes and much disillusion, but at the end of it all he returns to his hometown of Providence, Rhode Island, which remains a source of stability despite the passing of generations. McSorley's Providence is a world of tremendous loss, but not a 'world we have lost'.[2]

At the time of the publication of *Our Own Kind*, this world was very much alive in reality and in the popular imagination. The Irish who embraced *Reilly and the 400* instead of *Riders to the Sea* had much to occupy their attention well into the middle of the 1940s. Even as the passing of George M. Cohan brought an end to Irish dominance of the New York stage, Irish stories became the ethnic face of Hollywood during the golden age of the 1930s and 1940s.[3] As

Moynihan conceded in *Beyond the Melting Pot*, when Hollywood sought to portray 'the tough American, up from the streets, the image was repeatedly that of an Irishman. James Cagney . . . was the quintessential figure: fists cocked, chin out, back straight bouncing along on his heels' (Moynihan and Glazer, *Beyond the Melting Pot*, pp.246–7). This Irish–American moment in Hollywood would peak in 1945, when *Going My Way*, Leo MacCarey's sentimental story of Irish priests struggling to save a dying urban parish, swept nearly every major Oscar at that year's Academy Awards. Later generations of critics would follow Moynihan in dismissing the Irish achievement in film as yet another instance of Irish under-achievement in culture. With the suburban explosion still a few years off, 1946 was the perfect time for a novel of urban, working-class Irish life in America.

Even apart from its intrinsic literary merits, *Our Own Kind* benefitted from this broader Irish–American moment in popular culture. Reviews were in general very positive. The *New York Times* paid McSorley perhaps the highest compliment it knew how to give by comparing his writing favourably to that of John McNulty, the house Irishman at the *New Yorker*. Orville Prescott, the *Times* reviewer, praised McSorley for having 'the true novelist's preoccupation with character, the never failing miracle of human personality', as well as a 'sharp ear for the rhythms of human speech'. He noted that McSorley writes without 'fluster or pretense', yet nonetheless manages to produce a 'more truly a creative work of fiction than many a more highly touted novel by authors intent on documenting their sociological and psychological theories'. *Our Own Kind* clearly benefitted from a certain critical backlash against the experimental modernism and politically motivated realism of the past two generations of novelists, but Prescott's review also shows the persistence of some sense of a grand literary tradition in relation to which McSorley's subject matter would always appear provincial. For all of McSorley's craft, he presents not a generally human story expressed in a local idiom, but rather 'a convincing story of a racial community' (Prescott, 'Books of the Times', p.19). This assessment – that *Our Own Kind* is an admirable novel about an ultimately limited world – recurs throughout even the most favourable reviews.[4]

These criticisms reveal more than the obvious middle-class WASP bias as to the sort of social milieu necessary for truly great literature. The Irish modernists of the early twentieth century had long since overcome the charge of provincialism in milieu, but they did so largely by approaching their marginal culture from the perspective of the mainstream nineteenth-century traditions of European literature from Romanticism to modernism. Joyce's technical experimentalism transformed dirty old Dublin into the last stop on a journey of Western literature that began with Homer. In terms of literary politics, McSorley's mistake was one of method rather than subject matter. His writing has more in common with the urban folklore and dialect writing of a Finley Peter Dunne than any canonical European or American writer. At the end of *The Young McDermott*, the people of Providence remain the best guide to understanding the city of Providence. McSorley refuses to judge the city from the outside, a refusal that at the late date of 1949 can only be taken as wilful. With no romantic or modernist consciousness to serve as a *deus ex machina*, bringing order to the chaos of provincial Irish–Catholic life, the book reviewers at the *New York Times* found little to call their own in McSorley's writing.

This disconnect from the critical *zeitgeist* shows clearly in one of the few thoroughly negative reviews that *Our Own Kind* received in a major publication. The catty, anonymous reviewer for *Time* magazine contrasts McSorley's novel unfavourably to another best-selling Irish–American urban novel of the day, Betty Smith's *A Tree Grows in Brooklyn*:

> McSorley's kind of people are like Betty Smith's, but perhaps only Betty Smith can make a Tree.
>
> Author McSorley tells how a broth of a boy grows in Providence, where an Irish Catholic apparently can live and scarcely ever hear of Protestants. The boy's chief experiences involve neighbourhood toughs, his jolly dollop of a grandfather, and his dog, an old party who dies under a cloud (after biting a neighbor's daughter). All concerned murder the king's English, but in a grand, Gaelic manner.
>
> McSorley's 'own kind', the Irish, and Hollywood, which is currently underwriting a Celtic Renaissance, will probably lap it up.
>
> (*Time*, 'No Tree')

With Betty Smith as a foil, the reviewer is clearly not holding McSorley accountable to the standards of Joycean modernism. Stylistically, *A Tree Grows in Brooklyn* is very much in the conventional urban realist mode of the day – not as harsh as Farrell or Nelson Algren, but more than willing to confront the seamier side of working-class life. Smith won the hearts of the American reading public by ultimately telling a very American story of how book-reading and public school education bring hope to the otherwise hopeless life of a young Irish–American girl trapped in urban poverty, at the mercy of a charming-yet-drunken father and an overworked, long-suffering mother. McSorley confounds this narrative convention by presenting an Irish–Catholic world apart from the grand public school vision of America. For the sin of such parochialism, the reviewer dismisses *Our Own Kind* as a kind of literary equivalent of *Going My Way*.

The reviewer had time on his side. His dreaded Celtic Renaissance had already brought his beloved *Tree Grows in Brooklyn* to the screen to universal critical acclaim; among its many notable qualities, the film marked the directorial début of Elia Kazan, who would go on to be the leading American 'art' film-maker of his generation. Kazan would return to an Irish–American milieu for his greatest film, *On the Waterfront*, and once again he would tell a story of a lonely individual struggling to break free from the moral and cultural limitations of his urban, ethnic Catholic community.

McSorley's career, in contrast, peaked with *Our Own Kind*. He followed the money to Hollywood, but arrived just as the winds of fashion began to blow against his brand of community storytelling. *Our Own Kind* never made it to the screen. McSorley's only legacy to film history appears to be his brief but crucial mentoring of a young John Cassavetes, who has some claim on succeeding Kazan as the leading art film director of the 1960s and 1970s. A look at his brief professional relationship with McSorley helps us to place *Our Own Kind* in the context of the changing literary ideals of postwar America.

The details of McSorley's life remain sketchy. The *New York Times* introduced him as a man who 'in his time has played many parts, newspaper man, publicity man for movies, burlesque and vaudeville, fisherman, farmer and sailor' (Prescott, 'Books of the Times'). At some point in his Hollywood travels he crossed paths with Sam Shaw, a photographer and sometime film producer best known for his iconic shot of Marilyn Monroe standing on the subway grate. In 1953 Shaw met Cassavetes, then a budding young New York film director. He offered to produce a film for him, provided Cassavetes could come up with a workable script. The son of Greek immigrants, Cassavetes struggled with writing in English and had no idea whatsoever of how to write a film script. Shaw sent Cassavetes to McSorley – whom he described as 'the best novelist in the world' – for a crash course in script-writing. McSorley was then living fairly close by in Duxbury, Massachusetts, but was surprised when Cassavetes showed up at his door: he had not spoken with Shaw for over ten years. Despite this awkward introduction, McSorley agreed to teach him what he knew about writing (*Cassavetes on Cassavetes*, p.103).

Cassavetes acknowledged his literary debt to McSorley in a series of interviews with film scholar Ray Carney. McSorley defined good writing by three basic principles: character is more important than plot; the writer should let a story evolve naturally without explaining too much to the audience; and, 'style is truth' in the sense that the writer's primary duty is simply to write every scene true to the life and feelings of the characters he portrays (ibid., p.104). This anti-theoretical theory fit in perfectly with the existential ethos of postwar art film directors; McSorley's writing, however, points in a different direction. Cassavetes took McSorley's advice as a rationale for his rebellion against Hollywood narrative conventions. McSorley's own emphasis on character over plot suggests less rebellion against artistic convention than acceptance of the basic 'plot' of life as handed down by the traditions of his Irish–Catholic community: life is a day-to-day struggle to survive in which the innocent suffer and virtue goes unrewarded, yet God is merciful and allows enough love and laughter to sustain hope in the face of despair. These truths may not be distinct to the Irish, but among ethnic writers the Irish have given strongest voice to them. Cassavetes and McSorley worked on an adaptation of *Our Own Kind* that was to be called *The American Dream*, but nothing ever came of it (ibid.). In this brief partnership, two generations of ethnic artists met and went their separate ways.

The opening pages of *Our Own Kind* reveal a sensibility at odds with the dominant modes of ethnic consciousness in mainstream American literature. Ethnicity most often appears alternatively as a weapon with which to challenge the conventions of middle-class WASP culture or as itself an oppressive authority against which some young hero must struggle for independence. McSorley's hero, Willie McDermott, begins the novel waking from a night's sleep in the bed of his grandparents, Ned and Nellie McDermott. Sandwiched between the aging bodies of his grandparents, Willie appears perfectly situated for an early-morning Oedipal reflection on the oppressive weight of tradition. Instead, looking around the room, Willie's thoughts move effortlessly from horizontal, material connection to vertical, spiritual communion:

> Above their heads, yellowing and crisp, withered fronds of last year's palm sagged in dying blades from the varnished fleur-de-lis of the filigreed bedtop. Scummed over like a stagnant pool in the

mill lots, a mirror was braced on top of the broad-beamed dress-
er on his grandmother's side and near its edges drifted a host of
seraphs, cherubs, angels and archangels.   They mourned and
wept for James John, May He Rest in Peace; Margaret Mary,
Requiescat in Pace; and one brawny heavenly aide de camp to
Gabriel heralded the ordination of Michael Francis Ryan at the
Church of the Assumption of the Blessed Virgin, Providence,
Rhode Island, June 10, 1912.

(McSorley, Our Own Kind, p.1)

An orphan of sorts – his father died in an industrial accident, his mother
in childbirth – Willie nonetheless awakes to find himself firmly situated
in a community that extends beyond the living to the souls of the
faithful departed. These images inspire no particularly fervent early-
morning devotion, but serve the equally spiritual purpose of reinforc-
ing Willie's awareness of his place in the communion of saints.

McSorley gives his reader a Willie's-eye-view of his grandparents'
bedroom, yet against modernist conventions he privileges the objects
perceived over the process of perception. As McSorley follows Willie's
wandering eye, he clearly delights in the free mixing of the sacred and
profane achieved by the material culture of Irish–Catholic devotional-
ism. However challenged aesthetically, early twentieth-century
Catholic devotional art invested even the most mundane, disposable
objects with some intimation of immortality:

Tethered in the dry wastes of the wallpaper was the Agnus Dei
Qui Tollit Peccata Mundi and a more robust angel, snow
sparkling in the sweep of her wings of eagle feathers, who
brought the season's greetings from F. X. QUINN, CHOICE
MEATS AND GROCERIES, 132 Pine Street. The commode was
on his grandfather's side, sturdy squatting oak, or the next thing
to it, you might say, holding inside the Delft blue scrolled porce-
lain washbasin and a cracked pitcher that looked forever like a
little-necked duck. In the shelter of the bowl was his grandfather's black clay pipe, a plug of dark Mayo and a width of sulphur matches whose red tips, like the pears of the Precious Blood
dropping from the Sacred Heart of Jesus in its pearl shell frame
above, purpled in the damp morning light.

(Ibid., pp.1–2)

Such passages as this put flesh on the bones, if you will, of the much-
abused notion of a 'sacramental imagination' in Catholic writing.[5] Too

often, critics conflate sacramentality and romanticism, as if Catholics are instinctual Blakean poets, forever seeing eternity in a grain of sand. McSorley avoids such grand romantic leaps of imagination. Willie sees drops of the Precious Blood in sulphur match tips by virtue of the common colour of red. The analogy leads to no particular spiritual insight, but simply shows how the sacred and the profane reinforce each other through associational images. In the hands of another writer, the presence of the butcher's shop advertisement would be an occasion of ironic disjuncture or satire; in McSorley's work, it reflects only the seamless web of life.

It is a life, moreover, lived externally, with people in place. Willie's thoughts start to turn inward to 'his brief yesterdays' only to be interrupted by the thundering six o'clock bell of the Church of the Mediator that rouses his grandfather from sleep (ibid., p.2). The Church and his grandfather will remain the guiding influences on Willie throughout the novel, keeping him from withdrawing into himself – and out of the community. For Willie, Ned appears less as a font of wisdom than as a guide to people and places. In one significant passage, Willie recounts a typical Sunday with Ned, one that would begin with Mass, yet then move on to the race track, cock fights, Deignan's bar and Owen Teague's harbour master's shack. These Sunday jaunts would include visits to the extended family of the McDermotts throughout Providence. Significantly, Willie finds the family visits to be the only unsettling aspect of these excursions: his cousin Fred Kane invariably tries to embarrass Willie by talking about those 'things the boys knew but didn't talk about when their fathers and mothers were around' (ibid., p.19). McSorley celebrates the simple pleasures of urban ethnic life even as he acknowledges the darker elements that threaten to undermine this idyll. His association of adolescent sexuality and communal disorder would seem to place him firmly in the tradition of Irish Victorianism. Sex was, however, only one of a range of Victorian repressions – though perhaps the only repression consistently accepted by the Irish. The institutions and practices McSorley picks to represent communal stability – bars, race tracks and cock fights – suggests the huge gulf that remained between Victorian social norms and Irish, or at least, working-class Irish, life.

McSorley's handling of sexual themes is refreshingly free of the dynamic of repression versus liberation that has afflicted so much post-Romantic writing. His writing reflects an enduring folk wisdom that recognizes the destructive power of sexual passion and the stabilizing force of marriage apart from romantic love. These dangers lurk

not simply on the outer edge of Willie's extended family, but in the life
of the moral centre of the novel, his grandfather Ned. The communion of saints is a communion of sinners as well. As *pater familias*, Ned
presides over a home infused with the hatred and jealousy of Nell's
sister, Willie's maiden aunt Nora, who loved Ned and has never for-
given him for marrying Nell. The past is never past in the McDermott
home. Ned continues to agonize over the night he embraced Nora
following an evening of drinking in celebration of the birth of his first
child, Willie's father. McSorley writes of Ned's struggles with a profound sensitivity to the ambiguities of the moral life, but never gives
ambiguity the last word. Ned, a good man, sinned in a moment of
weakness and has been paying for it his whole life. Nora would eventually move in with the family, her presence 'like a sin repented but
unforgiven on his conscience' (ibid., p.16). Ned, for his part, can
muster no pity or forgiveness for Nora. He simply returns her contempt.

Ned's great hatred for Nora exists side-by-side with his great love
for Willie. This love itself is somewhat conflicted; Ned expresses it
most clearly by taking Willie along on his jaunts through the working-
class world of Irish Providence, and yet he desires nothing more than
that Willie escape the world of the iron mills and live the life of a
'scholar'. *Our Own Kind* differs significantly from a work such as *A
Tree Grows in Brooklyn* by rooting the quest for education within the
confines of Irish communal traditions. Though illiterate, Ned schools
Willie in the oral traditions of Irish–American nationalism, most significantly in his teaching of Robert Emmet's famous speech from the
dock. Ned sees art and learning as ways of putting Willie in touch
with his religious and ethnic traditions. At the end of a Saint Patrick's
Day celebration featuring nationalist songs and plays, Ned declares to
Willie, with pride: 'What the Irish can't do ... What scholars and
poets they are! What scholars, Willie! Ah, that was a grand thing!
My boy, the talents the Irish has is – is unspeakable!' (ibid., p.169).
Most important, Ned sends Willie to Catholic schools, the great fire-
wall against assimilation to WASP norms.

For Ned, education is a path to rising within, not away from, the
community – though the community itself presents certain obstacles to
Ned's dream for his grandson. Neighbourhood toughs, Joseph and
Eddie Riordan, persuade Willie to help them rob a drug store. The boys
are caught and escape reform school only when Ned and the Riordan
boys' father pay the drugstore owner (another Irishman) one hundred
dollars to drop the charges. Concerned for Willie's future, Ned moves

out of the neighbourhood. Like Ned's dreams of upward class mobility, this geographic move remains within the Irish world of Providence. Catherine Daly, the fiancée of Willie's uncle Chris, suggests the McDermotts move to her parish of St Malachi's in South Providence. The parish lacks a school, but Catherine puts Willie in touch with a pair of young, dynamic priests, Fathers James and Joseph McCaffrey, who provide the moral and spiritual guidance lacking in the public school. Ned is happy with the course Willie's education follows in South Providence – though he wishes that the public school paid more attention to Irish history and tends to favour a more radical Irish nationalism than that approved by Father McCaffrey.

Just as Ned seems to have put Willie back on the path to scholarship, everything falls apart. A series of family financial crises liquidate Willie's education fund. After a lifetime of back-breaking work at the foundry, Ned contracts pneumonia and dies. Chris succeeds Ned as the man of the house and quickly proves himself an unworthy successor. An accountant, Chris embodies all the worst traits of lower-middle class Irish Catholicism skewered by Moynihan and other Irish–American intellectuals of the postwar period: dull, listless and utterly lacking in spirit or imagination. Resigned to make the worst of a bad situation, he commands Willie to abandon his dreams even as he gives up his own: Willie must quit school and go to work to help support the family, while Chris himself breaks off his engagement with Catherine.

With the passage from Ned to Chris, McSorley would seem to prophesy the postwar cultural descent of the Irish into lower-middle-class mediocrity. But notably, he gives Willie, not Chris, the last word in the novel:

> Frantically, Willie dredged the waters of his memory for the indestructible words his grandfather and Father Joe had spoken to him, but he could not bring them up. Yet he knew they were there. He knew he could never run away from these people or from the house. He surrendered, knowing that the trellis of dreams, more than dreams, of faith and hope his grandfather had built for him was there for him to cling to and climb, even with the wicked little flames of hatreds and defeats and despair licking at his heels. Perhaps he might not realize in himself the great stranger his grandfather would have made of him, but, clinging and climbing, he would never have to know the bitterness, either, of having to say good-by to him.   (Ibid., p.304)

In many ways, the novel ends where it begins, with the communion of saints. James John and Michael Francis Ryan (with whom the novel opened) may have been only names on prayer cards, but Ned and Father Joe are living spirits that will guide Willie through the rest of his life. Rejecting the narrative trajectories – toward happiness or toward despair – of mainstream American literature, McSorley concludes *Our Own Kind* on a note of Christian hope. Looking to his future, Willie commits himself less to accomplishing a goal than to sustaining a relationship. He may not achieve success, but he will keep faith.

Much the same can be said for McSorley himself. His next novel, *The Young McDermott* (1949), follows Willie's story into young adulthood, but remains true to the spiritual and cultural vision forged in his account of Willie's childhood. Willie goes through all the motions of an urban coming-of-age story, but he finds no wisdom in the sordid experiences so often held up as paths to enlightenment in modern fiction. In the end, Willie comes neither of age nor to himself, but home to a place. *The Young McDermott* presents the city of Providence itself as the necessary material grounding for maintaining the fidelity Willie pledges at the end of *Our Own Kind*.

The novel picks up Willie's story as he begins his career as a journalist. McSorley himself began his writing career in newspapers, but for all of his presumably autobiographical inspiration, McSorley presents no standard portrait of the *artist* as a young man. Willie decides on journalism not to forge any distinct artistic voice, but simply to most closely approximate Ned's dream of education. He may not become a true scholar, but within the limits of his education, he will at least be a man of letters (McSorley, *Young McDermott*, p.7). At the Providence *Herald*, Willie is exposed to a very different kind of adult influence; though most of the editors and journalists are Irish, they tend to be free-thinkers who challenge Willie's faith and threaten his morals. Wary of their religious scepticism, Willie nonetheless respects their intelligence and tries to learn from them. Throughout, Willie draws support from Father Joseph McCafftey, the priest who guided him through his time of transition at St Malachi's and with whom he maintains a thriving correspondence. Still, temptations of the flesh ultimately prove more powerful than devotions of the spirit. An afternoon of drinking with a low-level reporter named Kavanaugh ends with a night at a brothel, where Willie loses his virginity to none other than Rose Riordan, the sister of the boys who had convinced Willie to help them rob Kelly's drug store. Even in sin, Willie cannot escape his roots.

McSorley's treatment of Willie's sexual experiences sets him against the grain of most modern writing. Despite his many experiences with prostitutes, Willie never falls into Studs Lonigan-style dissipation. Powerful physical and emotional longings drive him into sexual sin, but he never mistakes these desires for spiritual transcendence. McSorley's frank handling of sexual themes suggests that he was in fact dissatisfied with Irish–Catholic sexual repression. In a revealing scene, Chris and Nell come across a notebook in which Willie has written of his sexual struggles and accuse him of all manner of perversion: the joke is on them, however, for the writing they find so offensive is Willie's notes on his library copy of St Augustine's *Confessions*. McSorley critiques Irish–Catholic sexual repression even as he points to an alternative within the Catholic tradition itself. Augustine will prove an enduring guide for Willie as he sinks deeper into sin but never despairs of forgiveness.

In portraying Willie's descent into sin, McSorley draws on classical rather than Christian narrative traditions. Later in the story, Willie takes to sea after losing his job at the paper for refusing to cover up a story of the murder of a labour organizer by the police. Hoping to 'leave ... all his sins and troubles on the dock of yesterday and ride ... on ... to far, maybe happier tomorrows', Willie embarks on an odyssey that takes him deeper into the brothels and opium dens of post-World War One Europe (ibid., p.173). In this odyssey's most chilling passage, Willie nearly succumbs to the seductions of a modern-day Circe, a junkie prostitute who promises him the sweet oblivion of sex and drugs:

> he was afraid of the awful fascination of her nearness, her invitation never to let anything injure him again. Never to have to decide whether he was good or evil, or to have to achieve anything, even himself. He couldn't be more debased than he was ... He saw the beautiful face drawing closer to his own, the horrid, innocent blue eyes appealing to him. He was filled with loathing of himself and her. Yet, there was neither good nor evil in the eyes as he looked at them, only complete and debauched innocence. He felt as though he were sinking into the pit of some sordid dream which had no past and no future, only a wicked present.
>
> (Ibid., p.242)

Against this Circe, Willie ultimately turns to his Penelope, Catherine Daly. *Our Own Kind* had hinted at a mutual attraction between the two; with impediments of age and betrothal removed, their romantic relationship is free to develop in the early sections of *The Young*

McDermott. Following her rejection by Chris, Catherine too falls into sin, losing her virginity while drunk at a party hosted by the church organist. The two go their separate ways but always keep in touch. Stranded in Hamburg without a passport, Willie writes to Catherine to obtain his birth certificate. After surviving the temptations to cut himself off completely from his past, Willie receives a letter from Catherine containing both his birth certificate and a reason to return home – her pledge of love, despite all that has come between them.

Still, Penelope is not enough; a true Odysseus needs an Ithaca. Providence itself, as much as Catherine, Father Joe and Ned, has served Willie as a principle of moral and spiritual order. The newspapermen who cover the city hate it; the low-lifes of Hamburg have never heard of it. But Willie cannot make sense of his life apart from Providence. Even a brief stay in New York following the loss of his job at the paper places too much strain on Willie's sense of self: 'Why should I stay here when all I can think of is what happens there? Nothing can happen there now that hasn't been worse before. I never can do anything away from there' (ibid., p.202). On his voyage back from Europe he sings the praises of Providence to all the disbelieving sailors he meets on ship:

> You won't want to leave Providence in the spring … Spring can hardly wait for the snow to go before it gets to Providence. The crocuses push themselves right through the snow there and the forsythia is likely to throw out those yellow blossoms right in the middle of a blizzard. When May comes there are lilacs growing in nearly every yard you come to, sometimes when you are walking down a street the smell of the lilacs is so powerful it makes you drunk. You can walk in the park on Sunday afternoons and see the swans swimming in the lakes and flocks of ducks swimming after them and stretching their necks to look as big as the swans. You hardly take a step into that park when you see the prettiest girls you ever saw, they hate to see you alone. They like you to take them for rides in the rowboats you hire on the boathouse lake and you can drift around the islands in the lake and you're miles away from everybody else in the world. When some saint is having a birthday the streets are full of colored lights and music. Everybody drifts around under the lights listening to the bands play and watching the fireworks. Nobody is lonely and nobody worries about anything. Everybody has plenty to eat and drink.
>
> (Ibid. p.273)

This is, of course, only half of the story of Providence. Willie's – and McSorley's – strength lies in his ability to affirm the best of Providence after having experienced the city at its worst. Like a latter-day Augustine, Willie/McSorley understand that the City of God and the City of Man are inextricably bound together in this world; just as important, they understand that man was created to live in a city, to live in a community. In describing Willie and Catherine's reunion, McSorley writes: 'He told her everything he wanted; he knew he could find it in the shelter of St Malachi's; beyond it, he said, was nothing' (ibid., p.282). Ultimately, love and faith both take their meaning from rootedness in place.

The Young McDermott ends with the death of Nell, but the passing of the generations becomes an occasion for a final affirmation of the power of place. As Nell lays dying, Willie listens to Mick McDermott, Ned's brother, attack the Providence McDermotts for their lack of adventure. Mick has travelled the world with a circus and concludes: 'The trouble with the God-damn McDermotts is they never seen nothing nor knew nothing beyond the puddle where they were dropped. They never looked over the top of a hill to see was there anything in the next valley.' To this harangue, Willie, who has seen the world, can only reply with the damning rhetorical question, 'What's there to see there, Mick?' (ibid., p.286).

In the postwar era, such sentiments were not destined to win McSorley much of a following; sociological and literary trends ensured that his paean to place would fall on deaf ears. Suburbanization undermined the local attachments McSorley celebrates, while a new generation of Beat and existential writers celebrated the rootless freedom of life on the road. In his last novel, *Kitty, I Hardly Knew You* (1960), McSorley turned his literary sights on the experience of rootlessness, and found in it only despair. Kitty, the alcoholic prostitute protagonist, is an Irish immigrant girl who never finds her place in the Irish–Catholic urban villages of America. *Kitty*'s great literary crime against postwar literary culture is its refusal to see that failure as liberation. A culture that had an insatiable appetite for despair could not appreciate a character who is unable to see despair as insight into the existential condition of man. Kitty is no Sartre manqué. Though a habitual sinner, she consistently returns to the Church as the only alternative to her life of sin.

The novel ends in suicide, but even there the Church is present. It is Easter Sunday. Through a Dreiseresque accident, Kitty accidentally turns on the gas right after she resolves not to kill herself. In her gas-induced delirium, she speaks the language of Catholicism: 'I'll leave this place and its sin and the memory of its sin behind me. I must rest now, I can barely walk, I know, and I want to look my best going to Mass this day the stone's rolled away' (McSorley, *Kitty*, p.175). Kitty may or may not be saved, but Easter remains the only compelling story of salvation.

The secular literary establishment was not prepared to welcome McSorley's message, while Irish Catholics were not prepared to accept his medium. Subsequent developments in literature only pushed him further to the margins. Self-consciously Irish writers would reject their Catholicism, self-consciously Catholic writers would reject their ethnicity, and both would reject McSorley's integration of faith, culture, and place.[6] Still, McSorley's failure in his time may be what most commends him to our own. The Irish–American literary tradition has degenerated into an increasingly solipsistic pursuit of 'Irishness', while the quest for a Catholic literary imagination has degenerated into a bloodless exercise in theology. Against these trends, McSorley's writing stands as a model of storytelling within a tradition rooted in place. Beyond St Malachi's, there is nothing.

REFERENCES

Cassavetes, John. *Cassavetes on Cassavetes*, ed. Ray Carney. New York: Faber & Faber, 2001.

McSorley, Edward. *Our Own Kind*. New York: Harper & Bros, 1946.

—— *The Young McDermott*. New York: Harper & Bros, 1949.

—— *Kitty, I Hardly Knew You*. New York: Popular Library, 1960.

Moynihan, Daniel Patrick and Nathan Glazer. *Beyond the Melting Pot: The Negroes, Puerto Ricans, Jews, Italians and Irish of New York City*. Cambridge, MA: MIT Press, 1963.

'No Tree', review of *Our Own Kind*, *Time* magazine, 10 June 1946, http://www.time.com/time/magazine/article/0,9171,793031,00.html

Prescott, Orville. 'Books of the Times'. *New York Times*, 22 May 1946, p.19.

Present at the Creation: John V. Kelleher and the Emergence of Irish Studies in America

CHARLES FANNING

The American study of Irish culture came of age dramatically in the 1950s, and among literary scholars, three men – all of whom had returned from service in World War Two to promising academic careers – stand out as titans. David Greene of New York University published his pioneering two-volume *An Anthology of Irish Literature* in 1954, an achievement that went far toward making it possible to teach courses in Irish literature. He followed this with *J.M. Synge: 1871–1909*, the first scholarly biography of the playwright, in 1959. Richard Ellmann at Northwestern University published the influential critical biography *Yeats: The Man and the Masks* in 1948, followed by a pioneering study of Yeats's aesthetic, *The Identity of Yeats*, in 1954, and then by the magisterial biography *James Joyce*, which won the National Book Award for 1959 and effectively created the modern 'Joyce industry'.

The third figure, John V. Kelleher of Harvard, is, paradoxically, the scholar among these three whose contribution is both the least well known and the most wide-ranging. Kelleher was a renowned teacher for more than forty years, and his lectures, seminars and conference papers inspired and encouraged students and fellow-professors in the study of Irish history and literature. He trained numerous distinguished scholars, among them Philip O'Leary, Catherine McKenna and Helen Vendler. In a 1986 memoir, his former dissertator Roger Rosenblatt (later a prominent novelist, editor and journalist), recalled that 'as soon as I began listening to him, I realized that I had stumbled upon the goods: the teacher who loses sleep over ideas.' Rosenblatt continues,

> He would never speak of abstractions such as honor, loyalty, fairness, and reason. He believed in particulars, facts – that if a

decent mind paid attention to the facts, it might wind up worth
something someday. This attitude rested in a man not naturally
open-minded; when Kelleher changed his mind, you heard the
padlocks snap. Yet that was his underlying lesson: virtue requires
resistance. He used to quote an Irish proverb: Strife is better
than loneliness, which I came to understand as meaning that the
honest mind can never be lonely.

(Rosenblatt, 'Teachings of Mr Kelleher', p.264)

Kelleher's advocacy of interdisciplinary teaching and scholarship
became the crucial model for the emergent field of Irish studies. In
the late 1940s he also inaugurated the first serious consideration of
the literature and culture of the Irish in America.

Kelleher was born on 8 March 1916 in the mill town of Lawrence,
Massachusetts. His family's nearest connection to Ireland was his
father's mother, who had left County Cork for America in 1870.
After high school, Kelleher joined his father and uncles in the trade of
contract carpentry. In 1934 he visited a friend studying at Dartmouth
– the first college he had ever seen. A year later he enrolled there, supporting himself with scholarships and work as a waiter and fireman;
his freshman grades were two As and three Cs. But in the following
years he distinguished himself academically; as a senior in 1939, he
was allowed to work entirely on his own in the field that had become
his passion, the history and literature of Ireland.

After graduating with distinction, Kelleher went back to carpentry
for a year. Then, in 1940, he was invited to become a Junior Fellow
in Harvard's Society of Fellows, which grants its members fully subsi-
dized freedom to pursue their ideas. It is probable that he was nomi-
nated to this by Henry Lee Shattuck, an attorney and philanthropist
who that same year endowed (anonymously) a chair for Celtic studies
at Harvard, the first such position in an American university. Kelleher
and Shattuck soon became close friends. As a junior fellow, Kelleher
studied the Irish language with Kenneth Jackson and achieved wide
acclaim in 1942 by delivering the prestigious Lowell Lectures on the
subject of modern Irish literature. He was then 26 years old.

After wartime service in military intelligence, he returned to
Harvard. In May 1946 he travelled to Ireland for the first time with
his friend Richard Ellmann, staying more than three months. He
toured the country (mostly by bicycle) and met many Irish writers and
intellectuals, among them Frank O'Connor and Sean O'Faolain, who
became close friends. On Saint Patrick's Day 1947, Harvard

announced Kelleher's appointment to the position established by Shattuck. He held the Shattuck Chair until his retirement in 1986 (McKibben, 'Love of the Irish', n.p.). Although he later received honorary doctorates from Trinity College Dublin and the National University of Ireland at Cork, Kelleher's one earned degree was the Bachelor of Arts from Dartmouth. He died on 1 January 2004 in St Louis.

Kelleher's low profile probably derives from his preference for writing essays rather than books; though in his day a landmark essay could establish a scholarly reputation, in recent decades the book has become a near requisite for promotion and tenure in a major university. Further, Kelleher tended to publish in mainstream intellectual magazines – *Atlantic Monthly* and *New Republic* were favourites – rather than in scholarly journals. The essay form was perfect for Kelleher, in whom genius and perfectionism were at odds. In a book project, his nimble intellect would soon generate a geometrically progressing welter of ideas and observations – daunting and defeating in the long run. But his essays display a gem-like precision of thought and a striking conciseness of expression, leavened with wit, humour and colloquial directness. Appearing in the earliest days of Irish studies in America, these brief articles defined terms, set boundaries and opened doors for the future study of Ireland and Irish immigration.

The most remarkable feature of Kelleher's scholarship is his command of the entire range of Irish culture in both Irish and English. 'Matthew Arnold and the Celtic Revival', Kelleher's first major essay about Ireland, appeared in 1950. This piece assured his tenure at Harvard, which was granted in 1952. Here is the opening:

> When Matthew Arnold set out to describe the characteristics of Celtic literature and to analyze its effects, he paid the Celtic world the first valuable compliment it had received from an English source in several hundred years. However, the compliment, though enthusiastic, was guarded. Arnold noted this literature as the source of much of the lightness and brightness that rescued English literature from the heavy dullness of its Teutonic origin. He did not suggest that it rivaled English or classical literature in stature, or that any attempt should be made to revive it as a living mode. He took care, too, to be modest in his praise of its excellencies, to claim no more for it than could easily be justified – and this perhaps was his greatest service to the Celtic cause; for if he had shown too much enthusiasm, the audience he addressed would

likely have dismissed his entire essay as another example of crack-
pot philo-Celticism. So carefully did he seem to measure and bal-
ance his thesis that the lectures became a contemporary classic of
criticism, and in another generation had become the accepted doctrine, not only on Celtic literature, but on the literature of the
Celtic Revival which Arnold had not contemplated. For all practical purposes it is the doctrine commonly accepted today.

(Kelleher, *Selected Writings*, p.3)

The learning implied in this paragraph stretches from 'several hundred years' ago to 'the doctrine commonly accepted today'.

Kelleher also provides a balanced, appreciative placement of
Arnold's book, observing: 'We do not listen to him hoping for information. We listen for insight.' He continues:

Certainly, all the scholarly interpretation in the world, so long as
it is uncombined with the genuine critical faculty, can never by
itself give us the insights we need for an artistic valuation. The
field of Celtic studies has not been particularly blessed with the
critical gift. Arnold's book is still unique – a fact which he would
undoubtedly have deplored.   (Ibid., pp.20–1)

Kelleher's essay asks large questions involving much complexity: what
has been meant by 'Celticism' since the middle of the nineteenth century; where did these ideas come from; and what have been the mixed
blessings of these concepts for literature in the Celtic cultures? His
answers begin with Matthew Arnold's 1866 lectures, encompass
Arnold's reputation through the rest of the century, and limn his use-
fulness for Yeats and others who spearheaded the Celtic Revival in the
1890s and the shaping context of Irish nationalism and the fall of
Parnell. Along the way, the piece also discusses the Celtic scholarship
of Alfred Nutt, Whitley Stokes, Eugene O'Curry and Johann Zeuss;
the debate about nationalism among Davis, O'Leary, Davitt, Parnell
and Redmond; 'that quality of reserved emotion that gives the best
Gaelic poetry a whiplash sting' (ibid., p.20); Arnold's essays on Irish
politics and education; translations of the *Mabinogion* and other
Welsh texts; the 'fanciest hogwash' of Fiona MacLeod and Joseph
Campbell (the 'mountainy singer', not the scholar of myth);
MacPherson's *Ossian*; Shaw's *John Bull's Other Island*; and Joyce's
Portrait of the Artist as a Young Man. Amazingly, the essay is only
twenty pages long.

When, as the 1950s closed, Kelleher turned his attention to the fiercely challenging matter of bringing to greater coherence our understanding of the Irish annals and genealogies that comprise the abundant, contradictory and bewildering historical record of early Ireland, he was adhering to the interdisciplinary model of Irish studies that he had demonstrated in the Arnold essay. 'Early Irish History and Pseudo-History' helped to define the field of Irish studies as an interdisciplinary undertaking. Kelleher read it in 1961 at the inaugural meeting of the American Committee for Irish Studies. After surveying the preceding hundred years in Irish studies, he concluded:

> We have never visualized this field in its entirety. Our special areas of study are usually too small and are needlessly separated from one another, with the result that each of us is apt to depend upon too limited a body of information. Most of our historians know too little about Celtic and Anglo-Irish literature. Few of our students or critics of literature know much about Irish history. The Celticists and linguists, though their scholarship is generally the most professional within the field, all too seldom have shown sufficient interest in the historical or literary content of what they so skilfully edit. As a rule we do not know enough about the areas that impinge, or should impinge, on our own to ask relevant information from them ... We can rejoice then that a movement in the right direction, a movement towards unity and co-operation and the exchange of information and ideas, has at last begun. The formation of the American Committee for Irish Studies, and the unexpectedly large response it has evoked, is the most heartening and hopeful thing that has happened to us in years.
>
> (Kelleher, *Selected Writings*, pp.160–1)

Kelleher's earliest essays ranged widely across the developing field of Irish studies; they include a number of critical assessments of 'post-Revolutionary' Irish writing. 'Irish Literature Today' – published in 1945, the year before he first visited Ireland – casts a sweeping eye over the Irish cultural scene.[1] Though Celtic romanticism is dead and gone and literary realism in the ascendant, Kelleher asserts that the starting point for the Irish writer is the 'diminished reality' of 'a little country in the butter and beef business' (ibid., p.87). Much thought and artistry will be needed for the realist writer to get beyond the 'drabness of life in a restricted, semi-rural country without large ambitions'. He details at length the dire effects of literary censorship, reckoning that since 1928 'about fifteen hundred books have been proscribed, including just about every Irish novel worth reading' (ibid., p.91). As of 1945, three writers stand out to Kelleher – Liam O'Flaherty, Frank O'Connor and Sean O'Faolain.

In fact, Kelleher did much to create an American readership for O'Connor and O'Faolain. He introduced O'Connor's story 'Anchors' in *Harper's Bazaar* for October 1952, contending that its author was 'one of the major short story writers of our time' (Kelleher, 'Frank O'Connor', p.162), and in a vivid essay for the *Atlantic* in May 1957 he argued that O'Faolain was 'the most distinguished living Irish writer'. The essay ends with an image of O'Faolain's conversion to realism that itself reads like the conclusion of a story:

> When O'Faolain was twelve, and as yet an unalloyed romantic, he was plagiarizing so successfully from Robert Louis Stevenson that several of his tales were printed in the *Cork Examiner*. A career of graceful triumph was before him. But a year later he went one night to the theater to see the Abbey players in Lady Gregory's *Jackdaw*. There he saw something that shocked him. On the stage was a table, and on the table was a red and white checked tablecloth exactly like the one in the kitchen at home; and in a flash of wonder he realized that you could write about the life that merely lay around you. After that nothing came easy.
>   (Ibid., p.108)

Finally, springing from his own first reading (at age 20) of *A Portrait of the Artist as a Young Man*, Kelleher provided, in 'The Perceptions of James Joyce', a consummate short assessment of Joyce's novel in the *Atlantic* in March 1958. He judges *A Portrait* to be 'Joyce's one perfected work, evenly sustained and controlled from end to end by a talent in calm dominion over its theme, its instruments, and itself. The books that followed were quite different. Joyce saw no point in doing the same job twice' (ibid., p.79). Moreover, Kelleher acknowledges Joyce's 'innate stoicism', and goes on to an eloquent tribute:

> Joyce's heroism was partly this toughness and partly that his mind drove continually beyond itself in an ever-widening effort to define, through appropriate means, its own perceptions. The nature of those perceptions can be seen clearly in the *Portrait*: secret relationships, impalpable yet vitally communicative, sensed as existing between man and man, age and age, world and man, and, of course, between word and word. Most of them could be expressed only indirectly through symbol for they are

very curious relationships ... And suddenly all the individual strands of technique and attitude subsumed in Joyce's approach to his subject are seen moving together like muscles working under the skin, and the impact is multiple and one. We perceive what the adjective 'organic' is supposed to indicate in a work of art.

(Ibid., pp.80–1)

Importantly, these pieces from the 1950s laid the groundwork that Kelleher brought to full fruition in the next decade, in essays that led the way toward much valuable scholarship on the ways in which both Yeats and Joyce were distinctly Irish writers.[2]   This would prove an invaluable corrective to the wholesale appropriation of Yeats and Joyce into British Literature survey courses, a categorization that prevailed through the first wave of paperback anthologies used in the burgeoning college textbook market. (One indication of the extent to which Kelleher's insight ran counter to the prevailing critical consensus is the fact that the Modern Language Associate did not recognize Irish Literature as a specialty until the 1990s.)

Over the last half-century few developments have been more consequential for the content of Irish studies scholarship than the expansion of its purview to include the history and literature of Ireland's diaspora. Here, too, Kelleher was prescient. The scholarly discussion of Irish–American literature can be dated to the June 1946 issue of the *Atlantic Monthly*, where, in 'Mr Dooley and the Same Old World', Kelleher proposed Finley Peter Dunne as the first writer of genius to emerge from the culture of urban Irish America. 'Martin Dooley' was a fictional bartender in his sixties from the Chicago southside Irish neighbourhood of Bridgeport, who had first appeared in a weekly column in the *Chicago Evening Post* in 1893. The creation of a young Chicago journalist of Irish parentage, 'Mr Dooley' emerged as a celebrated American satirist when his hilarious commentary on the Spanish–American War of 1898 gained him national syndication. That he spoke in a brogue did not hinder his popularity. Kelleher's essay recognized both Dunne's satiric genius and his contribution to the understanding of Irish immigration and ethnic life in America.

Kelleher declares that 'Dooley is a unique invention: the only mythical philosopher I can think of with a philosophy.' He continues:

Like every writer worth his salt, Dunne had his vision of evil, profound and thoroughgoing, and what is less usual, balanced by an equally searching vision of decency. He could never write a *Utopia*. The complexity of the human spirit was his starting point, and his philosophy was bounded by an intensely felt perception that all souls are alike before man as before God ... It was, I think, largely because of this perception that people recognized in Dooley the peculiar authority of the man who has been there and knows. Applicability is an attribute of the classics. Dooley navigated in the world with his map of Archey Road; he traveled Archey Road by the signposts of the human heart. (Ibid., p.119)

Mr Dooley's prime target was hypocrisy – from the self-serving pretension of individuals in Bridgeport to global imperialism in the Philippines and South Africa – and his satire could be harsh, even Swiftian, as when mocking the slogans of empire: 'Hands acrost th' sea an' into somewan's pocket' or 'Take up th' white man's burden an' hand it to th' coons.'

And yet, Kelleher also notes that Dunne's 'natural kindliness' provoked the creation of a pantheon of heroes from everyday life:

They appear in different guises – a good cop, a hardworking father of a large family, a washerwoman whose tenderly reared only son turns out a bum, a Union veteran who never marches in a parade or waves the bloody shirt. In one of his finest heroic tales the hero is a fireman. It never disqualified a man, to Dooley's thinking, that he got paid for his bravery by the week.
(Ibid., p.122)

Kelleher explains that Mr Dooley 'remained fresh and alive to the last' because of his creator's 'objective sensitivity to social change'. Among other phenomena, Dunne chronicled vividly 'many of the most significant permutations of Irish life in America, as and when they took place'. At this point, Kelleher pauses to indicate a road ahead for prospective workers in the field of Irish–American literature: 'The whole process needs a history by itself, and none is yet written.' Dunne's columns indicate this process

by progressively relaxing the belligerence with which the characters, Dooley included, face the smug and wealthy world. More and more their angry sarcasm is softened by indifference, their irony by amusement. This is not growing weakness or old age or an access of gentleness – just that a battle has been won and the victors are letting down their stiffly assumed defense. (Ibid., p.116)

The next paragraph is vintage Kelleher, a miracle of compressed cultural history:

The pressure let up in numberless ways, about that time, as the first generation of American-born Irish took over from their parents. Think of it in concrete terms. Families that had struggled along for years – God knows how – on the father's uncertain wages of, say, eight to ten dollars a week suddenly found themselves with five or six times that amount as the boys and girls grew up and got jobs their parents could never dream of. They marched into Canaan land and the walls toppled in the onrush. The 'No Irish Need Apply' signs were broken up for firewood. It was a happy, marvelous time – a time for them to wonder at and enjoy – and it was enjoyed. (Ibid.)

Kelleher finishes up here by decrying the idea that the dialect could somehow be 'translated' out of the Dooley columns to gain new readers. Such tampering, he argues, would 'destroy their artistic compaction' and 'dissolve Martin Dooley altogether'. Not to worry, though, because 'there will, I believe, always be a scattering of people in whose estimation he will be secure. The need for study and a glossary to read it has rarely killed a specimen of wisdom, and of witty wisdom – never' (ibid., p.124). Sixty-plus years on, this remains true.

In November 1947 Kelleher published another trail-blazing piece in the Cork journal *Irish Writing*. 'Irish–American Literature and Why There Isn't Any' develops the outline of Irish–American life before and after the transforming turn of the twentieth century. The negativity of his title springs from Kelleher's observation of his own home place of Lawrence, Massachusetts, from which he concludes that the stories that have survived the watershed emergence of an Irish–American middle class are too distorted by the passage of time to reflect the realism needed for 'the great Irish–American novel, a trilogy, of course, which would tell the whole three-generation story from North Cork in 1847 or 1874 to Massachusetts in 1947' (ibid., p.126).

In this essay, Kelleher doubts the future possibilities of the Irish–American imagination. He recalls that his father

used to tell me I would never get what I was looking for. What I needed was the talk in the kitchens at night, when the old country friends came visiting. 'If you had the record of one night's talk, you'd have it all. But you wouldn't be able to understand most of it if you did have it.' Why, I asked; and he tried to explain how different it was from anything I could have heard at anytime after I was old enough to take notice. 'That talk vanished before the talkers. After the turn of the century it all died out; and especially after that you never heard them going off into Irish when they wanted to talk above the young folk's heads.' (Ibid., p.128)

And yet, Kelleher points to one obscure novel, *Annie Reilly, or the Fortunes of an Irish Girl in New York* (1878), by John McElgun, whose 'style leaves us something to desire – he seems to have quarried his language with a pick-axe; and his thought sometimes has the consecutive direction of a Mexican jumping bean, sometimes not' (ibid., p.133). Still, attention can profitably be paid to a hack such as McElgun, because

> very plainly he knew what he was writing about. Time and again, he gives us a chunk of realism ... He knew Ireland; he knew Queenstown and Liverpool and the passage agencies; he knew what the immigrant ships were like, what the Irish boarding-houses in New York were like, what happened to the Irish who fell away from the Church. All these things he mentions. (Ibid.)

By implication, there must be other such novels, maybe a lot of them – which the future historian can mine for valuable detail about this lost world.

The essay does praise two writers, 'both very substantial', Finley Peter Dunne and James T. Farrell, the latter of whom, Kelleher concedes, wrote well after the end of the old, vanished Irish America. In passing, though, Kelleher provides an original and central insight about Farrell's fiction:

> The significance of his work lies in his description and knowledge of the void into which whole myriads of our people have fallen, that modern, lower middle class, traditionless, urban void underlying industrially revolutionized society in Chicago, Liverpool, Paris, Milan, Dublin. The void has no national boundaries. The people in it have no essential nationality but modern barbarism ... *Studs Lonigan*, Farrell's trilogy, can be studied with profit by any politician or priest anywhere who feels that his particular institution has faced up to its responsibilities.
> (Ibid., p.135)

Two other of Kelleher's early pieces about Irish America deserve special note. 'A Long Way from Tipperary', published in *The Reporter* in May 1960, is his review of George Potter's history of Irish immigration, *To the Golden Door*. Four pages long, the piece contains this elegant summary paragraph:

Like most true history, the tale, fully told, is one from which almost nobody comes off well. Nearly all charges by and against the Irish are exaggerated and nearly all are true to one degree or another. This is clearest when Mr Potter is writing about New England, but it is not clear enough. Here his general impartiality is thrown out of plumb by his evident sympathy for the Irish and his tendency to see the Yankees even more in terms of settled characteristics. And that is too bad, for the Irish-Yankee confrontation is the richest still-unrealized tragi-comedy in American history. On the one side, the Irish, fleeing from a homeland where they had been racked, robbed, and demoralized by an imposed aristocracy of Protestant, Puritan, Anglo-Saxon derivation. On the other, a Protestant, Puritan, Anglo-Saxon people who had, when the Irish arrived, just about completed a city and a society made in their own best image. More thoroughly than ever before in history the sins of the fathers were visited on the second cousins once-removed. The mutual despair and hatred re-echoed from the welkin. No wonder that assimilation is not yet quite complete in and around Boston. Nor that the drama remains to be written. The dramatist would have to reimagine the tale with entire sympathy for both sides and full understanding of the two histories and unfailing consciousness of the irony.

(Ibid., pp.148–9)

The second piece, five pages long, was 'Irishness in America', which appeared in the *Atlantic* for July 1961. Here, Kelleher dates the emergence of an Irish–American middle class to the 1892 heavyweight title fight between John L. Sullivan, 'the Boston Strong Boy', and 'Gentleman Jim' Corbett, 'a prophetic figure: slim, deft, witty, looking like a proto-Ivy Leaguer with his pompadour, his fresh intelligent face, his well-cut young man's clothes'. Kelleher speaks of the 'heroic age' that ended with Sullivan's defeat:

Yet, of what was lost sixty-nine years ago, little would have lasted out the decade anyway, and there was less that the Irish really wanted to hang on to. Sullivan was lucky that he went when he did, while he was still the meaningful symbol of what the Irish here had perforce to be proud of: native strength, the physical endurance that made possible the 'Irish contribution to America' that orators and writers have since sentimentalized so much. What they really mean is that from the 1840s on, floods of Irish immigrants gave the country what it had not had before, a huge

fund of poor, unskilled, cheap, almost infinitely exploitable
labor, and that this labor force was expended, with a callousness
now hard to comprehend, in building the railroads and dams and
mills, in digging the canals, in any crude, backbreaking job. The
contribution was real enough, but it would be difficult to distinguish it from the drafthorse contribution to America, and it was
rewarded with about as many thanks.   (Ibid., p.151)

Seldom, if ever, has so much been suggested about the entire social
history of an immigrant culture in so few words.

In two hard-nosed, provocative essays that were meant to refute
romantic assumptions about the 'old sod' current in 1950s America,
Kelleher also made a significant contribution to American understanding of contemporary Ireland. In April 1954 he published 'Can Ireland
Unite?' in the *Atlantic Monthly*. The piece starts from one unambigu-
ous premise:

Partition is truly intolerable. Its effect is to reduce an entire
nation not merely to provincialism but to a queasy, suspicious
parochialism too often content with fourth-best because, lacking
whole strength, it might find the best unsafe to handle. Hence
emigration: that is no country for young men. Hence the literary censorship: good writers are known to reject the weak inspiration of the parish pump. Hence, too, the Orange lodges in the
North and the Knights of Columbanus in the South: to ensure
that the top parishioners profit most from the parish. Because
fear breeds every disease from bigotry to greed, Ireland will not
again be whole and sound till these fears are expelled.

('Can Ireland Unite?', p.61)

Asserting that 'at this late hour ... the history of the problem is nearly
irrelevant to its solution', he explains that 'three present factors count:
religious differences, the failure of either state to create within its own
borders a vigorously healthy society, and the bald fact that the division
between North and South aggravates with every passing year' (ibid.,
p.58). Politically, as the North has moved leftward thanks to 'British
social legislation', the 'formerly revolutionary South' has moved to the
right, and 'created a provincial, middle-class, somewhat reactionary
little republic'. In the North the Protestant majority fears that a
reunited Ireland will make them vulnerable to the same 'ugly record
of bitterness and discrimination' that they have visited upon their own
Catholic minority (ibid., p.59).

On the other hand, Eamon de Valera's 1937 constitution in the South – 'and if he had set it to music it could hardly be a more intimate reflection of his Roman-Calvinist personality' – begins, 'In the Name of the Most Holy Trinity, from Whom is all authority and to Whom, as our final end, all actions both of men and States must be referred, We, the people of Éire' ... ('Does this disenfranchise Unitarians?', Kelleher asks). And what of Article 44, with its recognition of the 'special position' of the Catholic Church? 'Would Protestants in the Twenty-Six Counties be allowed divorce, birth control, and so on, like their Northern coreligionists? Would the Six-County Catholics be left bleakly unprotected from these occasions of sin?' (ibid., pp.59–60). Kelleher goes on to enumerate the contrast between the two entities in education, social legislation, conditions of labour and population. He finds only one matching trait: 'the politicians on both sides of the Border are too much alike: old, cautious, querulous, and rather small-time' (ibid., p.61).

Hope for the future, Kelleher contends, lies primarily in the ticking clock. As young people come into positions of authority, the rigid orthodoxies on both sides of the border may crumble. A new constitution could be written, 'real politics' could emerge, and 'Ireland's great undeveloped potential' could be realized. 'There is no telling what upward limit might be reached if courage and initiative were equal to opportunity.' Kelleher ends with an anecdote from Frank O'Connor, who recalled that as a schoolboy in Cork, his new teacher, Daniel Corkery, wrote a phrase in Irish on the board for the class to memorize: '*Múscail do mhisneach, a Bhanbha!* ... Waken your courage, Ireland!' (ibid., p.62). Strong medicine – perhaps especially strong, coming from the United States – and yet the piece was reprinted (with only a few cuts) as the lead article in two issues of the *Irish Digest* in Dublin for December 1954 and January 1955.[3]

In the April 1957 issue of *Foreign Affairs*, Kelleher published 'Ireland ... and Where Does She Stand?', another wholesale condemnation of postwar Irish life that in many ways provided a transatlantic forum for the critique that his friend Sean O'Faolain had so sedulously offered in the *Bell*. He begins: 'Ireland is presently in serious trouble, with many indications of worse trouble to come' (Kelleher, 'Ireland ... and Where Does She Stand?', p.485). In the first place, no one looks to the government as the source of power and authority:

> In social, educational and cultural matters the Catholic hierarchy is felt to have greater and more effective authority. In economic

matters power is thought to be the monopoly of those owners, bankers, large shareholders, directors and managers who control the new industries and are linked fraternally in that anti-Masonic secret society, the Knights of Columbanus.

Second, 'Emigration is a comment, silent but explicit, on every Irish condition. It is a contributing cause of every Irish condition.' Furthermore, 'the prime causes of emigration are not economic'. Rather, 'The people emigrate because they do not like what they are offered and because they do not expect to be offered anything else.' In fact, Ireland's leaders are clueless and complicit in all this. 'What the people are offered,' Kelleher asserts, 'and what the emigrants reject is paternalism' (ibid., pp.487–93).

Above all, he blames de Valera for having governed for a generation by the assumption that 'he had only to look into his own heart to know what the Irish people wanted'. Kelleher says that

what Mr de Valera found in his heart was a burning desire for compulsory Irish in the schools and civil service; a thoroughgoing, or at least hardworking, censorship; efficiency and honesty in local government (achieved by taking all real powers away from the elected county and borough councils and killing such community initiative as there was): and in general a society based upon Catholic and 'Gaelic' principles of 'frugal sufficiency' and geared to the supposed tastes and interests of the small farmer, the truly representative Irish citizen.   (Ibid., pp.493–4)

In the event 'he and his successors have left Ireland a duller and, in spirit, a deader place than they found it. One has only to look at the literature, the theatre, the newspapers, the few magazines, the censored libraries for the proof – or listen to Radio Eireann – or spend a rainy weekend in a small town' (ibid., p.494). Although Kelleher prescribes a number of remedies, the essay concludes grimly. If the status quo remains unchanged, 'I can, however, imagine that Ireland may do what no other nation has ever tried, and perish by sudden implosion upon a central vacuity' (ibid., p.495). So much for diplomatic tact.[4]

In the last phase of Kelleher's career, most of his energies were directed toward pre-Norman Ireland, giving rise to a series of benchmark essays, many appearing in distinguished, but low-circulation journals of Celtic studies – a task that he called 'a lifetime affair with early Irish history, a matter of mistaking a mountain for a good-sized molehill, due to the surrounding fog' (Kelleher, *Selected Writings*, p.137).[5]   Once again his scholarship was breathtaking. And yet it is tempting to wonder, what if John Kelleher had not chosen this hardest and most remote of scholarly roads? Would Irish studies have been blessed with many more of the valuable analyses of Ireland and Irish America from the eighteenth through the twentieth centuries with which his career began?

It might be petty to think so, but, really, this is a bit like regretting the loss of the marvellous array of stylistically traditional renderings of Irish life that James Joyce might have produced, had he not conceived of *Ulysses* and *Finnegans Wake*. When Kelleher said that Joyce 'saw no point in doing the same job twice', he was talking about himself too. Inside a mind of genius, strife is indeed better than loneliness.

REFERENCES

Kelleher, John V. 'Eire and the Allies'. *New Republic*, vol. 110, 10 April 1944, pp.501–2.

—— 'Frank O'Connor'. *Harper's Bazaar*, vol. 86 (October 1952).

—— 'Can Ireland Unite?' *Atlantic Monthly*, vol. 193 (April 1954), pp.58–62.

—— 'Ireland ... and Where Does She Stand?' *Foreign Affairs*, vol. 35, no. 3 (1957), pp.485–95.

—— 'With Dick in Dublin, 1946', in Susan Dick et al. (eds), *Essays for Richard Ellmann: Omnium Gatherum*. Kingston and Montreal: McGill-Queen's University Press, 1989, pp.13–22.

—— *Selected Writings of John V. Kelleher on Ireland and Irish America*, ed. Charles Fanning. Carbondale and Edwardsville, IL: Southern Illinois University Press, 2002.

McKibben, William E. 'The Love of the Irish'. *Harvard Crimson*, 14 September 1981, n.p.

Rosenblatt, Roger. 'The Teachings of Mr Kelleher'. *Esquire* (June 1986), p.264.

Notes

CHAPTER ONE
Dance Halls of Romance and Culchies in Tuxedos:
Irish Traditional Music in America in the 1950s

1. Between 1946 and 1961, 531,255 people, almost 17 per cent of the population, left Ireland (Almeida, 'A Great Time to be in America', p.208). Forty per cent of people between the ages of 10 and 19 who were counted in the 1951 census were gone by 1961, the majority to Great Britain. Enda Delaney has noted that this was not a new development, but rather an acceleration of a pattern of emigration to Britain that had been in place since the 1930s and that had been reinforced by World War Two and its aftermath (Delaney, 'Vanishing Irish', p.80). During the 1940s, 26,967 immigrants arrived in the United States from Ireland, to be followed by another 57,332 in the 1950s (Kenny, *American Irish*, p.221).

2. The Victor recording company issued more than 15,000 foreign records during the 1920s and 1930s, ranging from Finnish fiddlers to Sicilian pipers. See Pekka Gronow, *The Columbia Listing 33000-F Series. A Numerical Listing* (Los Angeles: John Edwards Foundation, 1982), p.1, and also Smith, 'My Love is in America', p.227. Nicholas Carolan estimates that 3,000 Irish recordings were issued on both sides of the Atlantic during the 1920s and 1930s. The majority was issued in the US prior to the Wall Street crash (Carolan, 'A Discography of Irish Traditional Music', p.45).

3. In the half-century before Irish independence, such groups as the Land League, the Home Rule movement, Sinn Féin, trade unions and temperance groups all used fife and drum, and later, brass and reed bands at meetings and rallies. Between the Boer War and World War One British Army garrison towns shared bandmasters (many of them British, others German) with local musicians, both literate performers and oral-based traditional players. Leydon, interview with author, 1988; Ward, interview, 1986. See also Fleischman, 'Music in Nineteenth-Century Ireland', pp.41–2.

4. With their strong emphasis on technical brilliance, the recordings of the Sligo masters had a profound influence on Irish traditional music on both sides of the Atlantic. Tune sequences like Coleman's *Tarbolton Reel*, *The Longford Collector* and *The Sailor's Bonnet* are still regarded as sacrosanct today.

5. It is noteworthy that Irish and Cape Breton dancers joined forces in the Rose Croix Hall, a practice not always mirrored in the schismatic relationship between Irish and Cape Breton musicians in Boston. Despite a common Gaelic heritage, there was very little musical interaction between these two groups (Magone, interview with author, 2008).

6. Like musicians in other genres, Irish musicians working the professional circuit in the United States were subject to stringent regulations set by such unions as the American Federation of Musicians, which controlled wages, hours, orchestra sizes and working conditions in the music industry. In New York these regulations were relaxed during the 1960s as a result of anti-trust and right-to-work amendments initiated by Governor Nelson Rockefeller (O'Neill, interview with author, 2007).

7. Cork-born John Whooley was a key promoter of Irish culture in the Bay area for more thirty years. Kerry entrepreneur Bill Fuller owned twenty-three ballrooms around the world, including San Francisco's Fillmore West. Defying skeptics, he introduced Irish show bands to Las Vegas, a considerable feat given the tastes of the entertainment 'plutocracy' at the time. A mysterious and undocumented figure, Fuller shaped the careers of scores of Irish musicians in America. See 'Bill Fuller: The Man Who Built the Ballroom,' www.electric-ballroom.co.uk/history/history4.html.

CHAPTER TWO
Playing 'Irish' Sport on Baseball's Hallowed Ground:
The 1947 All-Ireland Gaelic Football Final

1. See also GAA, '1947-Final in the Polo Grounds', Cumann Lúthchleas Gael official website, www.gaa.ie/page/1947_final_in_the_polo_grounds.html (accessed 23 August 2007).
2. See, for example, the Official Guide of the GAA: 'The primary purpose of the GAA is the organisation of native pastimes and the promotion of athletic fitness as a means to create a disciplined, self-reliant, national-minded manhood' (Gaelic Athletic Association, 'Official Guide, Part 1' [Dublin: Central Council of the GAA, 2007], p.3).
3. See, for example, '50,000 Will Watch Irish Final Today'; and Pierce O'Reilly, 'Fans in flight: GAA officials concerned over shrinking Gaelic Park crowds', *Irish Echo*, 25–31 July 2001, www.irishecho.com/search/searchstory.cfm?id=9692&issueid=209 (accessed 14 February 2004).

CHAPTER FOUR
'Hibernians on the March': Irish–American Ethnicity and the Cold War

1. An earlier version of this essay originally appeared in *Éire-Ireland*, vol. 40, nos 1 and 2 (2005), pp.170–82. It appears here by kind permission of the publishers, the Irish American Cultural Institute, Morristown, New Jersey.
2. For more on the 'ethnic fade' thesis, see Waters, *Ethnic Options*.
3. The postwar emphasis on ethnic/religious pluralism is striking when presented in several American history textbooks. For an example, see Francis Brown and Joseph Roucek (eds), *One America: The History, Contributions, and Present Problems of Our Racial and National Minorities* (New York: Prentice-Hall, 1945). For a more critical, even suspicious view of Irish–Catholic Americans, see Adamic, *Nation of Nations*.
4. For another view on the origins of the Ancient Order of Hibernians, dating back to the organization's arrival in the United States in 1836, see Ridge, *Erin's Sons in America*, pp.11–2.
5. The widely held conclusion that the New Deal meant the inevitable decline of ethnic political machines fails to recognize the anomalous nature of James Michael Curley in Boston, and fails to appreciate the purposeful particularity with which Roosevelt treated the urban bosses of the time. See David Kennedy, *Freedom from Fear: The American People in Depression and War, 1929–1945* (Oxford: Oxford University Press, 1999), p.253. See also Charles H. Trout, *Boston, the Great Depression and the New Deal* (Oxford: Oxford University Press, 1977), pp.143–71; and Lyle Dorsett, *Franklin Roosevelt and the City Bosses* (Port Washington, New York: Kennikat Press, 1977).
6. For an excellent analytical survey of anti-Catholic intellectual thought in the mid-twentieth century, see McGreevy, 'Thinking on One's Own: Catholicism in the American Intellectual Imagination, 1928–1960', *Journal of American History*, vol. 84 (1997), pp.97–131.

CHAPTER FIVE
Shamrocks and Segregation: The Persistence of Upper-Class Irish
Ethnicity in Beverly Hills, Chicago

1. In his thesis, Greeley used pseudonyms for the neighbourhood and parish he studied. He notes, however, that the parish under study – 'St Praxides' – was his first parish as a priest, which from biographical information is Christ the King parish.
2. See also Waters, *Ethnic Options*.
3. See also Steinberg, Stephen. *The Ethnic Myth: Race, Ethnicity and Class in America*. New York: Atheneum, 1981.
4. See Ignatiev, *How the Irish Became White*, and Roediger, *Wages of Whiteness*.
5. Greeley, 'Some Aspects of Interaction', ch. 3. For a further discussion of the centrality of the parish to Irish–Catholic community life, see McMahon, *What Parish Are You From?*
6. In Chicago the Catholic Church largely allowed Irish immigrants to retain their distinctive identity. While the city housed Catholics of many different nationalities, the structure of the archdiocese allowed most ethnic groups to remain in separate parishes rather than uniting them in the same religious community. As English speakers, the Irish did not fit the structure of national parishes, but instead came to dominate the 'territorial' parishes: in practical

terms, territorial parishes became enclaves of Irish Catholicism. Even as late as 1980, St Barnabas and Christ the King were classified as largely Irish parishes in the official arch-diocesan history. See Koenig (ed.), *History of the Parishes of the Archdiocese of Chicago*, vol. 1, pp.100–2, 184–7. An examination of first communion and marriage records for St Barnabas and Christ the King also indicates that most parishioners were migrating from other traditionally Irish parishes on Chicago's South Side.

7. Minutes of Vanderpoel Improvement Association, 4 November 1947, Ridge Historical Society, Chicago. Though the BAPA is widely credited for ensuring calm, peaceful integra-tion of Beverly Hills in the 1960s and 1970s, in this early period the organization openly advocated restrictive covenants and keeping the area free from African Americans.

8. McGreevy provides an expansive discussion of Catholicism and race relations, particularly the role of Catholic organizations in addressing racial desegregation and the conflicts between working-class inner-city Catholics and an increasingly racially liberal clergy.

9. Msgr Gleeson responded to this letter in August 1965, providing a rough date of the orig-inal letter. Another letter by Herman J. Kelly, although undated, clearly responds to Msgr Gleeson's letter, thus indicating that Kelly wrote the original letter.

10. Historians who focus on the rise of white racial identities among ethnics in the postwar period include Eric Avila, *Popular Culture in the Age of White Flight: Fear and Fantasy in Suburban Los Angeles* (Berkeley, CA: University of California Press, 2004); Arnold R. Hirsch, *Making the Second Ghetto: Race and Housing in Chicago, 1940–1960* (Chicago, IL: University of Chicago Press, 1998); Thomas A. Guglielmo, *White on Arrival: Italians, Race, Color, and Power in Chicago, 1890–1945* (Oxford: Oxford University Press, 2003).

CHAPTER SIX
Irish New Yorkers and the Puerto Rican Migration

1. ADC is an acronym for 'aid to dependent children', a key part of the American welfare system.
2. The exact origins of the term *spic* are contested. The Puerto Rican writer Juan Pedro Soto, who spent a great deal of time in New York in the 1950s and 1960s, believes it derives from how Puerto Ricans mispronounced the English word *speak*. His 1956 collection of short stories, *Spiks*, begins with this explanation:

> Su mala pronunciación, de esa *i* que en la frase correcta de 'I don't speak English' debe ser aguda, no gruesa, hará que le endilguen, como hispanohablante, el término peyora tivo de spik.
>
> (The incorrect pronunciation [of the Puerto Ricans] of this i which in the correct phrase 'I don't speak English' should be acute, not grave and because of this, as Spanish speakers, the pejorative term spik was placed upon them.)

Soto also suggests that it possibly was derived from the insult word used for Italians, *spig*, which was short for *spaghetti*. Another theory is that the term evolved as a shortened version of the word *Hispanic* and, like Piri Thomas's use of *paddy* to include all white people, it has been transformed by popular use to insult anyone of Hispanic origin by many in the United States.

CHAPTER SEVEN
From 'Peace and Freedom' to 'Peace and Quiet': *The Quiet Man* as a Product of the 1950s

1. Especially valuable are Luke Gibbons, *The Quiet Man* (Cork: Cork University Press, 2002) and Michael Patrick Gillespie 'The Myth of Hidden Ireland: The Corrosive Effect of Place in *The Quiet Man*', *New Hibernia Review*, vol. 6, no. 1 (spring 2002), pp.18–32.
2. In the 1935 version this character is named Paddy Bawn Enright; in the 1933 version he is named Shawn Kelvin.
3. It is worth remembering that Samuel Beckett's *Waiting for Godot* was written in 1948 and premiered in 1953. In *The Quiet Man* we can find touches of linguistic disconnection like those in Beckett's play.
4. Trow's earlier book, *Within the Context of No Context* (Boston: Little, Brown, 1981), offers a broad argument that, since 1950, television in particular has worked to present its stories without any framing background or circumstance.
5. I am indebted to Patricia Monaghan, who pointed out how the film enacts the PTSD cycle, when I delivered a version of this essay at the American Conference for Irish Studies annual conference in 2008.

CHAPTER NINE
Ireland as a Past Life:
Bridey Murphy and Irish–American Tourism to Ireland, 1945–1960

1. The relative values of prices were calculated using the website www.measuringworth. com/uscompare, accessed November 2007. See Hugh G. Smith, 'Side Trip to Ireland; Comprehensive Tour List Set for Emerald Isle', *New York Times*, 17 February 1952, p.304, and James Doyle, 'Ireland Puts a Lot of Beauty in Little Space', *Chicago Tribune*, 8 June 1952, p.F17.
2. For example, the photograph headlined 'Ireland's Pastoral Serenity', showing a horse-drawn cart on a country road, in the *Chicago Tribune*, 29 January 1956, p.F5.
3. There did seem to be some dispute in Ireland about the meaning of the term 'An Tóstal'. During a Dáil debate on 16 June 1953 an opposition TD claimed that his dictionary translated the word into English as meaning 'arrogance, pride, envy', rather than 'at home'. See www.historical-debates.oireachtas.ie/D/0139/D.0139.195306160034.html for full details of the debate, accessed November 2007.
4. For much of the information on the production and distribution policies regarding the tourism films of this period, the author is grateful for the assistance of both Bill Morrison and Derek Cullen of Bord Fáilte.
5. For a detailed discussion of the influence of *The Quiet Man* on Irish tourism advertising, see Rains, *Irish-American in Popular Culture*, pp.114–16.
6. For a detailed discussion of Hinde's postcards of Ireland during this era, see Gibbons, 'Back Projections: John Hinde and the New Nostalgia', pp.37–43.
7. When the book was published, Virginia Tighe was given the pseudonym 'Ruth Simmons'. However, her real identity was soon revealed in the press, and is used throughout this chapter.
8. The 'reincarnation cocktail' apparently consisted of 'a jigger of vodka and a 1/2 jigger of maraschino liqueur shaken with lemon juice and crushed ice and topped with a cupful of flaming rum'. Perhaps fortuitously, the recipe for 'ectoplasm punch' does not survive. Brean, 'Bridey Murphy Puts Nation in a Hypnotizzy', pp.28–35.
9. In an odd incident from the mid-1950s, one first-generation Irish American appears to have taken the concept of Ireland as a refuge from the Cold War and contemporary American society to an extreme length. In January 1955 the *New York Times* reported that a US soldier believed by his military commanders to be one of a group possibly held prisoner by the Soviets was, according to his uncle, actually running a farm in Ireland. The paper explained that the soldier, Edward Hoban, 'came to the United States in 1948 ... and was drafted three months later. He served nine months and was released, but was recalled during the Korean hostilities'. 'GI Not Held By Soviet; AWOL Soldier Reported to Be Running Farm in Ireland', *New York Times*, 23 January 1955, p.39.
10. The Shannon Free Zone is still in operation and is currently administered by Shannon Development, an Irish government agency. See www.shannonireland.com, accessed November 2007.
11. This mail-order business continues to operate, now trading as Shannon Mail Order, a subsidiary of Waterford Wedgwood, and relying principally on Internet trading through its website, www.shopshannon.com (accessed November 2007).

CHAPTER TEN
Ignorable Irishry:
Leprechauns and Postwar Satire

1. An especially thorough discussion of these years is found in Dermot Keogh (ed.), *The Lost Decade: Ireland in the 1950s* (Cork: Mercier Press, 2004).
2. The Irishman as cross-cultural mediator proves a central role in *The Quiet Man*. Numerous contemporary reviews referred to Barry Fitzgerald in the part of Michaeleen Oge O'Flynn as a leprechaun. Though lacking the costume of a leprechaun (except for the cutaway coat during courting scenes), the Barry Fitzgerald role is given precisely the task of interpreting one culture for the other: it is he who teaches the outsider Sean Thornton (John Wayne) how things are done in Ireland. Des MacHale describes Michaeleen Oge O'Flynn as 'the chief leprechaun and Sean's guide throughout the movie' (MacHale, *Complete Guide to The Quiet Man*, p.58). Elsewhere, MacHale says, Michaeleen is 'no ordinary mortal, he is part human being and part leprechaun' and quotes the initial description of the character from Frank Nugent's screenplay:

'an impish man, bibulous, contumacious, locquacious [*sic*] and imperturbable. He is a master of all trades, none of which he follows. It can be said of him that he has his nose in everything, his heart in the right place and his mouth – by preference – in a large glass of potstill' (ibid., p.66).

3. Notably, Vivian Mercier remarks that 'Aodhg de Blacam, Gerard Murphy, and doubtless other writers too have suggested that the leprechaun material in the later material of *The Death of Fergus* was made available to Swift in some form, supplying him with hints for Gulliver's adventures in Lilliput and Brobdingnag' (Mercier, *Irish Comic Tradition*, p.29).

4. The Og character was played by David Wayne, who won a Tony for the part, the first ever given for a featured actor in a musical; *Finian's Rainbow* was also the first Broadway musical to be recorded on a Columbia LP.

5. In Stephens's book, the leprechauns dwell in 'Gort na Cloca Mora'. Many of the other place names in the musical are lifted from a seldom-performed 1937 play by Lennox Robinson, *Killycregs in Twilight* (Meyerson and Harburg, *Who Put the Rainbow*, p.234).

6. Another aspect of this postwar version of the leprechaun that deserves further consideration is the motif of something being lost or stolen. It was lobster pots in this book, the homeland in the Wibberley book, and the pot of gold in *Finian*. (The 1949 Bing Crosby movie *Top of the Mornin'* contains no leprechauns, but hinges on the plot device of American detective finds the stolen Blarney Stone.) Perhaps this, too, suggests that Americans of the time found in Ireland a refracted way to talk about some greater loss in the national life – Ireland and Irishness having come to encode a variety of ideas about lost genuineness, idealism and lost innocence.

CHAPTER ELEVEN
Unnatural Law: William McGivern's Rogue Cops

1. William P. McGivern (1922–82) was a native of Chicago. He served overseas in the US Army from 1943–46 and subsequently worked as a reporter and book reviewer for the *Philadelphia Evening Bulletin* from 1941 to 1951, before dedicating himself full time to writing. In 1948 he married the novelist Maureen Daly (born Castlecaulfield, County Tyrone, Northern Ireland; 1915–2006) and together they collaborated on a number of travel books and novels until his death in 1982. He won the Edgar Award for mystery writing in 1952 and was later President of the Writers Guild of America. In total he is credited (or co-credited) with thirty novels and five screenplays – all adapted from his own books.

2. For instance, *Where the Sidewalk Ends* (1950), *Detective Story* (1951), *On Dangerous Ground* (1951) and *The Mob* (1951).

3. The novel is dedicated to the writer, editor and later TV writer Howard Brown (1908–99), whose career move from genre pulp magazines to Hollywood anticipates McGivern's own. Brown's influence can be directly traced to the four 'Paul Pine' detective novels he wrote under the pseudonym of John Evans, particularly *Halo in Blood* (1946), which featured a cop villain. *Halo for Satan* (1948), by contrast, featured a corrupt Catholic priest, an example McGivern chose not to emulate.

4. The novel is dedicated to Earl Selby. From 1950, Selby wrote a column for the *Philadelphia Evening Bulletin* titled 'Our Town' and dedicated to exposing civil deficiencies or injustices, many of which led directly to institutional reform. The *Bulletin* was central to McGivern's formation and gave him his earliest writing employment as a crime reporter in the late 1940s. He took from this experience a strong sense of location – all his crime stories are set in Philadelphia – and a recurring interest in the theme of police corruption, which was clearly one of the paper's defining preoccupations. In 1964 former *Bulletin* colleagues James V. Magee (also an Irish–American US Army vet) and Albert V. Gaudiosi won the Pulitzer Prize for 'Local Investigative Specialized Reporting'. Their series of reports exposed an underground 'numbers racket' (gambling) that was taking place with the collusion of members of the Philadelphia Police Department. The articles led to arrests and a clean-up of the police department resulting in fifteen police suspensions and nine firings. Elizabeth A. Brennan and Elizabeth C. Clarage (eds), *Who's Who of Pulitzer Prize Winners* (Phoenix: Oryx Press, 1999), p.374.

5. An interesting comparative study in this regard might be found in Martin Scorsese's *Taxi Driver* (1976), which also posits a 'lonely figure' who takes up arms to 'clean the scum' off the streets of New York. Like *The Big Heat*, Paul Schrader's script also contains a strong religious subtext, which finally undermines the hero's redemption through violence and with it the larger status place of such heroism in American mythology.

CHAPTER TWELVE
Beyond St Malachi's There is Nothing:
Edward McSorley and the Persistence of Tradition

1. Charles Fanning devotes several pages to McSorley in his definitive survey of Irish-American literature, though he characterizes him merely as a 'regional realist', a transitional figure who helped to move the literary tradition on 'toward the considerable achievements of the slightly younger writers just ahead'. Charles Fanning, *The Irish Voice in America: Irish-American Fiction from the Eighteenth Century to the Present* (Lexington, KT: University Press of Kentucky, 1999), pp.303, 306. Lawrence McCaffrey has written of McSorley in a similar vein. Lawrence J. McCaffrey, 'His Own Kind: Edward McSorley and the Providence Irish', *Working Papers in Irish Studies*, vol. 6, no. 1 (Rock Hill, SC: Winthrop University Press, 2006), pp.3–20.
2. The phrase comes from Peter Laslett's classic study of everyday life in late medieval England, *The World We Have Lost: England Before the Industrial Age* (New York: Charles Scribner's Sons, 1965). The theme, however, can be found in at least one strain of urban American literature, particularly in writers influenced by the theories of modernization advanced by the Chicago School of sociology. See Carla Cappetti, *Writing Chicago: Modernism, Ethnography, and the Novel* (New York: Columbia University Press, 1993).
3. See my 'Public Enemies, Local Heroes: The Irish American Gangster Film in Classic Hollywood Cinema', *New Hibernia Review*, vol. 9, no. 4 (winter 2005), pp.48–64; for a more extensive treatment of this agument, see Christopher Shannon, *Bowery to Broadway: The Irish-American City in Classic Hollywood Cinema* (Scranton, PN: University of Scranton Press, 2008).
4. Writing for the *Saturday Review*, George Dangerfield praised the novel even as he used such terms as 'a limited work', 'a minor work' and 'a very narrow field'. See 'An Admirable First Novel', *Saturday Review of Literature*, vol. 29, no. 9, 1 June 1946, p.9.
5. On sacramentalism in art, see Andrew Greeley, *The Catholic Imagination* (Berkeley, CA: University of California Press, 2000), especially ch. 1, 'The Sacraments of Sensibility'.
6. Consider, for example, Lawrence McCaffrey's damning with faint praise: 'Irish-American readers will not discover much of themselves or their environment in *Our Own Kind*. They will, however, enjoy an entertaining, well-told, insightful glimpse at an important phase of Irish America's often tortured yet steady passage from impoverished working-class ghettos of mind and place to urban and suburban middle-class residence and status.' 'His Own Kind', p.18.

CHAPTER THIRTEEN
Present at the Creation:
John V. Kelleher and the Emergence of Irish Studies in America

1. 'Irish Literature Today' was reprinted in the *American Mercury*, vol. 175 (1945), pp.70–6 and in the *Bell*, vol. 10, no. 4 (1945), pp.337–53.
2. The landmark essays are 'Yeats's Use of Irish Materials', Kelleher, *Selected Writings*, pp.24–39, and 'Irish History and Mythology in James Joyce's "The Dead"', ibid., pp.40–56.
3. The piece was reprinted as 'Are We Facing the Facts about Partition?' in *Irish Digest*, vol. 52, no. 2 (December 1954), pp.5–8, and 'Steps to End Partition', in *Irish Digest*, vol. 52, no. 3 (January 1955), pp.5–8. Ernest Blythe, sometime politician and managing director of the Abbey Theatre, replied to Kelleher's analysis in 'Where Prof. Kelleher Goes Wrong', vol. 52, no. 4 (February 1955), pp.5–7, and in 'Have We Been Wrong About the North?', vol. 53, no. 1 (March 1955), pp.5–8.
4. Another notable contribution to an American understanding of Ireland is Kelleher's measured analysis, in the context of preparations for the Normandy Landings, of the failure of the US State Department to understand the roots of Irish neutrality in World War Two in history (both Irish and Irish–American) and character – specifically, the character of De Valera. 'Eire and the Allies', *New Republic*, vol. 110 (10 April 1944), pp.501–2.
5. Among these pieces are 'The Rise of the Dál Cais', 'Humor in the Ulster Saga', 'The Táin and the Annals', and 'The Battle of Móin Mhór', collected in Kelleher, *Selected Writings*, pp.159–245. See also 'The Pre-Norman Irish Genealogies', *Irish Historical Studies*, vol. 16 (1968), pp.138–53 and 'Uí Maine in the Annals and Genealogies to 1225', *Celtica*, vol. 9 (1971), pp.61–112.

Index

A

Acheson, Dean – and Sir Basil Brooke, 48
Adamic, Louis, *Nation of Nations*, 61–2
advertising industry (American), and brain-
    washing, 137–8
All–Ireland Football Final, 1947, **24–37**
    aftermath of, in US and Ireland, 32–4
    Cogley, Mitchell, 27, 28
    Comerford, James, 33
    commemorative replay game 1997, 35
    Daley, Arthur – description of game, 31,
        32–3
    de Búrca, Marcus, 28, 34, 35
    Durkan, Frank – description of crossing to
        US, 28
    Effrat's description of game, 32
    as Famine memorial, 24, 33
    Gaelic Athletic Association (GAA) –
    Ireland, 26–8, 33–5, 37; purpose of, 205
        (ch2, n1)
    Gaelic Athletic Association in United
        States, 26, 27, 29, 34, 35
    Gaelic Park (Innisfail Park), 26–7, 34–5
    immigration, 34–5
    importance of, 25
    Meagher, Wedger – description of game,
        30–1
    New York City, 24
    O'Donnell, John Kerry, 24, 27, 29
    O'Dwyer, Mayor William, 24, 26, 29, 31,
        35
    Ó Hehir, Micheál, 15, 26, 27 – description
        of game, 25
    O'Keeffe, Paddy, 33
    O'Rourke, Dan (GAA), 30
    objectives of, 34
    organization of, 26–9
    origin of, 26–8
    patriarchy, 29
    Polo Grounds, (New York), 24, 32
    Burkeville, 29
    Coogan's Hollow /Coogan's Bluff, 30
    history of, 29–30
    post–game commerce of, 33–4
    press reporting of, 29, 30–3
    profits, 33–4
    reaction in US, 34–5
    teams' return to Ireland, 34
    travel to, 28–9
    World War II, 26
America, Irish music in, *See* music, Irish – in
    America
American Airlines, 141
American Armed Forces Radio, 13
American Association for the Recognition of
    the Irish Republic, 40
American Committee for Irish Studies
    (ACIS), 193
American League for an Undivided Ireland,
    40–1
American Telephone and Telegraph Company
    – and tourism, 142
Ancient Order of Hibernians (AOH),4, **57–70**
    anti–bigotry, 63–4
    anti–communism, 58, 62, 62–3, 64–5, 66
    civil rights, 66
    Cold War, 57–70
    decline of, 59–60
    education, 67, 68
    Freedom Train, 63
    GI Bill of Rights, 68
    Great Depression, 59–60
    Hibernian Digest, 63–64
    Hibernians on the March (membership
        manual), 64–7
    history and purpose of, 58–60
    Independent Sons of Erin, 58
    Irish neutrality, 67
    Molly Maguires, 58–9
    National Hibernian, 59–60
    partition, 66
    postwar revitalization and recruiting, 62–5
    Protestantism, 63–4
    recruitment, 59
    redefining mission and purpose, 64–6

Reilly, George, 63, 64–7
revival of, 61–7
Rogers, Thomas (National Secretary), 62–3
social security, 59, 60
Anglo–Irish War, 40
Annie Reilly, or The Fortunes of an Irish Girl in New York (McElgun), 198
Anthology of Irish Literature (Greene), 189
Anti–Partition Campaign 1948–51, 38–54
assimilation, 51–2
Brooke, Sir Basil, and visit to America, 46, 47–50; British response, 49
Clann na Poblachta, 42
Costello, John A., Taoiseach, 45
de Valera, Eamon, 38, 39, 40, 41–3, 44, 45, 46; trip to US, 42–4
end of, 50
Evans, Sir Frank, 42–3
Fianna Fáil Party 41, 42; and partition, 42
Fine Gael, 42
Franks, Sir Oliver, 47, 48, 49
Gray, David, 38, 39–41, 43–4
Inverchapel, Lord (Sir Archibald John Clark Kerr), 42, 43
Ireland, Denis, 41
Irish–American response to, 45–6, 48
Irish–Americans, 38–9, 45, 46, 4
Irish Anti–Partition League, 41
McBride, Sean, 42, 44; visit to US, 45–6, 50
Marshall Plan, 44
Ormerod, Maj. C.B., 48
postwar Irish Americans, 39
reasons for failure of in the US, 50–1
Rugby, Lord (John Loader Maffey), 42, 43
Truman, President Harry, 43
Ulster Irish Society of New York, 47 in US 40–47
US and Irish relations, postwar, 39
Wilson, President Woodrow, 38
Arnold, Matthew, 191–92
assimilation, 2, 24, 87–99, 115, 119, 175; and anti–partition, 51–2; racial, 71, 72; and work, 118
Athlone Radio (Radió Éireann), 13

B

Baronet Cinema, (New York), 134
Barron, Milton, 60
Barton, Ruth ('It Came from Glocca Morra'), 146
Baruch, Bernard, 48
bean sí – and leprechauns, 157
Behan, Brendan – and image of Ireland, 148
Berlin, Ellin, *Lace Curtains*, 117

Bernstein, Morey (*Search for Bridey Murphy*), 4, 131, 136–8
Beverly Hills, Chicago, 4, 71–86
assimilation, 72
Beverly Area Planning Association (BAPA – and desegregation, 80–1; 206 (ch5, n7)
[Beverly] Improvement Association, 81–2; and Larosa, John, 81–2
Beverly Review, 73–4, 75, 76, 77
Christ the King Parish, 73, 74, 82; 205 (ch5, n11), 205–6 (ch5, n6); Herman Kelly letter to, 83
ethnic fade, 72
Irish ethnicity and Catholicism, 72–3
Irish influx, 72–3, 205–6 (ch5, n6)
Mothers of Longwood Academy, 73
Protestant – Catholic divide, 72, 79, 80–8
and Archdiocese of Chicago, 82
and Organization for a Southwest Community (OSC), 82–3
and Protestant–Catholic relations, 81
race / racial desegregation. 71, 79–82, 83; *See also* assimilation
and St. Barnabas Parish, Chicago, 82
and use of Irish language, 77
'whiteness' theory (racial), 2, 72, 162
Ridge Country Club, 76
St. Barnabas Parish, 73, 74, 75, 77, 79, 82; *See also* St. Patrick's Day, Shamrock Festival
St. Barnabas Woman's Club, 77; and desegregation, 82, 205 (ch5, n6)
St. John Fisher Parish, 74
St. Patrick's Day, *See also* Shamrock Festival, 73–9
Chicago's south side, 78
as community celebration, 76–7
Irish identity, 76–8
local business, 76
origins of celebration, 75
social class image, 78
United Irish Societies of Chicago, 78
St. Praxides Parish (Greeley), 205 (ch5, n1)
Shamrock Festival, 73–5, 77–9; upper–class image of, 79; *See also* St. Barnabas Parish
South Side Catholic Woman's Club, 73
Southtown Economist (Chicago), 76, 78
'whiteness', 72
Bevin, Ernest, 47
Big Heat (film and book, McGivern), 160–1, 166; *See also* McGivern, William P.
Catholic Church, 163–4
crime control and due process models (Packer), 167
Irish ancestry, 168
masculinity, 170

novel vs. film, 168, 169, 170

bigotry, *See* race / racism

Bildungsroman, *Family Installments: Memories of Growing up Hispanic* (Rivera), 89

Black and Tan War – and *Quiet Man*, 101, 109, 110

blackface, *See* leprechauns and blackface, race / racism

Blais, Madeleine, *Uphill Walkers* – and Catholicism, 121

Blanshard, Paul – and AOH, 64

Bogan, Louise, 116, 118, 124; and psycho-analysis, 124

Bord Fáilte, 133, 134, 141, 142, 148

Boston – and AOH, 58; social status of immigrants to, 14; music in, *See* Music Irish – in America

Brady, Sara, 3

Brainwashing, 137–38, 140; *See also* hypnosis

Brannigan (film, McGivern co–author) 161; *See also* McGivern, William P.

Brennan, Maeve, 114
   divorce, 124
   Irish heritage, 120
   marriage, 122
   professional life, 118
   Sneden's Landing, NY, 120
   Springs of Affection, 122

British Broadcasting Corporation (BBC), 13

Brooke, Sir Basil – and visit to America, 46, 47–50

Brown, Francis and Joseph Roucek, *One America: The History, Contributions, and Present Problems of Our Racial and National Minorities*, 60–1

Brown, Howard – influence on William McGivern, 208 (ch11, n1)

Burke, Eddie, 29

Byrne John (New York, GAA), 26

C

Cagney, James, 176

Canby, Henry Seidel, 63

Carney, Ray, 19

Carroll, Liz, 18

Cassavetes, John, 178–9

Catholic education – and Irish–American women writers, 118, 120–1

Catholic Messenger, 119–20

Catholic World, 64

Catholic–Protestant divide, *See* Protestant–Catholic divide

Catholicism / Catholic Church
   the arts, 174, 180; and Irish, 188

education, 177, 182, 183

ethnicity, 72–4

feminism, 119

immigration, Chicago, 205–06 (ch5, n6)

Irish and 1928 and 1960 presidential elections, 68–9

Irish American women writers, 118, 120–1; *See also* Irish–American women

McSorley, Edward, 188

postwar Irish–American, 61

tourism, 134

céilithe / feiseanna – in America, 12–3

censorship, 201–2

Chandler, Raymond, 161

A Charmed Life (McCarthy), 123

Chicago – Catholic Church and immigration, 205–6 (ch5, n6) ; music in, *See* Music, Irish – in America

Chicago Tribune, 133

Christ the King Parish (Beverly Hills, Chicago), 73, 74, 82, 83, 205–6 (ch5, n1, n6)

Churchill, Winston – serialization of memoir, 104

Circling My Mother (Gordon), 122, 124, 126

Clann na Poblachta Party, 42, 44, 50, 51

Cogley, John, 118–19

Cogley, Mitchell – and All–Ireland Final, 1947, 27–8, 29

Cohan, George M., 175

Cold War – AOH, 57–70; brainwashing, 137–8, 140, 207 (ch9, n9); Bridey Murphy affair, 138; hypnosis, 4, 137

Colon Lopez, Joaquin, 87, 88, 97–8; *Pioneros Ruertorriqueños*, 97

Comerford, James – and All–Ireland Final 1947, 33

Comhaltas Ceoltóirí Éireann, 11, 18

Communism and Irish America, 58, 62

The Company She Keeps (McCarthy), 117

Confessions (St. Augustine), 185, 187

Confessions of a Reluctant Catholic (McDermott), 119

Connery, Sean – and *Darby O'Gill and the Little People*, 158

Coogan's Hollow / Coogan's Bluff, *See* Polo Grounds

Corbett, 'Gentleman Jim' and John L. Sullivan fight, 199–200

Corkell, Bridie Murphy, 140

Corkery, Daniel, 201

Costello, John A., 42; and visit to US, 45

'Country People of Ireland' (photo essay, Lange), 136

Crime fiction, *See* McGivern, William, *film noir, noir* fiction

Crock of Gold (Stephens) – editions of, 149; image of leprechauns, 148–9, 150, 153, 154; place names, 208 (ch10, n5)
Cullinan, Elizabeth – and Irish heritage, 120
Curley, Mayor James Michael, 156
Curran, Mary Doyle (*The Parish and the Hill*), 117

D

Dáil Éireann, 50
Daley, Arthur – account of All–Ireland Final, 31–3
Daley, Mayor Richard (Chicago), 79
Daly, Mary E. ('Nationalism, Sentiment, and Economics'), 133
Dance Halls, Boston, 14–6, 204 (ch1, n5); New York, 15–16
Dance, Irish and Cape Breton, in Boston, 204 (ch1, n5)
Darby O'Gill and the Little People (motion picture and book), 146–7, 157–8
Darkest Hour (film, McGivern), 160; *See also* McGivern, William P.
'Daughters of the British Empire', 96, 97
Deasy, Mary, *Hour of Spring*, 117
de Búrca, Marcus, 28, 34, 35
de Valera, Eamon, 34, 38, 39, 40–5, 105, 201, 202; end of anti–partition campaign, 50; re–election of (1951), 50; tour of US, 42–6
Delaney, Enda – and immigration, 203 (ch1, n1)
Democratic Party, 69; in New York, 97–8
The Departed, 163; *See also* McGivern, William P.
DeWitt, O'Byrne, 12, 20
diaspora, *See* Irish diaspora
Diner, Hasia, 114
Dirty Harry (film, McGivern co–author), 161; *See also* McGivern, William P.
Disney, *See* Walt Disney Studios
divorce – Irish–American women writers, 124, 125–6; postwar rate in US, 125; *See also* individual authors
Donleavy, J.P. – and image of Ireland, 148
Donohue, Michael, (AOH president), 59
Donohue, Paddy – and All–Ireland Final, 1947, 31
Donohue, Stacey, 119
Dooley, Martin (Mr. Dooley), *See* Dunne, Finley Peter
Dougherty, Dr. Thomas G., 32
Down These Mean Streets (Thomas), 92–5
Dublin Records, 20
Dudley Street Opera House (Roxbury,

Boston), 14
Duffy, Charles, and *The Last Hurrah*, 156
Dugan, Harry (film director), 135
Dunne, Finley Peter (Mr. Dooley), 177, 195–7, 198
Durkan, Frank, 28
Duty Free (Shannon), *See* Shannon Airport

E

Effrat, Louis – description of All–Ireland Final, 32
Ellmann, Richard (*Yeats: The Man and the Masks, Identity of Yeats, James Joyce*), 189–90
emigration, 200, 202
Englewood Céili Band, 13
'ethnic fade', 2, 57, 72, 160
ethnicity, Irish / Irish–American, 57, 60, 61, 68, 143, 179, 188
AOH, 57–70
Catholicism, 71–7, 79, 83, 84
image, 95
Irish literature, 179
Quiet Man, 111, 121
racial desegregation, 71–9, 81, 83
sport, 25
Evans, Sir Frank, 42

F

Facts of Life (Howard), 119, 123
Fallon, Brian – and image of Ireland, 148
Fanning, Charles – and McSorley, 209 (ch12, n1)
Farrell, James T., 198
Feis, *See* céilithe / feiseanna
Feminine Mystique (Friedan), 122, 124
Fernwood Emergency Veterans Housing Project (Roseland, Chicago), 80 *See also* racial desegregation
Fianna Fáil Party 41, 42; and partition, 42
film noir, 161, 165, 166, 168, 169, 170; *See also* noir fiction
films, *See* motion pictures, *film noir*, individual titles
Fine Gael, 42
Finian's Rainbow (Saidy and Harburg), 149–51, 158
as comment on America, 149–51,
and *Crock of Gold*, 150
and image of leprechauns, 149, 150
and racism, 150
and US credit system, 150, 208 (ch10, n4)
Fitzpatrick, Fr. Joseph P., 87, 88, 93, 98
Flatley, Michael, 18

football, Gaelic, *See* All–Ireland Final 1947
Ford, John, 4, **100–13**, *See also* Quiet Man (film)
Foreign Office (British), North American Division, 46–7
Franklin Simon Department Store (New York), 141
Franks, Sir Oliver – and anti–partition campaign, 47, 48, 49
Freburg, Stan – and Bridey Murphy affair, 137
Freedom Train – and AOH, 63
Friedan, Betty (*Feminine Mystique*), 122, 124
Frost, Frances, *Then Came Timothy* – and leprechauns, 154
Fussell, Paul (*Wartime*, 1989), 103, 104

G

Gaelic American – and AOH, 68
Gaelic Athletic Association (Ireland) – appeal to for New York game, 27, 28; Dublin Central Council, 26, 35, 37; purpose, 205 (ch2, n1)
Gaelic Athletic Association (US), 26, 27, 29, 33, 34, 35
Gaelic League – and traditional music, 11, 13
Gaelic Park (Innisfail Park), 26–7, 34–5
Gaeltacht, 15
Gans, Herbert, 72
Garrett, George, 41, 44
Gender roles – and Irish–American women, 125
General Mills, Lucky Charms cereal – and leprechauns, 146
GI Bill of Rights, 119; and AOH, 68
Gimbel's Department Store (New York), 141
Goffman, Erving, 138
Going My Way (film), 176, 178
Gordon, Anna, 121
Gordon, Mary, 118; Catholicism, 121–2; *Circling my Mother*, 122, 124, 126; divorce, 126
Gray, David, 38, 39–41, 43–4
Great Depression, 9, 10, 100, 110; AOH, 59–60; immigration, 26, 27
Great Migration (Puerto Rican), 97
Greeley, Andrew, 68, 71, 80, 81–3, 164, 205 (ch5, n1); and 'sacramental imagination', 162, 163; *See also* Christ the King Parish
Green Rushes (Walsh), 101
Greene, David (*Anthology of Irish Literature, J.M. Synge, 1871–1909*), 189
Grimstead, David ('White–Black Humor'), 153
Grobe, William, 80–1
Gulliver's Travels (Swift), 149

H

Hamilton, Rev. Michael – and All–Ireland Final 1947, 26, 27, 28
Hammett, Dashiel, 161
Harburg, Yip (*Finian's Rainbow*), 149, 150, 151
Hartman, Susan, *The Home Front and Beyond*, 114
Hemingway, Ernest ('Soldier's Home'), 103
Hennessey, Capt William, 75–6
Herbert's Retreat, *See* Sneden's Landing (McCarthy)
Hibernian Benevolent Burial Society, 58
Hibernian Digest, 63
Hibernians, *See* Ancient Order of Hibernians
Hibernians on the March (AOH manual), 64–7
Hibernian Universal Benevolent Society, 58
Hickerson, John D. – and anti–partition campaign, 41, 42
Hills of Ireland (travelogue, 1951), 134, 135
Hinde, John (photographer), 135
Hoban, Edward – and the Cold War, 207 (ch9, n9)
The Home Front and Beyond, (Hartman), 114
Hour of Spring, (Deasy), 117
'How Hollywood Deals with the Deviant Male' (article, Thomas), 161, 170
Howard, Maureen, 114, 119–20
cultural heritage, 120
Facts of Life, 119, 123
marriage, 123
Not a Word About Nightingales, 120, 122–4
and psychoanalysis, 124
and religion, 120
Hypnosis, 131, 132, 136, 137–8, 140; *See also* brainwashing
'Hypnotizzy', 131, 132, 137, 138, 140

I

I, The Jury (Spillane), 161, 162
Ilich, Ivan, 98
immigrants – in Boston, social status, 14; gender roles, 14; music, 9–23, *See also* Music, Irish – in America
statistics, 204 (chI, n1,)
immigration, 174–75; decline in New York and US, 26–27; and All–Ireland Final 1947, 35
Independent Sons of Erin, 58
Innishfree (*Quiet Man*), 108–11; sports, 109–10; Riesman theory, 110–1
Innisfail Park, *See* Gaelic Park

Inverchapel, Lord (Sir Archibald John Clark
  Kerr) – and anti–partition, 42, 43
Ireland
  contemporary, 200
  cost of travel (1950s), 132
  exports, 141
  idealization of, 20, 138–40, 143, 146,
    147–48, 154–5; in *Quiet Man* 100, 105,
    112
  and image and economy, 140–42
  marketing of, 133
  merchandising, 141, 142
  neutrality in WWII, 43, 39, 60, 67, 101,
    110, 209 (ch12, n4)
  travel in – costs (1950s), 132
Ireland, Denis – and anti–partition campaign,
  41
Irish America – relationship with Ireland, 57
Irish America and postwar period, 5, 61,
  67–8, 174, 201
  Catholic influence on film, 171
  GI Bill, 68
  literature, 175, 183, 187
  San Francisco – resettlement of Irish, 19
  music in. *See* Music, Irish – in America
Irish–American image in film, 176
Irish–American studies, 1–6
Irish–American women and women writers,
  114–130; *See also* individual authors
    assimilation, 118
  Catholic influences on, 118–22
  divorce, 124, 125–6
  education, 115, 116, 118–9, 126
  employment, 115
  gender roles, 125
  influence of nuns, 115
  in labor force, pre–war, 114–5, 116
  in literary jobs, 116
  marriage, 117, 122–4, 125–6
  mothers, 118
  as nurses, 115
  pre– and postwar compared, 114–5
  professions, 118
  psychoanalysis, 124, 126
  as teachers, 115
Irish Anti–Partition League, 41
Irish diaspora, 5, 6, 131, 134, 136, 139, 140,
  142, 195
Irish Ethnicity, *See* ethnicity, Irish /
  Irish–American
Irish Folklore Commission, 136, 148
Irish Free State, 100
The Irish in Me (travelogue, 1959), 134, 135,
  139
Irish Institute of New York – and tourism,
  134

Irish Music Association of America (IMAA),
  18–9
Irish Press, 29
Irish Race Convention (New York), 41
Irish Republican Army, 101
Irish – political activities, 97
Irish studies, 189–203
Irish War of Independence (1919–21), 38
'It Came from Glocca Morra' (article,
  Barton), 146

J

J.M. Synge, 1871–1909 (Greene), 189
Jews – in the arts, 160
Jones, Guy and Constance, *Mr Peabody's
  Mermaid,* 151; *There Was a Little Man* –
  and anti–corporation comment, 151–3
Joyce, James, 176, 177, 203; *Portrait of the
  Artist as a Young Man* – and Kelleher,
  John V., 194–5, 203

K

Kavanagh, Herminie Templeton – and *Darby
  O'Gill* short stories, 157
Kazan, Elia (*On the Waterfront, Tree Grows
  in Brooklyn*), 178
Kelleher, John V., 190–203; and *The Last
  Hurrah*, 156
  Arnold, Matthew, 191–2
  Celticism, 192
  censorship, 201–2
  de Valera, Eamon, 202
  emigration, 202
  essay form, 191
  Farrell, James T., 198
  Irish neutrality in WWII, 109 (ch13, n4)
  Joyce, James, 203
  Last Hurrah, 156–57
  literary censorship, 193–4
  literature of diaspora, 195
  life of, 190–1
  McElgun, John, 198
  Mr. Dooley, 195–7
  O'Connor, Frank, 194
  O'Faolain, Sean, 201
  O'Flaherty, Liam, 194, 203
  partition, 200–2
  Potter, George, 198
  Rosenblatt, Roger, 190–1
  Yeats, W.B., 195
  WORKS (essays): 'Can Ireland Unite?', 200;
    'Early Irish History and Pseudo–History',
    193; 'Ireland . . . and Where Does She
    Stand?', 201–2; ' 'Irish American

Literature and Why There Isn't Any',
197–8; 'Irish Literature Today', 193;
'Irishness in America'. 199–200; 'A Long
Way from Tipperary',   198–99;
'Matthew Arnold and the Celtic Revival',
191–92; 'Mister Dooley and the Same
Old World', 195; 'Perceptions of James
Joyce', 194–5
Kelly, Anna, 29
Kelly, Herman – letter to Christ the King
Parish, 83
Kennedy, John F., 69, 148
Kennelly, Mayor Martin, 49
Kilfenora Céili Band, 13
Killanin, Lord, 101
Kinglake, A.W., 104
Kitty, I Hardly Knew You, See McSorley,
Edward: works
Ku Klux Klan, 69, 82

L

Lace Curtains (Berlin), 117
Lang, Fritz, (*Big Heat,* film), 168, 170
Lange, Dorothea ('Country People of
Ireland', photo essay), 136
Last Hurrah (O'Connor) – comment on
America, 156–7; and Kelleher, John V.,
156
Larosa, John – [Beverly] Improvement
Association, 81–2
League of Nations, 40, 51
Leprechauns **146–59**: *See also Mouse that
Roared*
blackface, 147, 153
as cultural immediary, 148
in *Darby O'Gill and The Little People,*
157–8
fairies / sídhe, 147
in *Finian's Rainbow,* 149–51, 158
image of, 146, 158; in *Crock of Gold,*
148–9, 150, 153, 154
infantilization of, 146–7, 15–55
and Jonathan Swift, 208 (ch10, n3)
and Lucky Charms cereal, 146
as malevolent figure, 146, 158
Michaeleen Oge Flynn as mediator, 207
(ch10, n2)
and racial stereotype, 146–7, 150
as symbol of Ireland, 146, 147–8
symbol of luck, 146
and theme of 'something lost and something found', 208 (ch10, n6)
in *There was a Little Man,* 151, 153
'Letter to Jackie', (Morris), 171
Life magazine, 135, 136, 137

Lomax, Alan – and Irish recordings, 20
The Lonely Crowd (Riesman), 108–12,
171–2; and McGivern's protagonists, 172
Lucky Charms cereal – and leprechauns, 146

M

McBride, Joseph, 101
MacBride, Seán, 42–4; and visit to US, 45,
50
McCaffrey, Lawrence, 72, 114, 123
McCarthy, Sen. Joseph, 61
McCourt, Frank, 87, 92;*'Tis,* 92, 95–7
McCarthy, Mary, 114, 116, 117–8
Catholic influence on, 119
A Charmed Life, 123
The Company She Keeps, 117
Edmund Wilson, 123, 124
Irish heritage, 120
marriage, 122–3
Partisan Review, 116
psychoanalysis, 124
McCormick, Robert – and Sir Basil Brooke,
49
McDermott, Alice (*Confessions of a
Reluctant Catholic*) – and Catholicism,
119, 121
McElgun, John (*Annie Reilly, or The Fortunes
of an Irish Girl in New York*), 198
McGillicuddy McGotham (Wibberley) – and
comment on America, 155–6
McGivern, William P., **160–72**
Brown, Howard – influence on McGivern,
208 (ch11, n1)
film noir, 161, 165, 166, 168, 169, 170
Irish ancestry, 168
Irish Catholicism, 162–9, 171
Irish–American masculinity, 171
Irish–American protagonists, 160
life of, 208 (ch11, n1)
Philadelphia Evening Bulletin, 208 (ch11
n4)
philosophy, 168–69
place names, 208 (ch10, n5)
'polluted protagonists', 163, 164, 166
protagonists and Riesman's theory, 172
and Selby, Earl, 208 (ch11, n4)
WORKS: *Big Heat,* 160–61, 166; and
Catholic Church, 163–64; and crime
control and due process models (Packer),
167; and Irish ancestry, 168; and masculinity, 170; and novel vs. film, 168, 169,
170; *Rogue Cop* (McGivern) , 160–1,
162–6; Cain and Abel conflict, 163;
Shield for Murder, 160; *The Departed,* 163;
and immigrant values, 165; and individual

choice, 163; and Irish Catholicism, 162–4, 166; and McGivern's protagonists, 172; novel vs. film, 164, 166; and redemption, 166; Riesman, David (*The Lonely Crowd*), 171–2

McKelway, St. Clair, 120

McKenna, Catherine, 189

McSorley, Edward, **174–186**
  assimilation, 175,
  Hollywood, 175
  Irish Catholicism, 179–80, 185
  Cassavetes, John, 178–9
  McNulty, John – reviews by, 176
  life of, 178
  literary theory, 179
  postwar period, 183, 187
  Prescott, Orville– reviews by, 176
  sexual themes, 181, 183, 184–5
  WORKS: *Our Own Kind*: 175, 176–82, 185; and Catholicism, 179–80, 182, 184; and education, 177; and *Going My Way*, 178; 178–84, 185; and Joyce, 176–7; and *A Tree Grows in Brooklyn*, 182; and Lawrence McCaffrey, 209 (ch12, n6); and sexuality, 184–85; and *A Tree Grows in Brooklyn*, 177, 178, 182; *Young McDermott*: 175, 184–7; and *Odyssey*, 185–6; and St. Augustine, 185, 187; *Kitty, I Hardly Knew You*: 187–8; and Catholic Church, 187; and Charles Fanning, 208 (ch12, n1); and importance of place, 187

Meagher, Wedger, 30–1

Maggie–Now (Smith), 117

Makem, Tommy, 10

'The Man in the Brooks Brothers Suit' in McCarthy, *The Company She Keeps*, 117

Man in the Gray Flannel Suit (Wilson), 153

Man Who Shot Liberty Valance (film), 106–7

Marlowe, Philip, 161

Marshall, George C. (Secretary of State), 42, 43

Marshall Plan, and partition, 44, 51

Marx, Karl, 149

Mauretania (ship), 28

Meerloo, Joost (*Rape of the Mind*), 137

Miller, Kerby, 114

Mister Dooley, *See* Dunne, Finley Peter

Modern Language Association – and Irish literature, 195

Molly Maguires, 58–9

Moore, Marianne, 116

Morgan Park (Chicago) – and desegregation, 80

Morris, Charles, ('Letter to Jackie'), 171

Moses, Robert, 91

Mothers of Longwood Academy, 73

Motion Pictures, *See also* film noir, individual film titles; McGivern, William; tourism/travelogues
  image of Irish, 175–6
  postwar image of Catholic Church, 171

Mouse That Roared (Wibberley) – and comment on America, 155

Moynihan, Daniel Patrick (*Beyond the Melting Pot*) – and literary modernism 174–6

Murphy, Bridey (Tighe, Virginia), 131, 136–7, 138, 139, 140, 207 (ch9, n7); *See also* Tourism to Ireland

Music, American, 10, 13, 20–21

Music, Irish – in America, **9–23**; *See also* music/musicians, music/bands, records and recording industry;
  American music, 10, 13
  in Boston, 9, 14–15; dance halls, 14–6, 204 (ch1, n5)
  céilithe and *feiseanna*, 12–13
  in Chicago, 9, 18–19
  Golden Age of, 10–11, 16, 21
  immigrants, 9–10, 11, 12–3
  influence of folk revival, 20–1
  influx of non–Irish musicians, 20–1
  influence of big band and jazz, 13
  Integration into American music, 11–2
  Irish Musicians' Association of America (IMAA), 18–9
  locales, 11–12
  in New York, 9, 12, 13, 15–8; All–Ireland Fleadh Cheoil (1960), 17–18; dance halls: 15–16; Fuller, Bill, 15; McNulty family, 15; postwar period, 9; range of influences in, 11, 12; Sligo fiddle style. 12; traditional and modern, 15; and traditional vs. dance bands, 17; vaudeville, 15, O'Neill, Francis, 18
  in San Francisco, 9, 19–20; dance halls and house dances, 19; Knights of the Red Branch – recordings, 19; post war period – resettlement of Irish, 19; and traditional music, 19

Music, Irish – in Ireland, 10; Clare, 12; and connection with American music, 13; Donegal, 12; Ennistymon, 13; European influence, 11; Galway, 12; Jazz influence, Kerry, 12; Kiloran Céilí Band, 13; Lisdoonvarna, 13; Roscommon, 12; Sliabh Aughty region, 12; Sligo, 12; Tulla Céilí Band 16, 17, 18

Musicians, Bands
  All–Star Céilí Band, 14
  Dan Sullivan's Shamrock Band, 14
  Diplomats, 14
  Four Provinces Orchestra, 14–5

Emerald Isle Orchestra, 14
Harp and Shamrock Orchestra, 18
Johnny Powell's Band, 14
New York Céilí Band, 17
O'Leary's Irish Minstrels, 14
Tara Céilí Band, 14
Tulla Céilí Band, 16, 17, 18
Musicians, Irish – Ireland and America
Canny, Paddy, 16
Carroll, Liz, 18
Clancy Brothers, 10, 21; and Tommy
Makem, 21
Coen, Jack 12
Cooley, Joe, 10
Cooley, Seamus, 17
Cronin, Johnny, 14
Derrane, Joe, 15
Flaatley, Michael, 18
Gillespie, Hughie, 10–11
Killoran, Paddy (New York), 12, 16, 20
Loughnane, Dr. Bill, 16–17
Leydon, Jimmy – and range of styles, 13
Lynch, Jerry, 13
McNulty Family, 15
Madigan, Pat – and range of styles, 13
Makem, Tommy, 10, 21
Morrison, James, 10, 12
Mulhaire, Martin, 17
Neylon, Frank, 10, 15
Noonan, Paddy, 16
O'Donnell, Danny, 19–20
Preston, Michael, 17
Rafferty, Mike, 13
Roche, Pat, 18
Ward, Brendan (orchestra director), 15–6
Whooley, John (music promoter), 204
(ch1, n7)
Musicians' unions, 13, 17, 204 (ch1, n6)
*My Pilgrim's Progress: Media Studies,
1950–1998* (Trow), 103–4
mysticism, Irish, 4

N

Naked City (film) – and crime control and
due process models (Packer), 168
Nation of Nations (Adamic), 61
National Geographic Magazine, 135
National Hibernian – decline of, 59–60
National Opinion Research Center, 68
New Deal, 69, 205 (ch4, n5)
New York – and All–Ireland Final 1947, 24;
music in, *See* Music, Irish – in America
New York Times, 133, 176
noir fiction, 161, 163, 166; and women,
168; *See also* film noir, McGivern, William

Nolan, Janet, 114
North Atlantic Treaty, 45
North Atlantic Treaty Organization, 51
nostalgia, *See* Ireland – idealization of
Not a Word About Nightingales (Howard),
120, 122–4
Notre Dame University – and mascot, 146
Novak, Michael (*Rise of the Unmeltable
Ethnics*), 2

O

O'Connor, Edwin (*Last Hurrah*), 156–7
O'Connor, Frank – and Kelleher, John V.,
194, 201
O'Donnell, John 'Kerry', 24, 27, 29
O'Donovan, Jer, 12
O'Dwyer, Mayor William, 24, 26, 29, 48,
91; and Sir Basil Brooke, 49; career of, 35
O'Faolain, Sean – and Kelleher, John V., 194,
201
O'Flaherty, Liam, 194
O'Hara's Holiday (travelogue, 1960), 135,
142
O'Hehir, Michael – and All–Ireland Final,
1947, 24, 25, 34
O'Keeffe, Paddy, 28, 33
O'Kelly, Seán T. (President of Ireland), 34
O'Leary, Philip, 189
O'Neill, Francis, 18
O'Rourke, Dan (GAA) – and All–Ireland
Final 1947, 30
On the Waterfront (motion picture), 178
Organization for a Southwest Community
(OSC, Beverly Hills, Chicago), 82–3
Ormerod, Maj. C.B. – and Sir Basil Brooke,
48
Our Own Kind, *See* McSorley, Edward:
works

P

Packard, Vance (*Hidden Persuaders*), 138
Packer, Herbert ('Two Models of the
Criminal Process'), and *The Big Heat,* 167;
and *Naked City,* 167–8
'Paddy'– as racist term, 93–5
Pan American Airlines – and An Tóstal, 142
The Parish and the Hill (Curran), 117
Partisan Review, 116
Partition, 200–201; *See also* anti–partition
campaign
American interest in, 38
Ancient Order of Hibernians, 66
Irish–American relations, 39
World War I, 38, 39

Philadelphia Evening Bulletin – and William
McGivern, 208 (ch11, n4)
Pioneros Ruertorriqueños (Colon Lopez),
97–8
place, importance of – in literature, 187
police, Irish–American and corruption – in
novels and film, 160–73
Polo Grounds, (New York), 24, 32;
Burkeville, 29; Coogan's Hollow
/Coogan's Bluff, 30; history of, 29–30; *See
also* All Ireland Football Final 1947
Portrait of the Artist as a Young Man (Joyce),
194–5
Post–Traumatic Stress Disorder (PTSD), 102;
110, 112
postwar period and Irish America, 5, 61,
67–8, 174, 201
Catholic influence on film, 171
GI Bill of Rights, 68
literature, 175, 183, 187
music, *See* music, Irish – in America
San Francisco – resettlement of Irish, 19
Potter, George, *To the Golden Door,* 198–9
Prescott, Orville – reviews of McSorley, 176
Potter, George (*To the Golden Door*), 198
Presentation of Self in Everyday Life
(Goffman), 138
Presidential election, 1928 and 1960 com-
pared, 68–9
Protestant – Catholic divide, *See* Beverly
Hills, Chicago
Puerto Ricans – New York, 87–99
and black americans, 94
Colon Lopez, Joaquin, 87–88; *Pioneros
Ruertorriqueños,*, 97–8
common experience with Irish, 88
cultural preservation, 97
and Democratic Party, 97
Fitzpatrick, Fr. Joseph P., 87–8, 93–8
infantilization of, 97
Irish discrimination against, 95–7
and Irish education, 89–91
and employment, 92
and gangs, 92–3
and neighborhoods, 91–2
and McCourt, Frank, 87, 92;*Tis,* 92, 95–7
negative image of, 95–7
'Paddy'– as racist term, 93–5
and racism, 93–5
Rivera Edward, 87,Edward, 87; *Family
Installments: Memories of Growing Up
Hispanic,* 89–91
'Spic' as racist term, 96, 206 (ch6, n2)
Tammany Hall, 97, 98
Thomas, Piri, 87, 92–5
Down These Mean Streets, 92–5

Seven Long Times, 92
Washington Heights, NY, 98

Q

Quiet Man (film) **100–13**, 135, 139, 140,
155, 156; *See also* Innisfree; Ford, John
Black and Tan War, 100, 109, 110
Danaher, Mary Kate (character), 100, 108,
109, 110, 111
Danaher, Will (character), 101, 102, 103,
107, 109, 111
fantasy vs. realism, 100
Flynn, Michaleen Oge (character), 101,
110, 111; as leprechaun figure, 207–8
(ch10, n2)
function of crowd, 111
and Fussell thesis, 104
Great Depression, 110
idealization of Ireland, 100, 105, 112, 155
Innishfree, 108–11; and sports, 109–10;
and Riesman theory, 110–1
Irish nationalism, 100, 101–2
Irish Republican Army, 101
Lonergan, Fr. (character), 100, 102, 107,
110, 111–2
and myth, 113
narration of, 105
play–acting, 107
Playfair, Mr. (character), 102, 109, 110, 111
politics, 101–02; silence about 10, 101–02
Post–Traumatic Stress Syndrome, 102, 110
112
Riesman theory (*Lonely Crowd*), 108–112
sports, 109–10
story versions and storytelling, 100, 101
105–7
Thornton, Sean (character), 100–5,
107–112, 155
Trow thesis, 104
Walsh stories, 100, 101 102–3, 110
war, 110; silence about, 100, 102, 103–4
'Quiet Man' (Walsh, story versions 1933 and
1935), 100–1, 102–3, 110, 206 (ch7, n2);
variations, 101

R

race / racism
Beverly Hills, Chicago, 71, 72, 79–80, 83,
84
bigotry, 63–4
blackface, 147, 153
desegregation, 71, 79, 80, 83
leprechauns, 146–7, 150, 176
Puerto Ricans, 93, 98; racial slurs, 93, 96,

206 (ch6,n2)
Radió Éireann, 13
Rape of the Mind (Meerloo), 137
Rebel Without a Cause (film), 154
Records and Recording industry, 10–11, 12, 19–20
Chicago, 18
Columbia World Library, 20
Copley Records, 20
Decca Records, 18
DeWitt, O'Byrne, 12, 20
Dublin Records, 20
Ennis, Seamus, 20
first LP of Irish music, 20
Lomax, Alan, 20
Loughnane, Bill, 17
O'Donovan, Jer, 12
San Francisco, 19–20
Victor label, 204 (ch1, n2)
Reilly and the 400, 174–175
reincarnation, 136–7, 140; parties, 137
'reincarnation cocktail', 137, 207 (ch9, n8)
Reilly, A.J., 61, 63
Reilly, George, and *Hibernians on the March*, 64–6
Republic Pictures, 101, 102
Riders to the Sea (Synge), 174
Ridge Country Club (Beverly Hills, Chicago), 76
Riesman, David (*The Lonely Crowd*), and *Quiet Man* (film), 108–112
Rivera, Edward, 87; *Bildungsroman, Family Installments: Memories of Growing up Hispanic*, 89–91
Rivers, Caryl, 118; Catholic education, 121; divorce and psychoanalysis, 124; gender rules, 125
Roediger, David (*Wages of Whiteness*), 147
Rogers, Thomas (AOH national secretary), 62
Rogue Cop (McGivern), 160–1, 162–66; *See also* McGivern, William P.
Cain and Able conflict, 163
The Departed, 163
immigrant values, 165
individual choice, 163
Irish Catholicism, 162–4 166
McGivern's protagonists, 172
novel vs. film, 164, 166
redemption, 166
Riesman, David (*The Lonely Crowd*), 171–2
Roman Catholic Church, *See* Catholicism / Catholic Church
Roosevelt, Eleanor – and dispute with Cardinal Spellman, 63

Roosevelt, Franklin Delano, 69
Rosenblatt, Roger, 189–90
Roucek, Joseph and Francis Brown, *One America: The History, Contributions, and Present Problems of Our Racial and National Minorities,*), 60–1
Roxbury (Boston). *See* Music, Irish – in America
Rugby, Lord (John Loader Maffey), 42, 43
Ruth, George Herman 'Babe', 30

S

'sacramental imagination' (Greeley), 162
Saidy, Fred (*Finian's Rainbow*), 149, 151
St. Barnabas Parish (Beverly Hills, Chicago) *See also* Shamrock Festival – Beverly, Hills (Chicago), 73, 74, 77
St. Barnabas Woman's Club (Beverly Hills, Chicago), 77; and desegregation, 82, 205–6 (ch5, n6)
St. John of the Cross, and *The Big Heat* (McGivern), 169–70
St. John Fisher Parish, Beverly Hills, Chicago), 74
St. Patrick's Day, *See* Beverly Hills, Chicago; Shamrock Festival
St. Praxides Parish (Greeley), 205–06 (ch5, n1)
San Francisco – resettlement of Irish, 19; *See also* Music, Irish – in America
Schloesser, Stephen – and 'polluted protagonists', 163
Scorsese, Martin, (*Taxi Driver*, film), 208 (ch11, n5)
Search for Bridey Murphy (Bernstein), *See* Murphy, Bridey
Selby, Earl – and influence on McGivern, 208 (ch. 11, n4)
Seven Long Times (Thomas), 92
Shamrock Festival, 73–5, 77–9; *See also* Beverly Hills, Chicago
Shannon Airport – and Irish tourist industry, 142–3; 207 (ch9, n10, 11)
Shannon Free Zone, 142
Shattuck, Henry Lee, 190, 191
Shaw, Sam, 178–9
Sheats, Dorothea ('I Walked Some Irish Miles'), 135
Shield for Murder (McGivern), 160; *See also* McGivern, William P.
Sligo fiddle style, 12, 204 (ch1, n4)
Smith, Alfred, 68–69
Smith, Betty, 117; *Maggie–Now*, 117; *Tomorrow Will Be Better*, 117; *A Tree Grows in Brooklyn*, 117, 177, 178, 182

Sneden's Landing, 120
'Soldier's Home" (Hemingway), 103
Sollors, Werner (*Beyond Ethnicity*), 163, 171
South Side Catholic Womens' Club
　　(Chicago), 73
Southtown Economist (Chicago), 76, 78
Spell of Ireland (travelogue, 1954), 134,
　　135, 139, 140
Spellman, Francis Cardinal, 29; and dispute
　　with Eleanor Roosevelt, 63
'spic' – as racial term, 96, 206 (ch6, n2)
Spillane, Mickey, (*I, the Jury*), 161, 162
sports – and Irish ethnicity, 24; Irish, in
　　New York, 35
Springs of Affection (Brennan), 122
State Department, US, 41
Steinberg, Stephen, 72
Stephens, James, See *Crock of Gold*
Stowe, William ('White–Black Humor'), 153
Stritch, Samuel Cardinal, 75
Sullivan, John L. – and 'Gentleman Jim"
　　Corbett Fight, 199–200
Swift, Jonathan, *Gulliver's Travels*, 149
'symbolic ethnicity' (Gans), 72
Synge, John Millington (*Riders to the Sea*),
　　174, 175

T

Tammany Hall, 35. 87, 97, 98
Taxi Driver (film, Scorsese), 208 (ch11, n5)
Then Came Timothy (Frost) – and lep-
　　rechauns, 154
Thomas, Deborah ('How Hollywood Deals
　　with the Deviant Male) and *film noir*, 161,
　　170
Thomas, Piri, 87, 92–5; *Down These Mean
　　Streets,* 92–5; racism, 93, 95; *Seven Long
　　Times,* 92
Thompson, Dorothy, 48–9
Thomson, Bobby, 30
Tighe, Virginia, See Murphy, Bridey
'Tis (McCourt), 92, 95–7
To the Golden Door (Potter), 189–99
Tomorrow Will Be Better, (Smith), 117
Tóstal Festival, See Tourism to Ireland
Tourism to Ireland, 1950s, 131, 132–3, 138,
　　148;　See also Murphy, Bridey
　　American Telephone and Telegraph Co.,
　　142
　　Americans vs. Europeans, 132 –3
　　articles, 135
　　Bord Fáilte, 133, 134, 141, 142, 148
　　costs of (1950s), 132
　　Bridey Murphy affair, 131–45
　　Catholic church, 134

demography – US, 132
government objectives, 141
Irish–American tourists, 132–3
Irish Government, 141
marketing and promotion of, 133, 135,
　　141, 142
motion pictures, 139, 140–43
nostalgia, 138–9, 141; See also Ireland,
　　idealization of
photographs, 135–6
postcards, 135–6
Shannon Airport – and Irish tourist indus-
　　try, 142–3, 207 (ch9, n10, 11)
Shannon Free Zone, 142
Tóstal Festival, as marketing tool, 77, 133,
　　142;　origins of, 142
tour groups, 134
travelogues – as promotional tool, 134–5
　　　Hills of Ireland (1951, 134, 135
　　　The Irish in Me (1959), 134, 135, 139
　　　O'Hara's Holiday (1960), 135, 142
　　　Spell of Ireland (1954), 134, 135, 139,
　　　140
A Tree Grows in Brooklyn (Smith), 117, 177,
　　178, 182
Trow, George W.S. (*My Pilgrim's Progress:
　　Media Studies, 1950–1998,* 1999), 103–4
Truman Doctrine, 51
Truman, Harry S., 43
Tulla Céilí Band, 16, 17, 18

U

Ulster–Irish Society (New York) – and
　　anti–partition campaign, 47–8
United Irish Societies of Chicago, 78
United States Gaelic Athletic Association
　　(New York), 26, 29, 35
United States International Trade Fair,
　　Chicago, 1950, 141
United States – diplomatic relations 39; spe-
　　cial relationship with UK, 40; United
　　Kingdom, 38
Uphill Walkers (Blaise), 121

V

Vanderpoel Improvement Association
　　(Beverly Hills, Chicago) – and desegrega-
　　tion, 81
Vaudeville, 15
Vendler, Helen, 189
Victor records, 204 (ch1, n2)
Vogue magazine – and Ireland, 139

W

Wages of Whiteness (Roediger), 147
Walsh, Maurice, and 'Quiet Man' stories , 100
Walt Disney Studios, 146–7, 157–8
Wartime (Fussell), 103
Waters, Maureen, 118; and Catholic education 121; and gender roles, 125
'whiteness' theory (racial) 2, 72, 94, 162
Wibberley, Leonard, *Mouse That Roared*, 155; *McGillicuddy McGotham*, 155–6
Wilson, Edmund, 123–4
Wilson, Sloan (*Man in the Grey Flannel Suit*), 153
Wilson, Woodrow, 38, 40
Women, and *noir* fiction, 168
A Word about Nightingales (Howard), 120
Working Women's Retreat Movement, 121–2

World War I, 40; and Irish nationalism, 38
World War II, 10, 26, 29, 33, 38, 39, 40, 41
  AOH, 59– 61
  immigration, 204 (ch1, n1)
  Irish ethnicity, 60
  naval bases in Republic of Ireland, 39
  neutrality and Kelleher, 209 (ch13, n4)
  silence about, 103–4
  Quiet Man, 100, 101, 102

Y

Yates, Herbert J. (Republic Pictures), 101
Yeats, William Butler and Kelleher, John V., 195
Young McDermott, See McSorley, Edward: works
Yunqué, Edgardo Vega, 92